THE STRIKE THAT CHANGED NEW YORK

THE **STRIKE** THAT CHANGED NEW YORK

Blacks, Whites, and the Ocean Hill–Brownsville Crisis

Jerald E. Podair

Yale University Press/New Haven & London

Printed in the United States of America

Library of Congress Cataloging-in-Publication Data
Podair, Jerald E., 1953–
The strike that changed New York : blacks, whites, and the Ocean Hill–Brownsville
crisis / Jerald E. Podair.
p. cm.
Includes bibliographical references (p.) and index.
ISBN 13: 978-0-300-10940-5

1. Strikes and lockouts—Teachers—New York (State)—New York.   2. Ocean Hill–
Brownsville Demonstration School District (New York, N.Y.)   3. Discrimination in
education—New York (State)—New York.   I. Title.
LB2844.47.U62 N4867   2002
331.892'813711'0097471—dc21   2002004315

A catalogue record for this book is available from the British Library.

The paper in this book meets the guidelines for permanence and durability
of the Committee on Production Guidelines for Book Longevity of the
Council on Library Resources.

For Caren and Julie

CONTENTS

ACKNOWLEDGMENTS

Many individuals helped me write this book. I thank them all: Benjamin Alpers, Adina Back, Kathy Baima, Wayne Barrett, Herman Benson, Ronald Bianchi, Pat Bonomi, Lizabeth Cohen, Cynthia Cupples, Ronald Evans, Henry Foner, Murray Friedman, Kevin Gaines, Jeffrey Gerson, John Giggie, Cheryl Greenberg, Judith Hanson, Herbert Hill, James Horton, Tamar Jacoby, Walter Johnson, Phil Katz, Leah Kopcsandy, Liz Lunbeck, Richard Magat, Martin Mayer, Hiram McClendon, Kenneth Mills, Carl Nightingale, Nell Painter, James Patterson, Darryl Peterkin, Norman Podhoretz, Wendell Pritchett, James Ralph, Jack Schierenbeck, Andrew Shankman, Fred Siegel, Jim Sleeper, Christine Stansell, Thomas Sugrue, Clarence Taylor, John Thomas, Don Tobias, Ben Toffolli, Brigitta van Rheinberg, Andrew Weiss, Benjamin Weiss, John Wertheimer, Sean Wilentz, and Henry Yu.

I also thank Mary George, reference librarian at Princeton University's Firestone Library, for her ongoing enthusiasm for this project, her unsurpassed expertise, and her friendship. Glenn Novarr and Alison Carper filled my research trips to Brooklyn with great food, conversation, and camaraderie. Robert Klein's generosity of spirit and dry wit have sustained me since we roomed together in college all these many years ago.

I met Bill Reel by chance ten years ago. Since then, he has become one of my dearest friends. His compassion, humor, and faith have helped me through difficult times. I'm privileged to know him.

Lucinda Manning, the United Federation of Teachers archivist, made the union's Ocean Hill–Brownsville papers available to me in a most generous and forthcoming manner. She has helped me with this project in every possible way. It would not exist without her. Also at the UFT, I thank Evan Daniel for handling my photograph requests with exemplary professionalism and care. The late Debra Bernhardt's knowledge, kindness, and dedication will be missed by all who study the history of New York City.

David Ment and Bette Wenech presided over my other major archival resource, the New York City Board of Education Papers at Columbia Teachers College, with efficiency, good humor, and courtesy. I truly enjoyed the months I spent with them on 120th Street, as, in David's words, their "best customer." They always made me feel like a guest, not a visitor.

I also thank the members of the Society of American Historians, not only for honoring me with their Alan Nevins Prize, but for the example of their historical writing. They inspired me to become a historian, and I hope that, like them, I can write books that matter.

I am grateful to my colleagues in the Lawrence University Department of History for their friendship and support, and for welcoming this expatriate New Yorker to the Midwest with patience and good humor. Brian Rosenberg, Dean of the Faculty at Lawrence, has been unstintingly generous in providing the funding necessary for the completion of this book. I thank him for the confidence he has shown in it, and in me. My weekly lunches with Gerald Seaman, Associate Dean of the Faculty, have been filled with wonderful conversation and laughter, especially when the "two Jerrys" sow confusion in restaurants and stores. Also at Lawrence, I thank Vicki Koessl and Joanne Johnson, who prepared the final manuscript with professionalism and skill, and Gina Pirrello, who provided prompt and expert research assistance.

I also thank Professor Anthony Grafton of the Shelby Cullom Davis Center for Historical Studies at Princeton University for his generous support of this book.

Gavin Lewis has been an extraordinarily helpful copy editor. His suggestions have made this a much better book than the one I turned over to him. I also thank Larisa Heimert, Keith Condon, and Heidi Downey at Yale University Press, as well as Chuck Grench, for their help in bringing this project to fruition.

My intellectual debts are many. Gary Gerstle believed in this book from the beginning. His advice, support, and friendship made it possible for me to see it through. James McPherson's sensible, calming words and counsel have meant a great deal to me over the years. I know I am not alone in considering him a role model. Daniel Rodgers helped me understand not only where this book should go, but also what a good historian must do, and, most importantly, why a life in history is the best life of all. Alan Brinkley has gone beyond the call of duty on my behalf on occasions too numerous to mention. He has always provided me with expert advice and criticism, as well as with an example of warmth, empathy, and respect that I hope to emulate with my own students.

My thanks, finally, go to my family. My brother, Lee Podair, gave me confidence from start to finish. My in-laws, Sidney and Florence Benzer, showed me patience and forbearance as this book developed. Simon Podair, my father, was the first to show me the delights of history. By the time I finished high school, he and I had visited virtually every important historical site on the East Coast — all, in the fashion of true New Yorkers, without the benefit of an automobile. I was able to write this book, in large part, because of those days, and because of him. My mother, Selma Podair, passed away in July of 1997. I wish she had lived to see this day. She would have been very proud, but then, she never needed a special occasion to be proud of me. On the subject of pride, I hope my daughter, Julie Podair, will always be as proud of me as I am of her.

My greatest debt is to Caren Benzer. She understood my passion for American history, and my need to make a life of it. Thanks to her, I was able to do so. She has contributed to this book in more ways than I can count. But, more importantly, she has shown me, every day of our lives together, love's truest meaning. With Caren, wherever I may be, I'm the richest man in town.

THE STRIKE THAT CHANGED NEW YORK

INTRODUCTION

May 9, 1968

Fred Nauman knew something was going to happen. He just didn't know what it would be. It would, however, involve him; he had no doubt of that. Nauman was a science teacher at Junior High School 271, in the Ocean Hill–Brownsville section of Brooklyn, New York, a thirty-eight-year-old German Jew whose parents had brought him to America on the eve of World War II. He was a chapter chairman for the union representing New York City's fifty-five thousand public school teachers, the United Federation of Teachers, known as the UFT. In that role, he had been locked in a year-long battle with the local school board in the Ocean Hill–Brownsville district over what it could and could not do. The local board, elected as part of an experiment in community control of the New York City public schools, had claimed sweeping powers in the district, including the sole right to determine curriculum, control expenditures, and hire and fire personnel.

To Nauman, these demands, especially the last, were outrageous: he was a union man, and the UFT had struggled since its founding in 1960 to give teachers a strong voice in just these areas. Now a local school board—composed of nonprofessionals—was trying to take away what the union had won. Even worse, it was accusing Nauman and the UFT of racism, since the local board, like the Ocean Hill–Brownsville neighborhood itself, was predominantly black, and Nauman, like most in his union, was white. Nonsense, thought Nauman: this wasn't about race, it was about labor rights. The local board just didn't seem to understand this. He considered himself a liberal, a civil rights supporter. Why didn't they understand?

The night before, he had gotten a tip from a UFT higher-up: expect the local board to try something in the morning. He was an obvious target. But would the board actually try to fire him? Firing a tenured teacher in the New York City school system was next to impossible, and only the Superintendent of Schools at central Board of Education headquarters could do it. The last time a local board had fired a teacher—or hired one, for that matter—had been before the city's schools were centralized in 1898. Nauman had been trying to get this through to the people on the local board all year. They just wouldn't listen. They seemed to him to go out of their way to provoke and confront. They wouldn't follow the rules, wouldn't listen to reason. Now, as he walked into Junior High School 271 on the morning of Thursday, May 9, 1968, he wondered what was next.

A few minutes into his first class, he was asked to report to the principal's office. When he got there, he was handed an envelope. He opened it and read:

Dear Sir:

The Governing Board of the Ocean Hill–Brownsville Demonstration School District has voted to end your employment in the schools of this District. This action was taken on the recommendation of the Personnel Committee. This termination of employment is to take effect immediately.

In the event you wish to question this action, the Governing Board will receive you on Friday, May 10, 1968, at 6:00 P.M., at Intermediate School 55, 2021 Bergen Street, Brooklyn, New York.

You will report Friday morning to Personnel, 110 Livingston Street, Brooklyn, for reassignment.

Sincerely,

Rev. C. Herbert Oliver, Chairman

Ocean Hill–Brownsville Governing Board

Rhody A. McCoy

Unit Administrator[1]

Nauman walked outside, and found a phone, and dialed the number of the UFT's headquarters in Manhattan.[2]

Three blocks away, one of the men who had signed the letter on behalf of the Ocean Hill–Brownsville local school board sat at his desk in a makeshift office in the lobby of a public housing project. Rhody McCoy was an early riser, and he had already been at work, omnipresent pipe in hand, for a few hours. He knew the

1. Rhody McCoy. United Federation of Teachers Collection, UFT Photo Collection, Robert F. Wagner Labor Archives, New York University.

kind of storm the letter Nauman and eighteen other white Ocean Hill–Brownsville educators were opening would cause, but he felt the UFT had given him no choice. McCoy was the "Unit Administrator" for the Ocean Hill–Brownsville district, responsible for the day-to-day operations of its eight schools. He was forty-two years old, a graduate of Howard University, who had spent his entire working career in the New York City public education system, first as a teacher and later as the principal of a school for emotionally disturbed children in Manhattan. The Ocean

Hill–Brownsville local board had hired him as Unit Administrator in July 1967, over the objections of the UFT. The union claimed he lacked the formal requirements for the position, but McCoy believed there was more to it than that. He was a black man with a reputation for quiet independence and an unwillingness to play by bureaucratic rules. This, much more than his lack of high examination scores and graduate credits, was what made the union nervous.

McCoy had taken the Ocean Hill–Brownsville job in large part because he saw it as a way to do something about the educational catastrophe he saw developing in the city's black community. Black children were not learning. Test scores were abysmal and dropout rates rising. White teachers did not want to teach in black schools. They transferred out to the "better" white schools as soon as they fulfilled the five-year service requirement. McCoy thought that most white teachers in New York, for all their protests about supporting civil rights and admiring Martin Luther King, didn't believe in the ability of a black child to learn just as well as a white one.

That was what so excited him about coming to Ocean Hill–Brownsville. The Ocean Hill–Brownsville project was premised on the argument that since the white-dominated educational bureaucracy had failed to teach black children, the black community itself should be given a chance. The central Board of Education had authorized the election of the Ocean Hill–Brownsville local, or "governing," board in July 1967, but then spent most of the 1967–68 school year telling it what it could not do. McCoy had spent the year wrangling with Nauman and the UFT teachers over the local board's powers. The union had objected to the board's choices for principals in the Ocean Hill–Brownsville schools. It had fought curriculum change. It had tried to stop the local board from controlling its own finances. And it had refused to allow the local board to choose its own teaching personnel. McCoy had begged union leaders to be more flexible. They wouldn't listen. He had told Nauman and his colleagues that this was an experiment in *community* control, and if this did not mean control over personnel, finances, and curriculum, what *did* it mean? They didn't understand. The union seemed to go out of its way to throw bureaucratic impediments at him. He was trying to be reasonable, but the white teachers wouldn't meet him halfway.

It was as if they didn't respect him. Perhaps that was it. He didn't have "proper credentials." Most of the sixteen members of the local board were women; many were on welfare. Nauman and the union didn't think they were "professional" enough. Or, maybe they just weren't white enough, perhaps that was the problem. In any case, a few days before, McCoy and the local board had decided to do something about it. They had met and made a list of the educators in the district who were the most hostile to community control. Nauman was one of them; so were eighteen others, many conspicuously active in the UFT. McCoy and the local board had drafted a letter ordering each out of the Ocean Hill–Brownsville district. They would run the schools in their community—not the union, the central Board of Education, or anyone else. The letter, which Fred Nauman was reading in the principal's office that morning, would see to that. And white people would respect them; the letter would see to that as well. Back at his office Rhody McCoy sat at his desk, puffed on his pipe, and waited for all hell to break loose.

The Ocean Hill–Brownsville school controversy, which began in earnest with Rhody McCoy's letter to Fred Nauman on May 9, 1968, was at its core the story of black and white New Yorkers who spoke different languages to each other, like strangers. Unlike many accounts of the civil rights movement during the 1960s, it offers few clear-cut heroes or villains. In a sense, this story is all the more troubling for its lack of a clear moral compass. The Ocean Hill–Brownsville controversy showed black and white New Yorkers to be profoundly at odds over the very shape and definition of human relations in the city. What did "racism" mean? What was "equality"? What cultural values would prevail in a "pluralistic" city? What did it mean to be "middle-class"? And, more broadly, what principles would govern the distribution of resources in a "fair," "just" city?[3]

The differences between blacks and whites over these questions that surfaced at Ocean Hill–Brownsville were not the work of unscrupulous demagogues or racial racketeers: they were too deep-seated and heartfelt for this. They would affect New York's social and class relations, electoral alignments, fiscal policies, labor negotiations, and political culture for decades to come. Indeed, they echo in the life of the city today. The idea that blacks and whites view the same circumstances and events in different ways is now something of a commonplace. Ocean Hill–Brownsville's historical significance for New York lies in the fact that this perceptual gulf first came into the open there, shaking a city that prided itself on its tolerance, open-mindedness, and humane liberalism.

It is also significant that New York's white population discovered at Ocean Hill–Brownsville that they and the city's black community were speaking different languages. Whites like Fred Nauman were genuinely shocked to find this to be the case. Nauman and thousands of white middle-class New Yorkers like him espoused a liberalism that was integrationist, cosmopolitan, and humanist. It assumed that a consensus existed in New York City built around a set of basic principles held by both blacks and whites: individualism within a broadly pluralistic setting, equality of opportunity, and a race-blind, meritocratic approach to the distribution of societal rewards. But Ocean Hill–Brownsville revealed a black community that was deeply ambivalent about those values. Indeed, many in that community—including many middle-class blacks—viewed them as fraudulent and hypocritical in their practical application. At Ocean Hill–Brownsville, blacks punished white New Yorkers for assuming they both believed in the same things, and for attempting to do their thinking for them. There was no consensus in New York in 1968—Ocean Hill–Brownsville made that abundantly clear to a shocked white community.

The anger with which whites reacted to this discovery had far-reaching consequences for race and class relations in the city. Politically, it led to a fundamental electoral realignment. For decades, New York's politics had been defined largely by a rivalry between Jews and Catholics. As recently as 1963, this rivalry had been one of the major themes of Glazer and Moynihan's seminal *Beyond the Melting Pot,* where they argued that "there is probably a wider gap between Jews and Catholics in New York today than in the days of Al Smith."[4] New York City's reputation as perhaps the nation's quintessential liberal city rested on a political alliance of Jews, blacks, and white Protestants arrayed against conservative Irish and Italian Catholics. During the bitter "regular vs. reform" battles of the 1950s and early 1960s, Jewish political acumen and electoral muscle were crucial in bringing down the Tammany Hall machine that had symbolized Catholic political power for almost a century.

Jewish-Catholic divisions during this period were rooted in culture, in sharply contrasting worldviews. Glazer and Moynihan described the two groups as separated by "two value systems": a secular, rationalist "Jewish" ethos, and a traditionalist, religious-based "Catholic" counterpart.[5] There seemed little chance, at the height of this rivalry in the early 1960s, of accommodation between the two. Yet, thanks in large part to the events of the Ocean Hill–Brownsville crisis, this is exactly what occurred.[6] By 1970, so-called "outer-borough" Jews—middle- and lower middle-class Jews residing outside of Manhattan—had bridged what only a few years before had appeared to be insurmountable political and cultural differences with white Catholics. Ocean Hill–Brownsville brought an end to the ambivalence of outer-borough Jews as to the extent and nature of their "white" identity, and they now viewed themselves almost wholly in "white" terms. Outer-borough Jews and white Catholics had begun to forge a race-based alliance that would shift the electoral politics of the city rightward. It would provide a popular mandate for the municipal spending reductions of New York's fiscal crisis of 1975–82 that disproportionately impacted the city's black community.

Before the Ocean Hill–Brownsville crisis, the city's political landscape was customarily described as a pluralistic mix of race, ethnicity, religion, and class.[7] Afterwards, Glazer and Moynihan observed in their rueful introduction to the 1970 edition of *Beyond the Melting Pot* that "race has exploded to swallow up all other distinctions." Ocean Hill–Brownsville destroyed the myth of New York as a pluralistic city; its identity now lay in stark shades of black and white. While "Jewish" and "Catholic" value systems still existed, they were now of secondary importance: "black" and "white" frames of reference had superseded them. Ocean Hill–Brownsville, which Glazer and Moynihan described as "the great divide in race relations in New York," had redefined the city's political and cultural landscape.[8]

The "black" and "white" perspectives or languages that the events of the Ocean Hill–Brownsville controversy illuminated clashed in three important respects. First, the controversy was the occasion for an angry debate between black and white educators over the operative definitions of the words "equality" and "racism" in the context of the city's public education system. The two groups offered sharply divergent explanations for the low level of academic achievement among black students, as well as for the relatively low number of black teachers and administrators in the system. The hostility of black educators like Rhody McCoy toward Fred Nauman and his white colleagues was fueled by their antipathy to the civil service examination system under which white teachers had advanced their careers. The attack by black educators on this system was, in effect, an argument for a definition of "equality" and "racism" that was institutionally based and results-oriented. The defense of the examination apparatus by white teachers as a guarantor of "color-blind merit" was emblematic of another, more individuated, understanding of these terms.

Ocean Hill–Brownsville was also the site of a dispute between black and white educators over the shape and definition of "pluralism" in city life. This dispute centered around different approaches to the teaching of black history in the city's pubic schools. Black teachers, notably those associated with the radical African-American Teachers Association, mounted a challenge to a UFT-endorsed treatment that sought to locate blacks within the historical trajectories of white immigrants, and generally, to downplay the consequences of group difference. Their challenge offered instead a radicalized version of pluralism, in which group identity—especially racial group identity—was accorded primary, formalized recognition, and which viewed groups, not individuals, as the defining units of American society.

Finally, the Ocean Hill–Brownsville controversy was the venue for a critique by black educators of the culture and values associated with the middle class in New York, notably individualism, competition, and materialism. The critique sought to link these values specifically to whites in the city, and generally, to the idea of "whiteness," in a significant departure from past practice. Black educators attempted to replace this "white middle-class" culture with an alternative one based on what they saw as traditional "black" values: mutuality, cooperation and community. Many whites, however, viewed this not as a search for a uniquely "black" middle-class culture, but as a rejection of middle-class values in their entirety. Once again, whites and blacks were divided in their understandings of and reactions to the same terms and ideas.

The Ocean Hill–Brownsville controversy, then, was about much more than whether Rhody McCoy, a black educator, could fire Fred Nauman, a white one. It was about how blacks and whites, with markedly different ideas about what equality, pluralism, and being "middle-class" meant, fought for their visions of a fair and just city, and what their different languages meant for the politics and culture of the city in the 1970s and beyond. Ocean Hill–Brownsville did not itself create "two New Yorks"—one black, one white, divided politically, socially, and culturally. It was, however, their most visible, palpable symbol.

Its significance lies in this symbolic quality, as a destroyer of illusions. Until Ocean Hill–Brownsville, many New Yorkers, especially whites, believed in New York as an exercise in cosmopolitan humanism, a pluralistic city broadly integrated along racial, ethnic, and religious lines. Indeed, by the early 1960s, this had become something of a civic mantra, to the point that Glazer and Moynihan, themselves pluralists, felt constrained to warn in *Beyond the Melting Pot* that New Yorkers still retained strong elements of provincialism and tribalism, and that the city was not a cosmopolitan paradise. But nothing they might have written could have prepared New York for the shock of Ocean Hill–Brownsville, and the discovery of the magnitude of the gulf that separated blacks and whites. Before Ocean Hill–Brownsville, Glazer and Moynihan argued that there were many New Yorks, and not just one. In its wake, as blacks and whites spoke past each other, it was clear that they had miscalculated: there were two.

To understand why a letter written to a junior high school science teacher in Brooklyn had such far-reaching consequences for New York City, then, it is necessary to understand how the two New Yorks the letter symbolized came to exist. During the two decades following World War II, the demographics, class structure, and economic base of New York City underwent profound shifts which affected blacks and whites in markedly different ways. By the mid-1960s, these shifts had created two distinct worlds in the city: a white one that was upwardly mobile, educationally successful, and culturally dominant, and a black one that was geographically isolated, economically undeveloped, educationally unsuccessful, and culturally marginalized. The road leading to Rhody McCoy's letter to Fred Nauman began with the creation of these racial worlds, and these two New Yorks.

1

TWO NEW YORKS

New York City, 1945–1965

In 1945, New York was a blue-collar, working-class city. In 1965, it was a white-collar, middle-class one. The economic, social, and cultural divisions that eventually caused the Ocean Hill–Brownsville conflict had their roots in this elemental shift. The face of New York changed profoundly in this twenty-year period; in many ways, it became a new city. New York's economic base shifted from manufacturing to service industries. Its corporate, financial, real estate, legal, insurance, and banking sectors boomed, expanding white-collar employment opportunities. The city spent prodigiously on state services, creating thousands of new government jobs. And government housing policies spurred an upsurge in the construction of middle-income rental and cooperative apartment units both in Manhattan and the outer boroughs of the city. This shift created a new middle class in New York. It was composed largely of those from working-class and impoverished backgrounds, who were the first in their families to work in a coat and tie. But New Yorkers did not share these new opportunities equally. The city's new middle class was composed primarily of whites, not blacks. The uneven black and white rates of participation in this process of middle-class formation between 1945 and 1965 would create the two New Yorks that the Ocean Hill–Brownsville controversy symbolized.

In 1945, New York City was the premier industrial city in the United States. It had more manufacturing jobs than any other American city; in fact, it had more such jobs than any two other American cities combined.[1] This industrial preeminence did not immediately meet the eye, however, overshadowed as it was by the city's reputation as an intellectual and cultural center. New York had no single dominant industry, equivalent to steel in Pittsburgh or automobiles in Detroit. Instead the city boasted thousands of relatively small, decentralized factories in a variety of fields—apparel, printing, small machinery, toys, and paper products, among others.

These industries were housed in buildings which often did not resemble "factories" in the commonly accepted sense. They were not self-contained and surrounded by fences and parking lots, but rather tenement-style buildings intermixed with residential housing and office buildings. Often, an industrial building contained a series of manufacturers in unrelated fields, reducing efficiency and snarling traffic on narrow city cross-streets.[2] While dirty, unsightly, and environmentally hazardous, these multistory factories provided employment to over a million New Yorkers, approximately 40 percent of the city's total working population.[3] Moreover, the vast majority of these jobs required little or no education. A New York City high school dropout in 1945 had options in semiskilled or unskilled employment—grueling, repetitive, and sometimes dangerous, to be sure—but viable employment nonetheless. Thousands of such dropouts poured into the city's economy each year, riding subways to midtown and downtown Manhattan, where many of these jobs were located.

Outsiders may have misapprehended New York's status as a manufacturing center, but city leaders did not. They took measures to protect and encourage industry, including keeping subway fares low to expedite the flow of workers to their jobs, and exercising a relative leniency in zoning practices that made downtown Manhattan an anarchic mix of factories, offices, and apartments.[4] New York City in 1945 may well have been an urban planner's nightmare, but for a man without an education who worked with his hands, it was a relatively hospitable place.[5] It was no workers' paradise, to be sure, but it was unquestionably a thriving working-class city.

All this changed after World War II, as the city's economy shifted from a reliance on manufacturing and port activities to one based on the provision of services. Municipal leaders began to view the tenement buildings that housed small factories as hazardous eyesores that destroyed the ambience of the city. The years after 1945 in New York were dominated by urban renewal.[6] High-rise office buildings and white-collar employees began to replace tenement factories and working-class New Yorkers. These were also years in which centralization as an operational and philosophical tenet of municipal governance went virtually unchallenged in city life. In this view, a decentralized series of small factories scattered around downtown Manhattan made no sense. They were "in the way," as were, for that matter, neighborhoods anywhere in New York that stood in the path of the city's new direction. Between 1945 and 1965, the man who did the most to bring this new vision of the city to fruition was Robert Moses.

Moses wielded unprecedented power during this period. He served at various times — and often simultaneously — as chairman of the Triborough Bridge and Tunnel Authority, head of the Mayor's Committee on Slum Clearance, City Parks Commissioner, and New York City Coordinator of Construction.[7] Moses' vision was that of an efficient and clean city that offered a high quality of life to its residents. "Quality of life," to Moses, meant most of all the absence of "slums," whether residential or commercial. Moses' New York would be a city of office buildings, not factories; of white-collar jobs, not blue. Under his influence, midtown New York underwent a high-rise office building construction boom in the late 1940s and 1950s. During this time, the city became the corporate headquarters of the world.[8] Changes in zoning regulations, subsidies, and tax incentives spurred private real estate construction. This public-private partnership changed the landscape of the city. High-rise offices, hospitals, university buildings, and cultural centers replaced tenement apartments and factories.[9]

More than just the city's physical landscape changed as a result of Moses' vision. The manufacturing jobs provided by the tenement factories began to disappear or relocate, replaced by those connected with the "service" industries housed by the new developments. Between 1945 and the early 1970s, New York lost almost half of its jobs in the manufacturing sector.[10] During roughly the same period, it added approximately 350,000 white-collar jobs.[11] Employment in finance, insurance, and real estate grew by almost 30 percent during the 1960s, with the securities industry alone adding 60,000 jobs.[12] Unlike those they replaced, these white-collar jobs required education — high school at a minimum, and often more.

The other growth industry in New York during the two decades following World War II was government. The city bureaucracy grew steadily, and with it opportunities for employment. The public sector added 155,000 jobs and grew by 38 percent during the 1960s, and by the latter part of the decade New York's proportion of government workers per 10,000 residents was higher than in any other American city except Washington, D.C.[13] Like the jobs created in the private service sector, these civil service jobs had educational prerequisites; most demanded the ability to pass written examinations.

The years between 1945 and 1965, then, saw New York shift from an economy based on manufacturing to one centered around service industries and government.[14] A 1960 Harvard University study of the changing New York economy bore this out. It predicted that the new service-oriented jobs being created in the city would counterbalance those lost in the manufacturing area.[15] Whether this would prove true or not—and the events of the 1970s would certainly call these forecasts into question—it was clear that New York's shift to a postindustrial economy was profoundly affecting class and racial relations in the city. It was, on the one hand, creating an upwardly mobile, mostly white, middle class, positioned by education and training to take advantage of the new opportunities offered by the expanding service and government sectors.[16] On the other hand, the city's growing black population, trapped by de facto residential and educational segregation, failing public schools, and a shrinking unskilled job market, was falling further behind, and separating out into social, political, and cultural isolation. These two parallel trends, both the result of the deindustrialization of New York, would define the racial politics of the city in the 1960s, and eventually lead to the Ocean Hill–Brownsville crisis.

The "new middle class" of New York City's postwar years had three major historical patrons. Fiorello La Guardia, mayor from 1934 to 1945, laid the initial groundwork for the development of this class. La Guardia was a political reformer in the New Deal mode. He established government operating through a centralized bureaucracy as the city's primary service provider, wresting this function from Tammany Hall and its allied political machinery, and paving the way for its eventual demise. La Guardia changed the political culture of the city to one based on the idea of the municipal government as central planner, distributor of resources, and major employer.[17] This last feature was most important to the growth of the city's new middle class after La Guardia's mayoral career ended. La Guardia established a ladder of upward mobility through government employment that thousands of New Yorkers would climb during the post–World War II years.

In addition to helping turn New York into a postindustrial city after 1945, Robert Moses was instrumental in changing its residential face. Moses' primary goal here was to provide housing for middle-class and middle-class–aspiring New Yorkers that was physically separated from that of the poor. His tool for this undertaking was Title I of the Federal Housing Act of 1949, which permitted government assistance to private land developers of "blighted and deteriorated" areas.[18] Moses used subsidies, tax breaks, and other benefits to induce these private developers to raze residential tenements and replace them with middle- and high-income housing. He also supported the Mitchell-Lama cooperative program, which provided subsidized "co-op" housing for middle-income New Yorkers; by the mid-

1960s, some eighty thousand Mitchell-Lama housing units had been constructed in the city.[19]

Robert Moses was a middle-class moralist at heart. He believed that tenement life sapped the respectable, sober virtues essential to middle-class living. He wished to separate the "responsible" working class from what he considered the "undeserving poor" through housing policy. In practice, this meant de facto residential segregation, since Moses essentially viewed the first group as comprising whites, and the latter, blacks. Under Moses, "slum clearance" consisted of constructing apartments for middle-class whites through private firms and shuttling blacks into physically separated public housing projects.[20] His preoccupation with whites and the middle class at the expense of the black poor was never in doubt. In 1966, a typical year, 4,851 low-income, 6,158 Mitchell-Lama, and 21,122 private rental housing units were constructed in the city.[21] Moses has been justly criticized for housing policies that reinforced residential segregation in New York.[22] He did, however, succeed in retaining much of the city's white middle-class population, preventing the mass exodus that befell most large American cities during the postwar years. At a high price—one that many would argue was exorbitantly high—Moses helped keep the new middle class in New York City.

If La Guardia provided the white middle class with jobs, and Moses with housing, Robert F. Wagner, Jr., mayor from 1954 to 1965, offered security and material largesse. Wagner's father, Robert, Sr., had sponsored the National Labor Relations Act in 1935 as senator from New York, and his son resolved to do the same for New York City municipal employees during his tenure. One of his first acts as mayor was to issue an executive order, which, for the first time, gave city workers the right to organize unions. In 1958, Wagner's Executive Order No. 49 awarded collective bargaining rights to these unions.[23] His negotiating posture with them was much more avuncular than confrontational. Wagner counted on municipal unions for political support, and he could usually be relied upon, after some ritual posturing and brinkmanship, to deliver generous wage packages. It was once said of Wagner that if a government employee in Brooklyn awoke with sore feet, the mayor's arches hurt.[24]

The ethnic, religious, and social makeup of the middle class that La Guardia, Moses, and Wagner helped create contrasted sharply with that of its heavily white Anglo-Saxon Protestant prewar predecessor. Largely second-generation Catholic and Jewish and of working-class parentage, its members were often the first in their families to attend college. After World War II, many of the social barriers that had hindered Jewish and Catholic advancement in New York's corporate world began to break down, the casualty of the wave of cultural pluralism that had swept the nation as a whole during the war.[25] Opportunities in government employment, with its examination-based, "objective" hiring criteria, were also expanding. By the early 1960s, when median family income in New York exceeded the national average by 8 percent, the city appeared to be entering a new era, one in which social status and inherited wealth mattered less than at any other time in its history.[26] To the New Yorkers who availed themselves of these heretofore unobtainable opportunities in the corporate and public service spheres, the city seemed to be well on its way to becoming a true meritocracy. To them, New York was an essentially fair place in which to live and work. It rewarded education, knowledge, and expertise, not group origins or personal connections, and promised opportunity and advancement to those who worked for it.

Perhaps no group better epitomized the city's postwar new middle class and its values than its public school teachers. Most were Jewish or Catholic, and educated either at one of the tuition-free city colleges or on the GI Bill.[27] They were the beneficiaries of the vast increases in government spending in public education in New York after World War II. Between 1948 and 1965, annual municipal spending on the city's public schools more than quadrupled, from $250 million to $1.1 billion, despite only a small increase in total student enrollment.[28] In the early 1960s alone, the number of educational personnel hired rose by almost 60 percent.[29] By the mid-1960s, per pupil expenditures in the New York public schools exceeded that of virtually every other major American city, and most suburban systems.[30] Thanks to this upsurge in available funds, the aura of flush times surrounded New York's public education system in the decades after World War II.

This had not always been the case. The New York City public schools were brought under the jurisdiction of a centralized, citywide Board of Education in 1898, after a failed half-century experiment with local, ward-based governance which became notorious for the buying and selling of teaching jobs, ethnic favoritism, and other forms of machine-based political corruption.[31] The Board of Education moved in the early part of the twentieth century to bring public educational personnel into the civil service framework, through the establishment of a Board of Examiners charged with developing objective written tests for available openings. This practice, however, did not fully take hold until the advent of the Great Depression, when, with teaching jobs in New York at a premium, virtually all positions were brought under the Board of Examiners rubric and made subject to competitive examinations. With the post–World War II upsurge in funding and job availability for public education in the city, the system opened up to Jews and non-Irish Catholics, who used Board of Examiners tests to end the Irish dominance that had prevailed since the early 1900s. Jews were particularly successful;

between 1940 and 1960, 60 percent of all new public school teachers in New York were Jewish.[32]

Teacher labor relations in New York were fragmented until 1960, when the UFT brought together some seventy separate teacher organizations into one bargaining unit. The UFT was an idea whose time had clearly come, thanks in large measure to Wagner's liberalization of New York's municipal labor policy during the 1950s. In addition, the teacher glut of the 1930s had become a relative shortage by 1960, and teachers who had previously feared for their jobs were now more secure and confident. The UFT obtained a representation election in 1961, and after it had been chosen as the teachers' collective bargaining agent, struck successfully for a contract in 1962. Thanks to the UFT, the 1960s were years of unprecedented gains for New York's public school teachers. The union negotiated contracts that raised salaries, reduced required workloads, provided for generous medical and pension benefits, and placed restrictions on involuntary reassignments of teachers to "undesirable" schools.[33]

By the mid-1960s, New York's public school teachers worked at jobs that Fiorello La Guardia had helped create, belonged to a powerful union that Robert Wagner had helped nurture, and quite possibly, lived in housing units that Robert Moses had helped construct. Fred Nauman—a child of poverty, the first member of his family to attend college, a charter UFT member, a beneficiary of the civil service examination system, and a resident of a middle-income, largely white neighborhood—may have best symbolized the New York public school teacher as member of the city's new middle class. For him, as for this class as a whole, New York appeared to "work." But this was only one face of the city.

The second great black migration to New York began during World War II, a result, as in the case of other major cities, of the curtailment of the sharecropping system due to the policies of the Agricultural Adjustment Administration, the mechanization of southern agriculture, and the job opportunities offered by war-connected industries in the North. In 1940, blacks had constituted only 6 percent of the population of New York. By 1950, this proportion had grown to 9 percent, by 1960 to 14 percent, and by the time of the Ocean Hill–Brownsville dispute in 1968, to 20 percent.[34] Brooklyn's black population increased sixfold between 1940 and 1970, from 4 to 25 percent of the borough's residents, as over five hundred thousand African-Americans in-migrated.[35] Southern blacks were drawn to New York, as white immigrants had been decades earlier, by the possibility of obtaining unskilled or low-skilled industrial jobs for which a formal education was not a prerequisite. But the black immigrants, unlike the earlier white ones, fell victim to the transformations that were taking place in the city's economy. With New York's industrial sector contracting, the jobs they sought were increasingly unavailable.[36] The areas of the city's economy that were expanding—white-collar service and government—demanded education and training, which most of the relocating black population did not possess.[37] During a period in which unprecedented opportunities for upward mobility were becoming available to the children of working-class whites in the city, most blacks found themselves on the wrong side of a seismic economic shift.[38]

Black economic vulnerability led in turn to geographic, political, and educational isolation from white society. Thanks in large measure to the policies of Robert Moses, options for housing were limited. Typically, black movement to the fringes of heretofore white neighborhoods would stimulate white withdrawal, leaving the area to the expanding black population. From that point on, the construction of segregated public housing projects and the practices of "blockbusting" (the use by real estate firms of racial fear among white homeowners to stimulate panic selling at depressed prices) and "redlining" (the refusal by banks to issue mortgages and loans to blacks for properties in white areas) completed the geographic containment of the city's black community. Many black elected officials, concerned with retaining a compact power base, contested this result only rhetorically.[39] Opportunities for interracial coalitions against residential segregation and other forms of discrimination, moreover, were limited during the 1950s by the excesses of anticommunism; black leaders were reluctant to ally with white liberals and leftists tainted by "Red" innuendo. Cut off as it was from crucial sources of support, the black community's political marginalization deepened.[40]

Residential segregation led in turn to educational segregation. By 1964, the average black student in New York attended a school that was over 90 percent nonwhite.[41] While the central Board of Education did not shortchange black-majority schools in terms of funding, spending as much on them as on white schools, two crucial characteristics distinguished the two: the number of experienced teachers and class size.

Although some experienced teachers voluntarily chose to work in black schools, the vast majority did not, transferring out as soon as possible. The UFT negotiated a "five year rule" governing the situation, under which teachers accumulating five years of service in any school could transfer. In practice, this stripped black-majority schools of teachers just as they were beginning to mature professionally. Moreover, the UFT leadership, pressed by its members, successfully opposed involuntary transfer of experienced teachers to black-majority schools, and even the idea of incentive bonuses known colloquially as "combat pay" to attract such teachers.[42] The result was a group of teachers in black-majority schools with a significantly lower level of professional qualifications than those in white areas, a disadvantage that could not be overcome by the idealism and enthusiasm of inexperienced educators.[43]

The other major disadvantage faced by black pupils in New York's public schools was large class size. The great number of black migrants to the city, combined with de facto residential segregation, created overcrowded conditions in black-majority schools that contrasted sharply with those in white schools. Between 1957 and 1967, the percentage of blacks in the public schools almost doubled, from 17.5 to 33.5 percent, while some 130,000 white pupils left the city system. This resulted in overcrowding in black-majority schools and relative underutilization of some white-majority schools.[44] Classes in black areas sometimes had as many as 55 pupils, a number that would have been unheard of in white-majority schools.

By the early 1960s, New York effectively had a dual public school system. In its "white" system, presided over by a cohort of experienced teachers, students read at or above the national average, and won a disproportionate number of National Merit and Westinghouse Science scholarships. In the "black" system, pupils in crowded classrooms, receiving instruction from teachers who were learning on the job, read an average of two years behind the city's white students, and dropped out of school at a rate double that of the city as a whole.[45] At a time when full participation in the economic life of the city was coming to depend ever more critically on educational achievement, New York's public schools were essentially predetermining outcomes based on race.

The Ocean Hill–Brownsville section itself symbolized the economic, geographic, political and educational isolation of New York's black community after World War II. Located in east-central Brooklyn, about eight miles from midtown Manhattan, the neighborhood had never been well-to-do. It was settled in the early 1900s, after the construction of the Williamsburg Bridge made it accessible, by Jewish and Italian immigrants seeking inexpensive living quarters from which to commute to jobs in Manhattan. Over the next half-century, it would become known as a birthplace of writers and intellectuals (Alfred Kazin, Norman Podhoretz, and Henry Roth, among others), community institutions (the Brownsville Boys Club, a pioneer in antidelinquency initiatives), and legendary criminals (the notorious Murder, Inc.).[46] Ocean Hill–Brownsville was predominantly white until the mid-1950s, when blacks from the adjoining neighborhood of Bedford-Stuyvesant, itself straining for space due to in-migration from the South, began to move in.[47] By the late 1950s, approximately twelve hundred blacks per month, from Bedford-Stuyvesant and directly from the South, were taking up residence in Ocean Hill–Brownsville.[48]

White flight followed swiftly. By the mid-1960s, the neighborhood's population was 95 percent nonwhite.[49] The new residents moved into the tenements and row houses formerly occupied by the departed whites, as well as a series of public housing projects constructed by the city as much to enforce residential segregation as to relieve overcrowding.[50] An informal "redline" border soon developed on Linden Boulevard, which separated Ocean Hill–Brownsville from the white middle-class neighborhood of Canarsie to the south. An unspoken assumption existed among Canarsie residents that blacks from Ocean Hill–Brownsville would not be permitted to move across Linden Boulevard in appreciable numbers; the economics of the rental and home market in this middle-income area did much of their work for them.[51] By the mid-1960s, Ocean Hill–Brownsville was for all intents and purposes geographically cut off from white New York.

Ocean Hill–Brownsville was self-contained, but it was not self-sufficient. It did not have many of the attributes of a "community," due to its relatively rapid shift in racial composition.[52] In the mid-1960s, only 40 percent of Ocean Hill–Brownsville residents had lived there for five years or more. Less than a fifth had been born in New York, an indication of the Southern roots of much of its population. There was relatively little home ownership.[53] There were also few established neighborhood institutions, again because of the recent arrival of most of its residents. Politically, it was dominated by Samuel Wright, a state assemblyman on friendly terms with the Brooklyn Democratic regular organization, who used Ocean Hill–Brownsville's low rate of voter participation to remain in power.[54] Although Wright paid lip service to the need for residential integration in New York, Ocean Hill–Brownsville's isolation actually worked to his benefit by furnishing a geographically compact and racially homogeneous electoral base. He knew any disturbance of the racial status quo could harm his political prospects, and conducted himself accordingly.

The relatively modest number of government patronage jobs Wright was able to dole out to reward his supporters, moreover, symbolized the economic isolation of Ocean Hill–Brownsville. By the early 1960s, these jobs, minor as they were, constituted one of its few sources of employment. Ocean Hill–Brownsville had never been economically self-sustaining; most of the whites who inhabited it until the 1950s worked in blue-collar jobs located outside its boundaries. But the neighborhood did have many small, locally owned businesses—retail stores, produce markets, and restaurants—along its main thoroughfares. Soon after the black migration to Ocean Hill–Brownsville began, however, the owners of these businesses moved out with most of the white population. The black newcomers lacked the capital, access to credit, and entrepreneurial experience to take over their operation, and by the mid-1960s the neighborhood's streets were lined with abandoned storefronts. The newly arrived residents of Ocean Hill–Brownsville were thus doubly isolated from the mainstream economy, unable to participate in either the local small business sector or the growing white-collar area that was serving as a route to upward mobility for so many white New Yorkers. And even government employment—except for friends of Samuel Wright—was, before the advent of the War on Poverty, primarily a matter of passing civil service examinations, which hinged on education and training that the newcomers in large measure did not possess.

Ocean Hill–Brownsville's social ills were a by-product of its boxed-in economic status. A contemporary observer was blunt: "Brownsville has no middle class. . . . There are no resident doctors, no resident lawyers; Negroes own less than 1 percent of the businesses."[55] "The great majority of Brownsville's citizens are poor persons who attempt to eke out a subsistence through a combination of welfare payments and temporary work," wrote another. Its welfare rate was twice the city average, and three-quarters of its population received some form of public assistance.[56] Only 16 percent of its residents worked in white-collar occupations.[57] Its unemployment rate was 17 percent, five times the city average; for young males, the rate was 36 percent.[58] Its crime, drug addiction, and out-of-wedlock birth rates were also among the highest in New York City. Most disturbing of all, however, in view of the city's changing economic structure, were conditions in Ocean Hill–Brownsville's eight public schools.

The neighborhood's flagship school, Junior High School 271, was typical. 271 was built in 1963 in response to the increased number of school-age children moving to the neighborhood as it changed in racial composition. Behind its modern facade lay a host of educational problems. Reading and math scores were among the lowest in the city, with 73 percent of its pupils below grade level in reading and 85 percent in math.[59] In a typical graduating class, only 2 percent went on to one of the city's specialized high schools, which required applicants to pass written entrance examinations and served as feeders to major universities and the city colleges.[60]

Since approximately one-third of Ocean Hill–Brownsville residents moved out of the neighborhood each year, the student population was highly transient; often there was as much as a 50 percent turnover among the pupils between September and June of an academic year.[61] Discipline was poor, with a rising number of assaults on teachers and acts of vandalism. Most teachers assigned to the school as their first job in the public system put their time in and transferred out at the first opportunity. Whether through the fault of disengaged teachers (as Ocean Hill–Brownsville parents charged), or uninvolved students and parents (as many teachers charged), it was clear that education of a very different sort was taking place in Ocean Hill–Brownsville and the white-majority schools of the city. Given the new requirements for economic success in New York, the potential consequences of this dichotomy were obvious, and ominous.

By the mid-1960s, then, Ocean Hill–Brownsville symbolized the isolation of dozens of poor black communities throughout New York City: geographically segregated, economically stagnant, politically weak, and educationally marginalized. It also symbolized the two New Yorks that had developed out of the economic and social changes that had swept the city over the preceding twenty years. The rival cultures that would grow out of these two New Yorks—one black and poor, the other white and middle-class, each with its own approach to and understanding of conditions and events in the city—would play a major role both in causing the Ocean Hill–Brownsville controversy, and in ensuring that it would continue to separate blacks and whites in New York for decades to come. They would cause Fred Nauman and Rhody McCoy, as well as countless other black and white New Yorkers, divided over understandings of equality, pluralism, and the content of "middle-class" values, to speak past each other.

It was fitting that the New York public school system would serve as the main battleground of this struggle. The crucial role education would play as a means of advancement—as a commodity—in the city's new economy was lost on neither blacks nor whites. Black leaders understood that education provided the only opportunity for their people to break out of their isolation in city life. Middle-class whites viewed it as the key element in their own enhanced status. The public education system, then, was a logical place for the two New Yorks to collide.

It is ironic that, for all their differences, both whites and blacks would be motivated by the same impulse during this battle: the defense of "community." This evocative word, at various times, animated every actor in the Ocean Hill–Brownsville controversy. Citizens of both New Yorks would turn to it as a weapon and a shield, for self-definition and self-protection, as they struggled over control of the educational system and the rules governing political, social, and cultural life in the city. "Community" would lead Rhody McCoy to write his letter to Fred Nauman, and, during the events of the Ocean Hill–Brownsville controversy itself, serve as a powerful symbol of black aspiration in New York. But it would be the city's white "community" that would have the last word on this subject, in an ending neither McCoy nor Nauman could have anticipated on May 9, 1968.

2

THE RISE OF "COMMUNITY"

The word "community" is a chameleon on the American ideological landscape. It is both liberal and conservative, an agent for both systemic change and the status quo. It is morally neutral, bending to the will of its master. During the 1960s and early 1970s, as blacks and whites in New York struggled over control of the city's public education system, it cast a powerful spell on both.

"Community" served first as the means by which white parents in the city's outer boroughs defeated efforts by civil rights activists to integrate the public schools. In response to white "neighborhood school" rhetoric, erstwhile school integration supporters changed direction and themselves took up the call for neighborhood control of schools and other local institutions in black areas, employing a new name: "community control." This challenge to the white teachers who worked in these schools, and to middle-class whites generally in the city, would climax in the Ocean Hill–Brownsville controversy itself, in 1968. Here, community control supporters would be joined by a set of allies with their own agendas—government, business, and foundation elites hoping to use it as a means of preserving social stability, as well as New Left–influenced intellectuals attracted by community control's link to participatory democracy.

Finally, during the early 1970s, middle-class, outer borough whites would turn the rhetoric of "community" they had heard at Ocean Hill–Brownsville in 1968 to their own uses, employing it to defeat busing and the construction of low-income housing projects in their neighborhoods. "Community" had traveled full circle on the ideological spectrum, from right to left and then right again. Those who had supported community control during the Ocean Hill–Brownsville crisis had not anticipated the possibility of more conservative uses of "community," and attacked the conversion of "their" doctrine to the purposes of the Right. But whether "fair" or not, whites were merely treading a path used by both the Right and the Left throughout American history. For all of community control's resonance in black areas such as Ocean Hill–Brownsville, whites in New York would be much more successful in making it their own.

In capturing control of this elusive idea, whites taught civil rights supporters in New York a painful, unanticipated lesson about the ideological malleability of "community" in city life. The events of the Ocean Hill–Brownsville controversy would ultimately force them into an untenable argument: that community control was the sole property of poor blacks and "progressive" whites, and that more conservative whites were not entitled to use it. Ocean Hill–Brownsville's ironic legacy was a civil rights movement in New York trapped by one of its own basic tenets.

The landmark 1954 Supreme Court decision in *Brown v. Board of Education,* which launched the first sustained, citywide effort to integrate the New York public school system, was as important for its line of reasoning as for its specific holding. By accepting the research of social psychologist Kenneth Clark showing that physical separation from whites produced lasting feelings of inferiority in black children, the court established the rationale for the school desegregation movement in New York, as well as for other northern cities, for the next decade. Only a few months after *Brown,* in December 1954, the New York City Board of Education issued a statement endorsing the Supreme Court's reasoning, stating that school segregation "damages the personalities" of black pupils.[1] But Linda Brown had asked only to attend her neighborhood school in Topeka; de facto residential segregation in New York made the achievement of *Brown's* objectives immensely more complicated. The idea that black children—no matter where they actually lived—needed to attend school with white children in order to receive equal educational opportunity, became the central tenet of civil rights activists in New York, including Clark himself, a City College professor.

After the *Brown* decision, under pressure from these activists, the New York City Board of Education unveiled a series of plans with the stated aim of placing black and white children in the same schools and classrooms. All failed. New York's schools were more segregated in 1966 than they had been in 1954. Each new initiative fell before counterattacks mounted by organizations of white parents, which melded a complex set of emotions—class anger, economic concerns, and simple racism—into the rallying cry of the "neighborhood school." The most significant of these groups was the Queens-based Parents and Taxpayers (PAT), which, between 1963 and 1965, a time when the flame of the city's school desegregation movement burned brightest, showed how a "community" could control its destiny, even in one of the most centralized cities and educational systems in the nation. PAT, however, may have been too successful by half; by 1966, its example would inspire its opponents in the city's civil rights movement to launch the campaign for community control of schools in black neighborhoods that climaxed at Ocean Hill–Brownsville.

The idea of community-based, grassroots organizing in New York was not new, of course, but it was not a particularly successful one until the 1960s. Community groups seeking to "fight City Hall" in New York after World War II faced a forbidding municipal bureaucratic apparatus whose inflexibility was often the stuff of legend. Emblematic was the attempt of a tenants' group in the East Tremont section of the Bronx between 1952 and 1954 to defeat Robert Moses's plan to construct a section of the Cross-Bronx Expressway through their neighborhood. Although the alternate route the group proposed would have shifted the route of the highway by only a few blocks, through a lightly populated area, their protest went nowhere. Stonewalled by Moses, elected officials, and the municipal bureaucracy, the East Tremont tenants were forced out of their homes.[2]

This culture of centralization may have been more entrenched in New York's public education system than anywhere else in the city. By the early 1960s, the system had become a classic example of top-heavy bureaucracy. Central Board of Education headquarters at 110 Livingston Street in Brooklyn housed some four thousand administrators, more than any other school system in the nation, and, indeed, more than the New York State Department of Education in Albany, which nominally governed it.[3] Virtually every educational policy decision emanated from "110 Livingston." It mandated curriculum, hired and assigned teachers, and determined budgets. Local school boards, having lost their substantive power when the New York City school system was centralized early in the twentieth century, existed in name only. Every requisition from an individual school, no matter how routine, was routed through central headquarters. Horror stories abounded. In one school, teachers ordered a movable blackboard for a special project. It arrived two and a half years later. Another school's library, unable to use fifteen hundred books because there were no shelves on which to place them, wrote to 110 Livingston requesting order forms for the shelves. Central headquarters replied that the forms could only be requested with yet another form—which was unavailable.[4]

PAT, then, appeared to be facing a formidable adversary in its fight to prevent the integration of the New York City public schools. But the Board of Education had exploitable weaknesses. All bureaucracies are cumbersome and slow-moving, but as one of the largest in the country, 110 Livingston was especially so. Board of Education files were replete with stacks of memoranda, minutes of countless meetings, and reams of correspondence—all concerning programs and projects that never saw the light of day. The Board of Education never had a leader like Robert Moses, who, for better or worse, got things done. Thus, a neighborhood group with the patience and determination to remain "in the way" for long enough could, like a judo practitioner, use the Board's size and weight against it. PAT employed this strategy successfully between 1963 and 1965, as it forced the wheels of the school integration movement in New York to grind to a halt.

The central figure in the effort to end segregation in New York's public schools during the decade after *Brown,* and PAT's main adversary, was the Reverend Milton Galamison. A graduate of Princeton Theological Seminary and one of the relatively few black Presbyterian ministers in the city, the Brooklyn-based Galamison began his struggle for integration soon after the *Brown* decision. In 1960, after three years as head of the Brooklyn chapter of the NAACP, he founded the Parents' Workshop for Equality in New York City Schools, an interracial organization of pro-integration activists from around the city, including many with ties to the Communist Party and pacifist groups.[5] Galamison was a radical egalitarian, who argued during this period that educational equality could not exist without racial integration. He did not seek compensatory education programs in isolated black communities. He demanded that blacks and whites be placed in physical proximity to each other, both in the city's schools, and—just as important in view of the prevalent system of "tracking" that separated out "slow" black pupils—in the classrooms themselves. Ultimately, he wished to see the ratio of blacks to whites in each of New York's individual school districts correspond to that in the city school system as a whole. To achieve this goal, he advocated a number of mechanisms. Whites might be convinced of the moral force of the arguments for desegregation and move their children voluntarily. That failing, the Board of Education might redraw school district lines to encompass adjoining black and white neighborhoods. But Galamison did not put much faith in these remedies. Ultimately, he believed, large-scale, involuntary shifts of populations, through busing, would be needed to achieve his goals.

Galamison and his allies gained an initial measure of success in 1960 when, prodded by his threat of a black student boycott of the city's schools, the Board of Education adopted an "Open Enrollment" integration plan.[6] Under the plan, black children from seriously overcrowded schools would be permitted to attend a selected number of underutilized white-majority schools. Open Enrollment was an entirely voluntary program, involving no transfers of white pupils. Thus, for Galamison, it represented only a first step toward his goal of complete integration, and he continued to press the Board of Education for stronger measures.

The record of participation in the program, however, might have given him pause. Between 1960 and 1966, only about 5 percent of the eligible black pupils availed themselves of the opportunity to transfer to white-majority schools under the Open Enrollment program.[7] Some black parents were quoted as charging that busing gave their children "the feeling that to receive anything good you must leave Negro neighborhoods." "[T]he parents," an observer noted, "believe that the effort should be placed primarily on quality of education in the local schools," and were "not as interested in busing as they are in improving the neighborhood schools."[8]

Undoubtedly, the Board of Education's inability or unwillingness to properly publicize the Open Enrollment program helped cause the low level of participation in it.[9] Although white parents complained more about the possible busing out of their children than the arrival of a limited number of bused-in black pupils under Open Enrollment, Board administrators feared their reaction and moved with their usual caution. But the program did receive favorable mention in the city's newspapers, as well as publicity from Galamison and his allies in the civil rights community. There was undeniably an element of conscious, voluntary choice in the failure of black parents to take advantage of the Open Enrollment program in appreciable numbers. To some degree, the city's civil rights leadership and the average black parent worked at cross-purposes during this period. While the former pressed ahead with a campaign to integrate the public schools as an end in itself, many of the latter implicitly questioned the central assumption of that campaign: that black children needed their white counterparts to avoid the stigma of inferiority. In so doing, they were expressing, at least implicitly, a preference for the community-centered approach to education that would prevail in black neighborhoods after 1965. In this instance, then, the city's black population may well have been ahead of its own leadership. At the very least, the tepid reaction of black parents to the Open Enrollment program in the early 1960s evinced an ambivalence about the value of integration for its own sake that the city's civil rights leadership ignored or misapprehended.[10]

In August 1963, responding once again to Galamison's threat to organize a citywide public school boycott, the Board of Education announced a new integration plan. It merged the already existing Open Enrollment program into a broader "Free-Choice Transfer" plan, under which any student in an overcrowded, predominantly black school could transfer to any white-majority school in the city with available space. The other provisions of the plan, however, departed from the board's voluntarist approach to school desegregation. It announced its intention to begin the "pairing" of adjoining black and white schools in the fall of 1964, adopting what was commonly known as the "Princeton Plan." Black and white students in the same grade would be placed together, in one school. White students would be required to attend schools in black neighborhoods, and vice versa, although most would be within walking distance of their homes. If distances were too great, however, busing would be instituted.[11]

The board also confirmed its prior decision to redraw some school district lines with the aim of promoting racial balance, most notably combining the white East Flatbush area of Brooklyn and a portion of heavily black Brownsville. It situated virtually all school pairings and redrawn districts in the outer boroughs outside Manhattan, and in neighborhoods that contained significant numbers of the city's new middle class.[12] East Flatbush was one such neighborhood. There, the board redrew district lines to ensure that the student population of its Junior High School 275 would be one-third white, one-third black, and one-third Puerto Rican. Another such neighborhood was Jackson Heights in Queens, where the board announced plans to pair two elementary schools, approximately six blocks apart, beginning in September 1964: PS 149, with an almost entirely white student population, and the overwhelmingly black PS 92. This decision inspired the formation of PAT.

Although its residents preferred to use the word "neighborhood," the area of Jackson Heights that surrounded PS 149 was a prototypical new middle-class "community." Its residents, primarily Jewish and Italian, were civil servants, small businessmen, salesmen, and solo practice lawyers and accountants. They lived in small private homes with tiny front yards, and in Mitchell-Lama cooperative apartments—"self-contained colonies, neat, sterile and uniform," as one newspaper reporter put it.[13] Observers often remarked on their passionate desire for upward mobility and their contempt for those whom they perceived as lacking in this quality. More often than not, the objects of their disdain were black. A Jackson Heights priest captured this sentiment in describing his parishioners:

> By most standards, these are good people, endowed with many of the great American virtues. They are hardworking and thrifty. They're honest and devoted to their families. But many have worked their way out of real poverty and in the process haven't had much time to worry about other people's problems or think about the Negro and why . . . they make out and the Negro hasn't. And they're not secure enough socially or economically to add to their American virtues the great human virtue of understanding, tolerance and compassion.

People come to me and ask 'Why does integration have to begin with *our* children?' And I tell them it has to begin somewhere. But they're not very satisfied with my answers.[14]

PAT was founded in Jackson Heights in September 1963, shortly after the Board of Education announced its school pairing plan. Its leadership reflected the neighborhood's ethnic, racial, and class makeup: Bernard Kessler, a Jewish lawyer, Joan Addabbo, an Italian housewife, and Rosemary Gunning, an Irish community activist. Three major impulses motivated them and the organization's rank and file. The first impulse, as much as they sought to deny it, was race-related. PAT attempted to defuse charges of bigotry by announcing that it opposed only the forced transferring out of their children, and not the transferring-in of black students under the Open Enrollment or Free-Choice Transfer plans.[15] "The racial issue doesn't have anything to do with what we want," argued one PAT leader. "We believe in Open Enrollment. If Negroes want to go to the white schools where there's room, they should be allowed to." But the comments of other members reflected their feelings toward blacks, and particularly their work ethic. "I wouldn't live in Harlem for anything in the world," said one. "I'd scrub floors. I'd take in laundry. I'd get any kind of job and I know I'd succeed because in the United States anybody can do anything if he tries hard enough. . . . If a Negro lives in Harlem it's because he doesn't want to work hard enough to get out of that environment." "Color?" asked another sarcastically. "It wasn't color holding them back. It was the kind of people they were. I worked with Negroes. . . . They don't work hard or help their children in school or care about their families or keep their homes clean." A third spoke even more bluntly: "If I was God, what would I do to improve the lot of the Negro? I'd make everybody white."[16]

PAT members also linked their opinions about blacks to their unapologetically middle-class culture, one that stressed work, family, and advancement, and which had a strong individualist tone. Asked about school integration as a moral issue, a PAT-er replied, "I don't think I have a moral obligation to anybody—to my family, husband and child maybe, but no one else."[17] "Just sitting next to each other is not going to change things," said another. "I don't know why the Negroes are behind, but they are, and I don't want them hurting my child's chances in school." PAT members used this concern with education as a marketable route to material security as a consistent theme, as they sought to justify their opposition to school pairing: "I don't like [my son] with a lot of slow readers who will pull down his IQ. . . . I don't want nothing going wrong with my son's education."[18] "You can't take children from different educational levels and put them together," argued another.[19] PAT also supported ability-group tracking—determined by the use of intelligence tests—in the public schools, and the continuation of competitive, examination-based "specialized" high schools for gifted students.[20] Other PAT-ers cited economic concerns, worrying aloud about the consequences of a large influx of black children into their schools: "Eight years ago, we paid $12,000 for this house. We scraped together every penny we had. . . . My husband and me, we worked hard to get it and it's all we have. And now if the Negroes start coming, it won't be worth a cent."[21]

Finally, a strong sense of neighborhood drove PAT members. This impulse was conservative in nature, a reflection of PAT-ers' definition of "community" as a stable, safe haven from a hostile outside world.[22] PAT "community" was insular and anticosmopolitan. "I want my children to go to school where I went to school and that's just two blocks away," said one PAT'er. "This is my neighborhood." Another described the difference between Jackson Heights and Manhattan: "I was born and raised here. Just like my folks. There's a lot of second and third-generation families out here. It's a real neighborly place—not like New York City where nobody cares who lives next door and nobody owns their own home. You buy a house because you want your kid to go to a school nearby and the church is just around the corner. And then, here comes the government or the school board and they say, 'Mister, you can't send your kid to a school near you'. . . . I ask you, is that right? We're losing our freedoms in this country." A third captured the spirit of angry independence that animated the Jackson Heights community. He attacked school pairing as "most of all a moral issue. What right does anybody—anybody—have to tell me what to do? Where does it all end?"[23]

Driven by this mix of racism, middle-class anger, and "community" sentiment, PAT quickly spread beyond Jackson Heights and into other white outer-borough areas. By late 1963 there were over a hundred chapters in Queens, Brooklyn, and the Bronx, and the group claimed three hundred thousand members.[24] PAT-sponsored rallies at City Hall consistently outdrew similar demonstrations staged by pro-integration forces.[25] At one rally, in March 1964, some fifteen thousand white parents—six times the number that would march at a Galamison-sponsored rally four days later—called upon Mayor Wagner and the Board of Education to abandon pairing and race-based school district zoning. In addition to the customary speeches, PAT members expressed themselves musically. Their choice of lyrics—sung to the tune of "Music, Music, Music"—said much about them and their world view: "We've got troubles of our own/So why not keep us close to home/Please, oh, please leave us alone/Stop zoning, zoning, zoning."[26]

PAT gathered forty-two thousand signatures on a petition to put busing to a citywide referendum in the November 1964 election, which failed only because an appeals court ruled that education was technically a state, not a city, function.

The organization warned politicians "if just one child is bused out, we will hold you responsible." PAT also filed suit against the Board of Education's attempt to re-draw Brooklyn school district lines to bring whites from East Flatbush and blacks from Brownsville together at Junior High School 275.

East Flatbush was another neighborhood typical of the city's "new middle class." A *New York Post* profile described its residents as obsessed with education and up-ward mobility for their children. The newspaper traced a traditional white middle class "path of progress," which forced transfer to JHS 275 would disrupt. The "path" began at a local elementary school, and continued on to 90 percent white JHS 285, then to Samuel Tilden High School, and, finally, to nearby Brooklyn College. The typical East Flatbush student came from a home with a substantial family library and in which parents regularly supervised the completion of homework assignments. JHS 285 contained thirteen "special progress," or "SP," classes for gifted students, well above the city average. Virtually all of the school's black pupils were assigned to "slow" or vocational tracks. "Most of the white parents are very stable, very settled," said JHS 285's principal. "Why should they seek trouble?"[27]

Given this background, it was not surprising that East Flatbush PAT-ers viewed the Board of Education's plan to transfer their children to JHS 275 as "trouble." Their lawsuit sought to make use of the race-neutral language of the Fourteenth Amendment's Equal Protection Clause, as well as the New York State Education Law's provision that "no person shall be excluded from any public school on ac-count of race," to attack racially based rezoning.[28] PAT's broader objections to re-zoning were a reflection of their members' perspectives on individual merit, ini-tiative, and equality. "The very nature of a quota system," wrote one, "violates the American principle of liberty. The slightest compromise with equality of opportu-nity would open the way for restrictive and discriminatory practices. [Rezoning] sets up an artificial situation that retards rather than encourages . . . [and] affects a person's desirability as an individual."[29] Another East Flatbush protester combined PAT's core themes—race, middle-class anger, and community—in justifying the lawsuit: "We lived in Brownsville for a long time, and we worked to get out. Now that we're here and they're there, we don't want to go back."[30] The case eventually reached the United States Supreme Court, where a majority upheld the Board of Education's rezoning plan.

The climax of PAT's anti-integration campaign came in September 1964, when, on schedule, the Board of Education instituted its pairing plan in Jackson Heights. For the first time in the history of the modern civil rights movement, white par-ents in a northern city established a private school to avoid the consequences of a desegregation plan. During the entire 1964–65 academic year and a portion of the next, PAT operated a separate elementary school for children whose parents refused to send them to PS 92, the paired school some six blocks away.[31] PAT members and sympathetic neighborhood residents served as teachers at the school, whose curriculum generally tracked that of PS 92. Although the Board of Education gradually wore down the resolve of the Jackson Heights boycotters through threats of truancy action against their children, it was not able to close the unaccredited school until 1966, thanks in large part to the support the private academy received from other PAT chapters around the city. While Jackson Heights was the only neighborhood to take the extreme step of establishing a separate school to oppose pairing, many PAT members in other areas voted with their feet: during the 1964–65 academic year, 35 percent of white students in paired schools left for other neighborhoods, three times the percentage for non-paired schools.[32]

Ultimately, PAT lost battles, but won its war. Despite adverse court rulings, unsuccessful referendum campaigns, and failed attempts at alternative pedagogy, not to mention the opposition of virtually the entire city media corps, PAT had stymied the effort to integrate the New York public schools by 1966. Fearful, almost traumatized, by the threat of massive white resistance, the Board of Education cut back on the number of paired schools, and even curtailed the less controversial Open Enrollment and Free-Choice Transfer plans.[33] Busing, PAT's bogeyman, in the end became a nonissue; thanks to the group's pressure, only about a thousand of the one million pupils in the city system were ever involuntarily bused by the Board of Education.[34] By 1966, the New York City public schools were as segregated as they ever had been. "Community"—white community—had won out.

New York's school integration activists embraced community control, in large measure, because of PAT's success with it. During PAT's heyday between 1963 and 1965, these activists had been forced by practical necessity to rely on the force of centralized authority—the Board of Education—to realize their goals. They had little choice, because their attempts to defeat PAT through counter-organization on a community level in white neighborhoods failed. In March 1964, Galamison and other veterans of the pro-integration coalition formed a grassroots organization to carry the fight to PAT, which they named EQUAL. Like its predecessor, the Parents' Workshop for Equality in the New York City Schools, EQUAL was an interracial group composed of black civil rights activists and white leftists. In addition to its pro-integration stand, EQUAL also sought to counter what its members considered PAT's educational elitism with a radical egalitarianism that rejected tracking, intelligence testing, and any school, whether the elite Bronx High School of Science or the so-called "600" schools for "slow" or "disruptive" pupils, that differentiated based on ability. "Is our education system as now set up used to bind some of our children so that others can succeed?," asked EQUAL leader Ellen Lurie, referring to ability tracking. "If this is what we must do to keep white middle-class families in our schools, is it worth it?" EQUAL members stressed an appreciation of the "richness in human differences," and the "need to bring together in one classroom those who are different if we are to achieve our democratic goals."[35] While EQUAL did not reject the ideas of upward mobility and material success out of hand, it sought to redefine the market rules governing them to reward "currencies" other than high grades and test scores.

EQUAL attempted to replicate PAT's community-based organizational structure by establishing affiliated groups in white outer-borough neighborhoods affected by school pairing. Despite receiving favorable attention in the local media, their results were disappointing. EQUAL's total citywide membership was a small fraction of PAT's.[36] In Jackson Heights, the center of the school pairing struggle, EQUAL's affiliate organization, the Citizens Committee for Balanced Schools, made little headway in its recruiting campaign against PAT, attracting only 150 members. EQUAL fared no better in the other white middle-class outer-borough neighborhoods where it sought to spread its message.[37] Galamison and EQUAL responded to this failure by writing off pro-PAT sentiment as exclusively racist in character, ignoring its class dimension, and dismissing its "community" argument as an insincere rationalization of school segregation.

Galamison and EQUAL also criticized the Board of Education's school pairing plan itself as ineffectual. It would, by definition, affect only black pupils living in areas adjacent to whites, and thus not the great majority deep inside ghettos.[38] They demanded the mass transfer of students so that each local school district would reflect the citywide proportion of black and white students. When the Board of Education stalled on its promise to provide Galamison with a "timetable" for full school integration in the city, including plans for busing, he organized, along with Bayard Rustin, a public school boycott on February 3, 1964. It was 44 percent effective among students, although there was a wide disparity between black areas, in which 75 to 80 percent of the pupils stayed out of school, and outer-borough white areas such as Flatbush and Bensonhurst, where the percentages dropped to 16 and 18, respectively. A City Hall rally held in conjunction with the boycott drew twenty-six hundred protesters, short of Galamison's goal of eight thousand and far below PAT's total of fifteen thousand at its rally one month later. The UFT leadership, while rhetorically committed to school integration, angered Galamison by refusing to officially endorse the boycott, fearing Board of Education reprisals against its members; only 8 percent of the city's teachers stayed out on February 3, a figure only slightly above the normal daily absence rate.[39]

Galamison also reacted angrily to any argument that smacked of "neighborhood school" rhetoric, associating it reflexively with PAT and racism. When, on the eve of the February 1964 school boycott, the president of the Board of Education, James Donovan, called for programs to help black pupils "in their own communities," Galamison was dismissive: "That's just raising standards in segregated schools to make segregation more bearable. . . . The cause of [black pupil] retardation in the first place is segregation. I don't advocate spending one nickel in support of segregated schools." Integration supporters also criticized the Free-Choice Transfer plan on the grounds that it permitted the central Board of Education to "abrogate its responsibility for integration, shifting it to the individual parent."[40] But despite other school boycotts, fasts, and vigils, it was clear by 1966 that Galamison and EQUAL could not rely on the central authority of the Board of Education to integrate the public schools of New York. The politically attuned board could count heads. The disparity in membership between PAT and EQUAL was obvious, and while blacks represented about 30 percent of New York's public school enrollment in 1966, they were only 20 percent of the city's total population, and about 15 percent of its registered voters.[41] Given a choice between angering politically potent white voters or a marginalized black community, the board, predictably, took the path of least resistance. By 1966, with the campaign to integrate the city's public school at a dead end, Galamison, EQUAL, and New York's civil rights activists searched for new goals and strategies.

They would find their answer in the same kind of community organizing in black neighborhoods that PAT had perfected in white ones. With school integration essentially a dead issue, their new goal would be local black institution building and empowerment. This new strategy dovetailed with the simultaneous emergence of black power ideologies in New York's black neighborhoods. The Black Power movement in the city was led by a diverse group of intellectuals, politicians, and street activists. These included Stokely Carmichael and Charles Hamilton, co-authors of *Black Power;* Harold Cruse, whose *The Crisis of the Negro Intellectual* called for a new black cultural nationalism; tenant organizer Jesse Gray, who used his Harlem rent strikes to promote black economic self-sufficiency; and Congressman Adam Clayton Powell, the flamboyant practitioner of "black power" in the political arena. The idea of "community"—black community—was a perfect vehicle to express both disgust with white New York and faith in the political, economic, and cultural regeneration of black New York. But the shift from integration to "community" carried with it a potential conundrum for blacks and progressive whites, one whose ironies appeared lost on Galamison, EQUAL, and other critics of PAT and the "neighborhood school." They could not—or would not—acknowledge community control's applicability to conservative white neighborhoods. To be sure, EQUAL leader Rosalie Stutz did attempt to distinguish between the white "neighborhood," which she viewed as stagnant and reactionary, and the "community," which she saw as vibrant and progressive. "There will emerge new forces and alliances," she wrote, "leading to the destruction of the so-called 'neighborhood school', which does not serve the neighborhood at all. In its place will arise the community school, which will truly serve everyone in the community."[42]

Yet this might have been a distinction without a difference. EQUAL may have confused the substantive goals of its members' idea of "community"—egalitarianism in the distribution of social resources and a rough intergroup equality in rates of achievement—with its procedural mechanisms. Whites with very different substantive goals could, and did, employ the procedural mechanism of "community" to achieve their own ends, as PAT had so recently shown. Rather than come to grips with this, EQUAL, Galamison and other supporters of community control in black neighborhoods argued that conservative white groups such as PAT which also employed the idea of "community" were in fact doing something else, since "true" communities could never be "reactionary."[43] Alternatively, when they did discuss the relevance of community control to whites, they offered cosmopolitan, politically liberal Manhattan neighborhoods such as Greenwich Village and the Upper West Side as potential staging grounds. Most often, however, they were silent on the issue, as if it were irrelevant.

It is, however, not difficult to understand the eagerness of community control supporters to embrace the idea of community as a means to black empowerment, even with the warning signal of PAT blinking in their eyes. Their long struggle to integrate New York's public schools, into which they had poured so much political and emotional capital, had ended in defeat. Central authority, here in the form of the Board of Education, had failed them. White communities had rejected them and their message. Conditions in black-majority schools were worsening, and the gap in achievement between black and white schools was growing each year. Clearly, something had to change, or an entire generation of black schoolchildren would be lost. It was this sense of political exhaustion and impending catastrophe that led EQUAL, Galamison, and the other survivors of the school integration wars in New York to embrace community control of education with such fervor. Whether or not they understood the full implications of their decision for the long term, in the short run, with ghetto education in crisis, there seemed no other choice.

The mid-1960s, moreover, were propitious times for the ideology of "community," in New York and elsewhere in America. The 1964 Economic Opportunity Act's mandate of "maximum feasible participation" of the poor in the programs of the War on Poverty had ushered in an era of community action in the nation's urban centers.[44] New York, like other cities, established a network of community corporations in designated poverty areas. They funneled money through elected boards composed of local residents to "delegate agencies"—grassroots groups engaged in social and economic activism, often outside traditional political structures.

Harlem's official community corporation was HARYOU-ACT, which in 1964 had published a groundbreaking study of the area's social problems under the supervision of Kenneth Clark, entitled *Youth in the Ghetto*.[45] The study paid special attention to Harlem's educational problems, so it was not surprising that HARYOU-ACT emphasized education in its distribution of community action funds. By 1966, it supported Clark's own Northside Center for Child Development, which studied conditions in Harlem's schools; MEND, or Massive Economic Neighborhood Development, a Galamison-affiliated group which also concentrated on local education; and the Harlem Parents Committee, an educational activist organization with ties to EQUAL. That year, these and other local groups would begin the struggle for community control of education in New York's black neighborhoods at a newly constructed Harlem school, Intermediate School 201.

IS 201 represented a dividing line between the dying school integration movement in New York and the nascent community control impulse. The Board of Education had once held high hopes for the school, planning it in the early 1960s as a state-of-the-art model in integrated education. It intended to build it close to the East River, on the far edge of Harlem, where it would be accessible to whites from the Astoria and Long Island City sections of Queens across the river.[46] The Board of Education actively recruited these white students for 201, inundating their neighborhoods with flyers touting the opportunity to obtain an education for "successful living in a democratic, multi-cultural and multi-racial city," as well as the school's modern design and services.[47] Although over ten thousand of these flyers were distributed and a strenuous recruiting drive was undertaken, virtually no white students agreed to attend.[48] Giving up, the Board of Education shifted 201's location to Harlem proper. Upon its completion in the spring of 1966, it sat squarely in the middle of that neighborhood, at 127th Street and Madison Avenue, a windowless, air-conditioned fortress with the latest in modern equipment, and no white students.

IS 201 was the last gasp of the integration impulse in the New York City public school system. In 1964, newly appointed State Education Commissioner James Allen had issued a report on segregation in the New York schools that called for the construction of "intermediate schools" covering the fifth through eighth grades on the borders between white and black neighborhoods, as a means of promoting integration without large-scale busing or pairing.[49] He believed that since students at these schools, at ages ten through fourteen, would be older than most of those who had been the subjects of pairing experiments, there would be less cause for objection from white parents about traveling the relatively short distances to school.

But Allen was wrong. White parents were no more willing to send their children to intermediate schools with blacks than they had been to paired elementary schools, as the failed effort to attract white students to IS 201 illustrated. Thus, when Schools Superintendent Bernard Donovan announced in the spring of 1966 that IS 201's first principal would be Stanley Lisser—a white, liberal integrationist, but a white nonetheless—Harlem parents were furious. At a meeting with EQUAL to plan a protest of this decision, a Harlem Parents Committee leader, Isaiah Robinson, first articulated the idea of community control of education in black neighborhoods. His words closed the door on one phase of the civil rights movement in New York, and began another. A white EQUAL member recalled the bittersweet moment: "Isaiah Robinson [a black activist] suggested, almost as a joke, that since white children would not be sent into Harlem schools and black children were not being invited downtown in any meaningful numbers, maybe the blacks had better accept segregation and run their own schools. A jolt of recognition stung all of us: Isaiah's joke was a prophecy. It is hard to get across the sudden sadness we all felt. We were close, loving friends. Now we had to agree to separate because the society would not recognize our marriage and, one way or another, the black children had to be legitimized."[50]

On September 12, 1966, IS 201's scheduled opening day, demonstrators from the Harlem Parents Committee, EQUAL, MEND, and HARYOU-ACT, as well as CORE, SNCC, the Organization of Afro-American Unity, and the African-American Teachers Association, picketed outside, seeking for the first time not an integrated school, but a community-controlled school. They demanded not only that a black principal be appointed in Lisser's place, but that the Harlem community, through a board composed of local residents, control the operation of all neighborhood schools. The protesters formed a "Parent-Community Negotiating Council" for that purpose. While the protesters lost on the immediate issue at 201, with Lisser retaining his position thanks in large part to UFT pressure, the controversy at IS 201 symbolized the new direction of the civil rights movement in New York City. Community control supporters could argue, somewhat disingenuously, that it "should not be construed as resignation in the face of continued educational segregation or acceptance of the neighborhood school," but the idea of "community" had indeed emerged as the black version of the "neighborhood school."[51]

"Community"—now defined in black, not white terms—would be the axis around which new racial and class alliances would revolve in the New York of the late 1960s and early 1970s.

The movement for community control of black schools which the IS 201 controversy launched produced an unlikely alliance of government, business, and media elites; New Left–influenced intellectuals; radical teachers; and civil rights activists. Each had their own reasons for supporting community control. The most visible member of that alliance was John Lindsay, who had succeeded Robert Wagner as mayor in 1966. Community control in black neighborhoods dovetailed with Lindsay's personal beliefs and spoke to his political realities.

If Robert Moses was a middle-class moralist, Lindsay was an upper-class one. A graduate of St. Paul's and Yale, a "good-government" liberal from the Upper East Side, he combined the best and worst attributes of the Anglo-Saxon Protestant ethos that he personified: a sincere concern for the underprivileged and a moral certitude that bordered on sanctimony. As vice chairman of the National Advisory Commission on Civil Disorders which produced what was popularly known as the Kerner Report in 1968, Lindsay would be responsible for its best-known passage: "Our nation is moving toward two societies, one black, one white—separate and unequal."[52]

Lindsay's mayoral career, between 1966 and 1973, represented an attempt to prevent this dire prophesy from fulfilling itself in New York. His aide, Barry Gottehrer, captured the tenor of the Lindsay administration's operative philosophy when he wrote, "those who have nothing or those who have the least should get the most even if it is everything you have."[53] All too often, however, Lindsay behaved as if he believed that "you" referred solely to New York's white middle class, whose racism and self-interestedness stood in the way of racial progress.[54] His attitude toward it, and especially toward municipal unions, lay poles apart from that of his predecessor, Robert Wagner. "Lindsay just doesn't seem to understand the life of a mailman or a cop," observed one civic leader. "They feel he is buying racial peace for Park Avenue by giving away to Harlem what the middle class needs."[55] The charge by Lindsay's city planning staff that black problems were the result of "the callous disregard of the white middle class" epitomized the mayor's attitude.[56]

Lindsay was haunted by the Watts riot of 1965, and he feared above all the possibility of a comparable racial conflagration in New York. Community control of schools in black neighborhoods thus had enormous appeal to him as a means of keeping New York "cool" while other American cities burned.[57] It would shift power away from a hostile white middle class–dominated educational bureaucracy, and toward a group that made up a major part of his political constituency.

In a June 1968 exchange with Kenneth Clark on one of his weekly television programs Lindsay articulated both his support for community control and his impatience with white New Yorkers who objected to it:

CLARK: Mr. Mayor, my views on the subject of decentralization, I think, are very similar to yours. That it has to be. It has to come. . . . The central Board of Education has certainly not been responsive to the initial cries of Negroes and other deprived groups in the city for desegregation. After the deprived people stopped asking for desegregation, they just asked for the same degree of control over the quality of their schools which people in the suburbs have and which middle class people even in our city have. . . .
LINDSAY: Of course it goes without saying that I agree very profoundly with what you've just said. And that's why you and I together have supported, without overwhelming success, I might say, a meaningful decentralization program. But one of the reasons we were not successful is that we ran into a storm of protest from the very middle class that you were just talking about . . . who were fearful of decentralization. . . . I had the impression from the mail and the telegrams we received that the opposition to decentralization had to some extent succeeded in frightening the middle class in our community. That decentralization meant black power, black control. And then somehow some kind of iron-fisted violence on top of it all.[58]

Similar sentiments drove New York's business community. By the late 1960s, many business leaders had become increasingly concerned about the possibility of racial violence in the city. They began to advocate both increased levels of social services to the black poor and community control, to forestall Armageddon. While these leaders believed that community control could serve as a route to a more educated and productive workforce, they were primarily motivated by fears of social dislocation. Random House editor Jason Epstein, himself a community control advocate, captured that sense of fear when he wrote in the *New York Review of Books* that "if the children of the ghettos are trapped in a dance of death, their dancing partners are the holders of the city's mortgages, the owners of its utilities, and the rulers of its commerce. For the ideologists of Black Power to talk of coalitions with the working class seems beside the point. Their appropriate allies are the city's power elite."[59]

New York's corporate leaders viewed community control as a hedge on their economic investments, a down payment on social stability. It also had the advantage of costing them little. Community control redistributed power much more than it did economic resources. Furthermore, it did not even redistribute power from them. Most of the city's business leaders either lived outside the city or sent

their children to private schools, and were not personally affected by the consequences of community control of education in black neighborhoods. Thus, the
bill for community control would be paid by others. Business elites shared with
Lindsay a view of the white middle class as being most responsible for racism
in the city, despite the fact that in the late 1960s seventy of New York's hundred
largest corporations reported no significant black employment at any level.[60]

The business community's two major vehicles of support for local control of
education in black neighborhoods were the New York Urban Coalition and the
Ford Foundation. The Urban Coalition, whose slogan exhorted businessman to
"give a damn," attempted to link minorities and the city's corporate world. It provided pro–community control grassroots organizations with funding and advice
through its Education Task Force. The Task Force, which received financial support
from the Carnegie Corporation, the Rockefeller Brothers Fund, and the Taconic
and Ford Foundations, drew its corporate membership from the ranks of the city's
top business executives. They met regularly with the Task Force's minority members, which included representatives from EQUAL, the Harlem Parents Committee, and HARYOU-ACT.[61] No representative of the city's fifty-seven thousand public school teachers, however, appeared on its roster. The Task Force, in fact, had no
substantial contact with the UFT until after the McCoy-Nauman letter of May 9,
1968.[62]

The Ford Foundation had been involved in community organization since the
early 1960s, through its "Gray Areas" program, which sought to provide services
to urban black neighborhoods. But under the leadership of McGeorge Bundy, who
became its president in 1966, the foundation began a close and active identifica-
tion with the idea of community control in American cities, particularly New York
City. Bundy, who had served as national security adviser to presidents Kennedy
and Johnson before coming to Ford, arrived with the stated intention of making
the achievement of racial equality the foundation's top priority. Community control, with its promise of black empowerment, appeared to be a means to that goal.
Bundy asked Mario Fantini, an educational policy expert and community control supporter, to identify projects that merited the foundation's support. In 1967,
Fantini would recommend the Ocean Hill–Brownsville experiment to Bundy, beginning Ford's controversial involvement with community control of education in
New York.

Fantini was a product of the group of social workers, academics, and urban
planners that sprang up in the early 1960s around "opportunity theory"—the idea
that poverty and its related behaviors were not the products of individual failure, or even socially constructed pathologies, but of blocked routes to economic
and political advancement. Fantini and his colleagues, many of whom were active

in planning the War on Poverty, believed that grassroots community action in ghetto neighborhoods would unlock these routes to upward mobility by redistributing resources downward. Thus Fantini and "opportunity theory" activists, like the members of EQUAL, believed that the rules for success in the American marketplace had to be changed to reward currencies, such as skill in community organization, that they believed the black poor possessed in abundance.

Fantini viewed himself, with good reason, as a subversive of sorts in the bastion of corporate largesse that was the Ford Foundation. But community control served both Fantini's and his corporate employers' agendas. Fantini desired black political and economic self-sufficiency. The business community wanted social peace. Community control, especially in education, offered the possibility of both. If Fantini felt any qualms about employing perhaps the nation's quintessential corporate philanthropy to accomplish his goals, he did not let them show.

Community control also attracted the interest of white, New Left–influenced intellectuals and activists, who were intrigued by its link to a key New Left tenet, participatory democracy. They viewed community control as an antidote to the excesses of mass society in 1960s America: bureaucracy, rationalization, and impersonality. And in New York, few more vivid examples existed of institutional tyranny than the bloated Board of Education administrative apparatus. The board was a particularly inviting target for intellectuals who coupled this idea of bureaucratic pathology with one borrowed from theories of progressive education: that the school was uniquely suited to the task of social regeneration.[63]

Community control, then, was as much a political idea as an educational one. Marilyn Gittell, a professor of sociology at Queens College, whose Ford Foundation–supported Institute for Community Studies would play a major role in the Ocean Hill–Brownsville controversy, viewed community control of education in such expansive terms. Demand for community control, she argued, "far transcends the right to elect school boards . . . it reaches into the democratic ethos, projecting a communal involvement through the public school and making the school the agent for transforming the ghetto into a community. . . . Essentially, the question is one of making democratic theory work, because what distinguishes a democratic system is its participatory character, and inherent in the democratic concept is the individual's right to take part in the formulation of policy if he so chooses."[64]

Other New Left–oriented intellectuals, including Paul Goodman and Jason Epstein, shared these sentiments. Epstein, writing in the *New York Review of Books,* the leading forum for community control advocates in the city, linked it to "participatory democracy, which follow[s] from traditions of community anarchism and radical populism," and "a spontaneous and apparently irresistible surge of democratic fundamentalism, arising from a revulsion toward established social and political institutions."[65] Thus did community control create one of the stranger set of bedfellows in the city's history, with corporate leaders and left-wing intellectuals—McGeorge Bundy and Dwight Macdonald—on the same side of the barricades. It would not be the last time community control demonstrated its capacity for producing unintended consequences and paradox.

Community control also received support from radical New York City public school teachers, many of whom were veterans of the recently disbanded Teachers Union, or TU. For decades, the Communist-leaning TU had fought a bitter, ideologically charged battle with the UFT's lineal predecessor, the socialist Teachers Guild, before losing a representation election to the UFT in 1961. TU veterans had often spent their teaching lives in black schools—unlike many of their colleagues, by choice. They were also steeped in traditions of grassroots organizing that led naturally to the community control movement. This combination of antiracism and neighborhood-oriented activism made ex-TU members among the most passionate supporters of the community school movement.[66]

Another, younger group of radical New York City public school teachers that would be among the most prominent supporters of community control had ties to the New Left, and had been profoundly influenced by participation in the 1964 Freedom Summer black voter registration project in Mississippi. There, they had taught in "Freedom Schools," which brought an alternative, socially conscious pedagogy to southern black students. These teachers were inspired to bring the philosophy of the Freedom Schools, which emphasized grassroots participation, antiauthoritarianism, and racial identity, to the urban north. There, they were drawn to a community control impulse that promised to replicate the educational successes of the southern phase of the civil rights movement.[67]

Much of the city's mainstream media, notably the *New York Times,* also embraced the idea of community control. The *Times's* education editor, Fred Hechinger, a frequent critic of the Board of Education and "business as usual" in the public schools, mused in 1966 that if "a foundation . . . could select the principal and give him free rein to select and train his staff, to evolve his educational ideas and shape his plan of action . . . especially in a 'difficult' area—the example would be difficult to resist."[68] For him, as well as for the *New York Post* columnists James Wechsler, Jimmy Breslin, and Murray Kempton, the public education system was a disaster, and any change, especially one which shifted power downward from the bureaucrats at 110 Livingston Street, was preferable to the status quo. Editorial writers at the *Times,* the *Post,* and local television stations WCBS, WNBC, and WABC also found the community control idea promising, for similar reasons. Community control was an issue almost tailor-made for a media corps naturally hostile to bureaucratic sloth and institutional arrogance, traits which the Board of Education appeared to possess in abundance.

Black educators in New York had reasons of their own for embracing community control by 1966. Some, like Milton Galamison and Kenneth Clark, came to it in frustration, out of the ruins of the public school integration movement. For others, with less invested in the integration movement, it was no less a gesture of frustration. To the members of the African-American Teachers Association, or ATA, which had been founded in 1964, community control represented a chance to reverse the downward spiral in ghetto education, as well as, on a more practical level, to increase employment opportunities for black educators, who comprised only about 8 percent of the city's teaching staff at mid-decade.[69] The ATA began as a component organization of the UFT, but split off from it in 1967. At the peak of its influence, it claimed to represent half the black teachers in New York. The ATA was inspired more by economic and cultural nationalism than by any integrationist ideal and had embraced community control during the IS 201 controversy. Its leaders, Albert Vann and Leslie Campbell, headed a picket line of ATA members protesting the Lisser appointment, carrying signs reading "We Want Black Teachers in Black Harlem."[70] Community control fit the agenda of the ATA perfectly by 1966. It linked the organization's radical and careerist members, offering a sense of racial identity to the former and the possibility of expanded job opportunities to the latter.

The community control idea, finally, was immensely attractive to black intellectuals and activists in the city by 1966. Preston Wilcox, an adjunct professor at the Columbia University School of Social Work who rose to prominence during the IS 201 controversy, became one of the city's leading community action theoreticians. Wilcox believed the events at 201 were about much more than the racial identity of its principal. He wished to show "that a community can organize effectively around the process of educating its children." He created the "Parent-Community Negotiating Council," through which the Harlem community spoke during the IS 201 dispute, for this purpose. Wilcox envisioned the council as effecting "a fundamental restructuring of the relations between school and community based on a radical redistribution of power," which would redefine the rules governing the public educational system in all black neighborhoods. It would not only select educational personnel and screen curriculum, but as the primary locus for movements aimed at social change in minority areas, it would "concern itself with those larger issues such as police brutality and public safety and the operations of the welfare system, which impinge so critically on the lives of schoolchildren in the ghetto." He also viewed the school as a potential conduit for social services, center for adult education, and source of employment and upward mobility. "For parents," Wilcox argued, "active participation in positions of influence in the school should help change their positions in the larger community."[71]

In 1967 and 1968, Wilcox's vision would serve as the blueprint for the Ocean Hill–Brownsville local school board. By 1966, it had already attracted the support of a broad spectrum of black intellectuals, including Charles Hamilton, Harold Cruse, and Stokely Carmichael. Like the members of the ATA, they admired community control's combination of racial self-realization and upward mobility. After decades of reliance on whites in economic and political life, there was a refreshing quality to an idea that promised both empowerment and uplift, and independence. But this tantalizing vision of self-sufficient black redemption, so deeply embedded in the ideology of community control and so attractive to black intellectuals, would prove something of a chimera. If, as the Kerner Report argued, whites were "deeply implicated" in the growth and life of the ghetto, they would be as intimately involved in any attempt to solve its problems.[72] Eventually, black intellectuals in New York would be frustrated by one of community control's many paradoxes: the realization that blacks needed to rely on white assistance in order to become independent of them, assistance that, in time, whites would be increasingly reluctant to give.

By 1966, then, a coalition of government, business, and media elites, white leftist intellectuals, radical teachers, and black activists and educators, had, for diverse reasons, formed around the idea of community control of education in black neighborhoods. The UFT, however, absented itself from this coalition. The union viewed community control as a serious threat. Its leaders had both self-interested and philosophical reasons to be wary of it.

The men and women who founded the UFT in 1960 had deep roots in the democratic socialist movement. The Teachers Guild, out of which the UFT grew, had been the voice of democratic socialism within New York teacher unionism since the 1930s. Albert Shanker, who became union president in 1964, had been active in the Socialist Party–controlled Student League for Industrial Democracy as a graduate student at Columbia University in the 1950s. He was also a member of the Young People's Socialist League, led by Max Schactman, the ex-Trotskyist who by the fifties was a leading democratic socialist spokesman.[73] A steady stream of democratic socialists moved through the UFT hierarchy during its early years, including Charles Cogen, the union's first president; organizer Tom Kahn, later head of the League for Industrial Democracy; Sandra Feldman, a future UFT president, whose then-husband Paul Feldman edited the Socialist Party newspaper *New America;* and Bayard Rustin, whose A. Philip Randolph Institute was subsidized by the UFT.[74]

In keeping with its socialist antecedents, the union leadership during the UFT's early years encouraged a confrontational, outsider image—what one observer termed "a scrappy readiness to take on the power structure."[75] In the context of the early 1960s, the "power structure" meant the central Board of Education, with which the fledgling union battled over recognition and contract issues, and the principals, whom the class-conscious teachers identified as "the bosses." This anti-employer attitude, however, was doomed to a short life, largely because all but the most socially committed teachers aspired to careers as administrators themselves, either as principals or Board of Education bureaucrats.[76] The desire of so many "workers" in the city's public educational system to become part of "management," almost by definition, exerted a chilling effect on long-term expressions of working-class identity. By the time of the Ocean Hill–Brownsville controversy, the UFT and the principals would be allies, even suing the Ocean Hill–Brownsville local board together as co-plaintiffs.

By 1966, with its early battles for recognition won, the UFT had entered a consolidationist period typical of more mature unions.[77] For all practical purposes, it co-managed the public school system. President Shanker's relations with Schools Superintendent Donovan were familiar and cooperative. Each knew how far the other could be pushed, and acted accordingly. The superintendent and the Board of Education, in fact, served an important purpose for Shanker. The union leader could invoke their opposition to avoid taking actions demanded by Galamison and EQUAL with which he and his membership were uncomfortable. For example, Shanker refused to give the union's official endorsement to Galamison's February 1964 pro-integration school boycott on the grounds that the Board of Education would retaliate against teachers who publicly supported it.

By 1966, the UFT was more concerned with institutionalizing its power than with confronting the Board of Education across the class divide. With a growing administrative structure of its own, it now bore more than a passing resemblance to its heavily bureaucratized negotiating partner at 110 Livingston Street.[78] A dissident UFT leader commented on the changed union: "[U]nion activists had [previously] been pro–trade union, antisupervisor, and socially progressive. This type of activist has been replaced by right-wingers, teachers who are in supervisory or quasi-supervisory jobs, and anti–trade unionists. . . . The organizing staff fell victim to applied attrition. Socially concerned and independent staff were replaced with technicians whose role was simply to tell teachers what is or is not a grievance, how much money they should be receiving in their paychecks, and how and why to avoid political or philosophical questions."[79]

The UFT and the Board of Education were now bound together by ties of expediency and habit, closer to being partners than class rivals. The centralized framework of the city's educational system cemented this relationship. A shift to a local-ized, community-based structure endangered the UFT's co-managerial role in the public schools. It had the potential to disrupt labor relations, forcing the union to deal with a panoply of disparate local school boards. It also threatened the prac-tice of central assignment of teaching personnel through which the UFT prevented involuntary transfers from one district to another, a major issue for rank-and-filers terrified at the prospect of working in black-majority schools. And, finally, it meant giving up control over curriculum content to local boards, a further loss of influence, since the UFT now played a major role in the preparation of the Board of Education curriculum guides that governed the content of instruction in the city's schools.

UFT leaders took pains to avoid phrasing their concerns over community con-trol's inroads into union prerogatives in racial terms. Shanker, for example, at-tacked community control of curriculum by arguing that it would allow localities to harass his members for "teaching about the U.N.," a reference to conservative white neighborhoods calculated to revive memories of McCarthyism.[80] But in a practical sense, Shanker had much more to fear from community control in black neighborhoods than white ones. By 1966, the former was on the political and intellectual front burner in the city. And while the white version of community control aimed essentially at preserving the status quo, black neighborhoods sought an educational transformation with few discernible limits. Community control in black schools threatened the labor edifice Shanker and the UFT had constructed, one that would crumble without centralized control of schools.

The UFT, however, feared community control for more than just self-interested reasons. Union leaders, many of whom were active in the southern phase of the civil rights movement, were troubled by the ways in which arguments for com-munity control in black neighborhoods seemed to echo those of southern "states rights" proponents, not to mention PAT supporters closer to home. "Local activity," the union argued, "has almost always involved parochialism and frequently big-otry. Innovation [has] not come from local control—quite the opposite, it emerged from state and federal control overriding local provincialism."[81] "We don't hap-pen to believe that the little old hometown is a warm, nice place," said Shanker, explaining his philosophy. "We think that the smaller area, the more provincial, the more bigoted, the more narrow; that the smaller the group, the more homo-geneous, the more there's an appeal to a primitive type of tribalism."[82]

Philosophically, community control was almost guaranteed to trouble UFT leaders. Both socialists and mainstream liberals had come to appreciate the value of centralized government initiatives on both the national and local levels. This

placed them on the opposite side of the ideological divide from the decentraliz-
ers of the community control movement. In addition, Shanker and his colleagues
never forgot the example of conservative "community" offered by PAT. The UFT
hierarchy supported the idea of integration long after most blacks and whites in
the city had, for their own reasons, given up on it, and PAT symbolized to them
the intolerance and rigidity that lurked behind the idea of community control. A
decade of dealing with conservative parents in white middle-class areas of the city,
including Jackson Heights, had disabused union leaders of any romantic notions
about the virtues of "participatory democracy"; to them, community control was
a dangerous, double-edged sword.

The UFT hierarchy also knew that much of the union rank and file rejected
their liberal views, especially regarding racial issues. The contrasting reactions of
the union leadership and the rank and file to Mayor Lindsay's proposal for the
creation of a civilian review board to adjudicate citizen complaints against members of the police force served as a reminder of this internal division. The proposal, placed on the November 1966 ballot as a referendum issue, split the city as a
whole along racial, class, and geographic lines. Blacks and a majority of Manhattan
whites supported it as a deterrent to police brutality and racism. Outer-borough
whites opposed it, arguing that it shackled the police unnecessarily and protected
criminals.[83] Shanker and the UFT leadership threw their weight behind the civilian
review board proposal. The union's Executive Committee, composed only of high-
ranking officials, adopted Shanker's resolution of support for the board by a vote
of 30 to 2. A different result, however, occurred in the UFT Delegate Assembly,
made up of chapter chairmen from individual schools, and thus more representative of the membership body as a whole. Here, the resolution passed by only 486
to 375, despite Shanker's strenuous attempts to impose discipline.[84] The civilian
review board proposal, opposed by a large majority of outer-borough whites, went
down to defeat in the November referendum.

Shanker's inability to get his rank and file to make a strong statement in favor
of the civilian review board reminded him of their more conservative views, especially on racial issues, a lesson he never forgot. He would rarely make the mistake
of getting too far out in front of them again. In the words of a high-ranking union
official, "if it were not for the UFT [leadership], the teachers would take the same
position on desegregation and other race issues as all civil servants. They would
want to remain as tied to the status quo as PAT."[85] Such a rank-and-file body—
careerist, upwardly mobile, and skittish about blacks, both inside and outside the
school system—could hardly be expected to be sanguine about a community control doctrine that threatened their professional lives and promised, in the words of

Preston Wilcox, "a radical redistribution of power."[86] The UFT membership would serve as a consistent rightward brake on Shanker and his union leadership as the controversy over community control developed.

UFT leaders, finally, also opposed the community control idea because it challenged the brand of pluralism that prevailed in New York City during the 1960s, one that the UFT hierarchy supported wholeheartedly. This pluralism encouraged the interplay of overlapping economic, associational, and to a much lesser extent, ethnoreligious interest groups, with an emphasis on strong, top-down leadership. But community control supporters argued that this elitist, "top-down" pluralism had failed the average citizen, especially the black citizen, in New York. Community control ideology also challenged traditional pluralism's attempt to subsume racial identity under a host of other, nonracial cues and ties. "Standard pluralist rhetoric about how one individual is many things, an American, a teacher, a veteran, a family man, a citizen of Philadelphia, and a Negro," wrote a community control advocate, "is replaced by the all-abiding 'I am a black man'. There is a shift away from multiple role identifications and toward a more compelling monochromatic role definition . . . which operates as a determining and preemptive factor in the individual's other role performances; hence one thinks of oneself as a black teacher, a black father, a black citizen. Ideally the ordinary life roles are now endowed with a special expectation and commitment."[87]

In addition, an implicit assumption existed among community control supporters, especially black ones, that the "community" would be essentially of one accord, and that there would be little difficulty in reaching a consensus on major issues. When Rhody McCoy averred that the Ocean Hill–Brownsville local school board had "an unrelenting duty to interpret the will of the people of the community"; when a Brooklyn community control supporter referred ritualistically throughout his autobiography to "The Community" and "The Black Community"; or when a black teacher spoke of "the collective community"; they were endorsing a pluralism in which the "community," bound together by a shared racial identity, had one will.[88]

This monolithic aspect of community control troubled UFT leaders. Their approach to pluralism assumed the existence of conflict, albeit foreshortened ideologically, and diversity of opinion, although contained within a framework that accepted existing political, social, and economic structures in the city. They saw community control as antipluralist, antidemocratic, and even totalitarian in its implications. Community control supporters, for their part, viewed the UFT's brand of pluralism as itself limited and exclusionary. They questioned just what the union accepted. Community control, to them, would test "the limits of liberal pluralism" in the city. "Diversity is encouraged," wrote a community control supporter, criticizing the UFT's approach, "so long as consensus on the legitimacy of the existing social framework is maintained. Tolerance of other interests is the rule, so long as those interests can be met within the existing legal structure. But if the articulated demands of a disaffected group can only be met within a changed social framework . . . too bad for pluralism then. . . . That, then, is [community control's] distinctive revelation: the iron fist of undeviating authority in the velvet glove of liberal pluralism, Hobbes' ferocious eyes peering out from behind tolerant Madison's skull."[89]

Thus, aside from matters of self-interest, the UFT leadership and supporters of community control of the New York City schools held sharply clashing opinions of "community's" potential for good or evil. To the union, it was a cover for small-town provincialism, racial chauvinism, and political and social arrangements that mocked prevailing concepts of democracy and pluralism. To its supporters, community control provided the very essence of democracy—participation on the widest possible scale—as well as the opportunity to break through the limits of liberal pluralism to challenge discriminatory social, cultural and political institutions in the city.

More broadly, by the end of 1966, the idea of "community" had crystallized the differences between the two New Yorks that had developed over the preceding twenty years. It had become the means by which groups of New Yorkers of different races, classes, and cultures defined themselves against each other. It had created an alliance of blacks and elite whites arrayed against the city's white middle class, and of Manhattan against the outer boroughs. It was also pushing the largely Jewish rank and file of the UFT ever closer to their Catholic neighbors in outer-borough areas such as Jackson Heights, subordinating almost a century of religious animosity to the shared imperatives of race and class. And finally, it framed a developing debate between black and white New Yorkers over the values that would govern the city's public culture, one that would climax at Ocean Hill–Brownsville.

3

"BLACK" VALUES, "WHITE" VALUES

Race and Culture in New York City

During the 1960s

The Ocean Hill–Brownsville dispute would become the defining battle in a cultural war that raged in New York City during the 1960s, and continues to affect the city today. As the events at Ocean Hill quickly swept beyond the immediate protagonists into the public discourse of the city as a whole, so did the cultural questions associated with it. The debate began with a basic educational question: why did black pupil achievement levels in the New York public school system lag behind those of whites? It soon grew to embrace the legitimacy of black lower-class culture, the validity of "middle-class" values and their relevance to the black community, and the ability of traditional models of cultural pluralism to speak to all segments of the city's population. Responses to these issues, along with the question of how to define the words "equality," "racism," and "merit," divided largely along racial lines. Black and white New Yorkers stared across a cultural divide, interpreting the same phenomena in markedly different ways, and offering vastly dissimilar solutions to the problems faced by the city. Ultimately, their competing versions of what constituted a "fair," "inclusive" city would place whites and blacks on opposite sides in mayoral elections, labor negotiations, and arguments about municipal spending and taxation levels. The legacy of these disagreements would be two hostile, culturally separated New Yorks.

Beginning in the mid-1960s, the same coalition of black and white educators, activists, and intellectuals that had organized around the idea of "community," also mounted a challenge to the prevailing civic values in New York City, and to the actors it associated with them—the majority wing of the UFT, the city's educational bureaucracy, and, more generally, most of the middle-class whites living in the city. The challenge was threefold. First, it attacked the idea of the "culture of poverty" as an explanation for low black student achievement, and defended the validity of lower-class black culture against attacks by white critics. Second, it questioned what it saw as the shallowness and fraudulence of the core "middle-class" values of the city—"race-blind" individual merit, unbridled competition, and materialism—associating them specifically with whites. Finally, it rejected the moderate cultural pluralism that had come to prevail in New York by the mid-1960s—one which stressed the primacy of individual identity within a host of overlapping ethnic, racial, religious, class, and civic group affiliations— and sought to replace it with a radicalized version based almost exclusively on racial status.

The challengers were a diverse group. They included black cultural nationalists, notably members of the ATA, who spearheaded opposition among black teachers to the UFT before, during, and after the Ocean Hill crisis. There were also black intellectuals such as Harold Cruse and Charles Hamilton, and a group of writers and activists centered around the black cultural journals *Freedomways* and the *Liberator.* In addition there were black leaders with ties to the white community, such as Kenneth Clark, and Milton Galamison, who had moved from leadership of pro-integration public school boycotts in 1964 to support of community control as a member of the city's Board of Education by 1968. They were joined by antipoverty, community action, and grassroots activist organizations with ties to the city's lower-class black community, notably Brooklyn CORE, headed by street organizer Sonny Carson. New Left–influenced whites, including Ford Foundation–financed intellectuals, and writers centered around publications such as the *Village Voice* and the *New York Review of Books,* also joined this cultural challenge. Finally, there were dissident radical teachers within the UFT, including veterans of the Communist-influenced Teachers Union and of the southern phase of the civil rights movement, as well as activists connected with the educational gadfly organizations EQUAL and United Bronx Parents.

The members of this coalition were animated by a belief that culture was central to an understanding of the problems faced by the black community in New York, and a desire to use it as the primary engine of black advancement in city life. To them, government spending was important, but not sufficient in and of itself. Social progress would come not when government programs elevated the incomes of the black poor so that they might become black versions of the white middle class, but when they came to understand and appreciate their own unique culture. Blacks could then use culture as a unifying force, organizing around it as a community to change the institutions that governed their lives. The world around the poor, and not the poor themselves, needed to change. This approach, rooted in the "opportunity theory" which served as the philosophical underpinning for the War On Poverty's community action programs, accordingly demanded the recognition of values and behaviors that had heretofore been denigrated or ignored by white society, and their use as currency for black advancement both within the public education system and in city life generally. As such it was almost predestined to clash with the views of the UFT and its allies in New York's white middle-class population.

By the mid-1960s, white UFT members had carved out a culture that in many ways was emblematic of large numbers of middle-class whites in New York City as a whole. New York was now a middle-class city, if one went by statistics. Approximately 67 percent of its households earned between $5000 and $25,000 a year (national household income averaged $7400 in 1967).[1] New York was also a predominantly white city: approximately 75 percent in 1960, 72 percent in 1965, and 66 percent in 1970. The city ranked only thirteenth of the fifteen largest American cities in percentage of nonwhite population during the decade.[2] Because of the city's large geographic area, moreover, much of the white middle class continued to live within its borders, a trend running counter to what was occurring in most other major American cities at the time.[3] New York had also become, by the mid-1960s, a white-collar city, the result of the shift from industrial to service and government jobs as the base of the city's economy after World War II; by the end of the 1960s, 59 percent of the city's labor force worked in the white-collar sector.[4] The government sector jobs went in large measure to the white children of working-class parents, from Jewish and Catholic backgrounds, many educated on the GI Bill. By the 1960s, the new middle class they had formed was typified in many ways by the members of the UFT.[5]

Between 1945 and 1965, New York public school teachers used the competitive testing system of the city Board of Examiners as a powerful engine of upward mobility. Passing examinations and accumulating graduate credits and advanced degrees, however, were more than just a path to material success for the teachers. By the mid-1960s they gave expression to a distinct culture. This culture was built around an ideology of marketplace competition between self-reliant individuals, who were judged by standards of "objective merit" divorced from considerations of racial group origin. It preached the virtues of work and delayed gratification. It was, in fact, a collection of what many Americans had come to regard broadly as "middle-class" values.

The complex array of tests administered by the Board of Examiners, a relic of the Progressive era that prided itself on applying objective standards to applicants rewarded according to ranked lists, defined the parameters of the public education market in New York City. The tests demarcated the professional life and career expectations of the average teacher. While a teacher might quibble over an individual test or Board of Examiners' decision, few questioned the system's overall fairness. By the mid-1960s, the idea of "merit," as embodied in this civil service apparatus, was a fundamental part of the average teacher's worldview. It rewarded individual initiative, hard work, perseverance, and, with its slow pace, a willingness to forego present pleasures for the promise of future rewards. It resembled, in many ways, a modern-day Protestant ethic for a dogged, upwardly mobile group of largely non-Protestant New Yorkers.

In 1963, New York University School of Education Dean Robert Griffiths conducted a comprehensive study of the Board of Examiners teacher recruitment and promotion system. He found teachers concerned to the point of obsessiveness with passing tests. Everywhere in the system, he reported, there were "almost frantic efforts to take tests. [Teachers] appear either to be preparing to take a test, taking one, or waiting for the results of one." Griffiths described a system which measured success by the rapidity with which a teacher rose to become an administrator. He traced the career of a hypothetical teacher entering the public school system fresh out of one of the city colleges, the traditional feeder institutions for New York public school teachers. The teacher's career was a marathon race that rewarded diligence and obedience, not creativity. If the new hire passed the requisite number of examinations and accumulated the required graduate education credits, he or she could make the long climb from probationary status to tenured faculty, department chair, assistant principal, principal, and, finally, Board of Education bureaucrat. While Griffiths himself advocated the complete revamping of this system, including the abolition of the Board of Examiners, most white teachers viewed it as "fair" and "open to all." The consensus, among white teachers at least, was that while individual tests could be improved, "we must have them" in the interest of a fair system. But black teachers disagreed: less than half believed the system was "fair," and twice as many blacks as whites thought promotional opportunities were not "open to all."[6] There was good reason for this. In addition to short answer and essay components, many examinations tested oral expression, and the examiners were notorious for eliminating black candidates for allegedly poor pronunciation.[7]

Most white teachers were also committed to a competitive, merit-based ethos for their students. The New York City public schools had long operated on a system of "homogeneous grouping," or "tracking," for its pupils. Judgments on the relative abilities of students were made as early as kindergarten, where teachers were encouraged to identify children with high potential. In the early grades, the results of standardized tests—IQ tests until 1963, and reading tests thereafter —were combined with teacher evaluations to place pupils into ability-grouped classes, often designated by number, e.g., 3–1 for the "bright" class, 3–3 for the "slow" class. Once "tracked," a pupil often remained roughly in the same relative position throughout his or her career. Tracking continued even into high school. Promising students were steered toward courses that led to the "academic" diploma required for college admission, while others were placed in a "general" program which awarded a diploma that was little more than a certificate of attendance.[8]

Parents of children in the New York public schools were closely attuned to this system, and, for many, the attainment of a high "track" for their child was an openly-stated, unapologetic goal. White middle-class parents, especially, accepted the competitive nature of tracking as an article of faith. For them, education was largely commodified. Writing in 1965 of white middle-class parents in the Jackson Heights section of Queens, who opposed the integration of their children's elementary school, sociologists Kurt and Gladys Lang observed that "the residents in this area are very concerned about the progress their children make through the grades, about possibilities for acceleration, about admission to special programs and to college, as partial insurance against future insecurity." Education, they found, "is valued not so much for its content as for its marketability. Education is necessary if children are to retain the same relative position as their parents. . . . [T]he high valuation placed on learning is essentially that of the middle class; education is not the magic key to the kingdom sought by the children of immigrant parents before them."[9] Another white parent, who claimed to support racial integration in his Manhattan school district, nonetheless argued for tracking within his desegregated school. "The homogeneous grouping system," he wrote to a neighborhood newspaper in 1963, "allows each child to move at the level of his intelligence and needs. If homogeneous grouping were abolished, we would sacrifice the excellence of white and nonwhite alike to the dubious assumption that mixing complexions can advance (or hinder) the education of children. Excellence, interracially: this is what we want."[10] While some white parents groups, like EQUAL, opposed tracking, they were clearly outnumbered; most white parents accepted it and its ethos as legitimate for their children.

Nor did the majority of white teachers object to the values that underlay the tracking system. Indeed, most were themselves its products. While not as vocal as the principals, who had objected to the end of IQ testing, they worked comfortably within the tracking system, identifying "gifted" pupils, and vying among themselves for the prestige that went with teaching the "fast" classes.[11] The UFT leadership, for its part, never seriously challenged tracking.[12] It also opposed the forced transfer of experienced teachers to ghetto schools, implying that "good" students in white schools were a reward for years of satisfactory service.

The Board of Examiners and tracking systems, then, were of a piece for the majority of white teachers in the New York City schools by the mid-1960s. They were complementary parts of a competitive, individualist culture, which was presumed to apply objectively measured standards of merit, without respect to group origins, to educators and students. Its currencies were grades, test scores, and advanced degrees. The manifestations of this culture were not lost on its critics. The Harlem community action group HARYOU's 1964 study of that area, *Youth in the Ghetto,* which was supervised by Kenneth Clark, described it as follows: "Public school teachers in New York City come largely from the city colleges, which have a dominant pupil population from a culture which prepares the child from birth for competition of a most strenuous type. . . . The competitive culture from which the bulk of the teachers come, with the attendant arrogance of intellectual superiority of its members, lends itself readily to the class system within the school."[13]

Arrogant or not, however, this culture was one that many middle-class white New Yorkers, inside the school system and out, accepted as legitimate. Nathan Glazer, writing in December 1964, noted the hold the competitive culture had on Jews in New York, but he also understood how it also resonated generally. "The liberal principles . . . the newer ones arguing the democracy of merit—that have been so congenial to Jews and so in their interest," he wrote, "are also being increasingly accepted by everyone else nowadays under the pressure of a technological world. We are moving into a diploma society, where individual merit rather than family and connections and group must be the basis for advancement, recognition, achievement." "The ideologies that have justified the principles of measurable individual merit and the logic of the market place," he concluded, while particularly beneficial to Jews, also "coincide with the new rational approaches to the distribution of rewards."[14] Thus by mid-decade the competitive individualism of the majority of the white teachers in the New York public school system reflected to a great degree larger cultural trends in the nation and city that had developed after World War II.[15] The meritocratic culture—a product of the Cold War, the technological and knowledge revolution, and cultural pluralism—fit the lives and aspirations of the white teachers perfectly, and they embraced it as their own. But as they would discover, the "marketplace" had a very different logic in the city's black community.

The second element of white teacher culture in the mid-1960s revolved around the idea of the "culture of poverty" as a critique of lower-class black behaviors in New York. Here too, the attitudes of white teachers reflected broader trends. A product of post–World War II social psychology, the culture of poverty theory was, unlike the genetic-based racialism it replaced, rooted in environmental determinism. During the 1960s, three of its most important interpreters were cultural anthropologist Oscar Lewis, who popularized the general theory; sociologist and sometime presidential assistant Daniel Patrick Moynihan, who applied it to black lower-class culture; and education scholar James Coleman, who used it to explain low educational achievement among impoverished pupils.

Lewis, in *La Vida* (1966), as well as in an influential article in *Scientific American* appearing in October 1966, described the culture of poverty as "a reaction of the poor to their marginal position in a class-stratified, highly individuated, capitalist society." This culture was characterized by rejection of, or indifference to, the dominant values of the surrounding society. It could include, among other traits, nontraditional family structures, strong present-time orientation, propensity to violence, and lack of sexual inhibition. By the age of six or seven, Lewis argued, the values of this culture—or subculture—had taken hold of a poor youngster, making it almost impossible for him to take advantage of opportunities for upward mobility. The culture of poverty, to Lewis, was a "comparatively superficial" one, filled with "pathos, suffering and emptiness." "Poverty of culture," he observed, "is one of the crucial traits of the culture of poverty."[16]

Lewis emphasized that the culture of poverty was not unique to any race, and, indeed, could be found wherever capitalism and poverty coexisted. Moynihan, however, in his 1965 policy paper "The Negro Family: The Case for National Action," applied the culture of poverty theory specifically to black Americans. Drawing on the work of E. Franklin Frazier and Stanley Elkins, Moynihan drew a portrait of a deeply flawed lower-class black family structure and lifestyle.[17] While the scope of his research was national, Moynihan, a New Yorker, was already familiar with the workings of the culture of poverty in his native city. His 1963 study of race and ethnicity in New York City, *Beyond the Melting Pot,* co-written with Nathan Glazer, had articulated the concerns regarding the "pathology" of black institutions that would later appear in "The Negro Family."[18]

Finally, James Coleman's 1966 report to the United States Commissioner of Education, "Equality of Educational Opportunity," moved the culture of poverty theory into the debate over low black educational achievement. After conducting an exhaustive study of the American educational system—mandated by the Civil Rights Act of 1964—Coleman concluded that funding levels, quality of facilities, and even class size had little effect on academic achievement. Summarizing his findings for the general public in an article in *The Public Interest*, he wrote that "the sources of inequality of educational opportunity appear to lie first in the home itself and the cultural influences immediately surrounding the home." It was essential, he argued, "to replace this family environment as much as possible with an educational environment," by, for example, extending school hours or enrolling pupils in the Head Start program, in which they would start school at an earlier age.[19] The solution, in so many words, was to remove poor children from the "culture of poverty" of their homes and communities, and immerse them in the saving, middle-class, and predominantly white world of their school and teachers.

Thus, by mid-decade, Lewis, Moynihan, and Coleman had placed the issue of the legitimacy of lower-class black culture, and its effect on educational achievement, on the national agenda. The issue was no less compelling in New York City, where white UFT teachers had made the culture of poverty an article of faith. The culture of poverty idea served a number of purposes for the teachers. Since the theory, at least as Lewis articulated it, applied to the poor of all races, it provided a defense against accusations of racial bias when used to "explain" low levels of black educational achievement in city schools. It appeared enlightened in comparison to older theories based on genetic determinism. It shifted the blame for academic failure away from the school and teacher and toward the pupil's family and community. And, not least, it permitted lower-class black students to be classified as "culturally deprived," creating the need for compensatory education programs to expose them to the culture they were missing at home.

The culture of poverty idea, then, was the perfect white middle-class lens through which to view the behavior of the black urban poor. To many white UFT teachers in the 1960s, the lives of their black students were classic examples of the theory in action. The reason for low black achievement, wrote one, "is indissolubly bound up with the character of the parents, their view of life, their aspirations, their sense of moral values and the cohesion which exists in the given family. . . . [T]here is a definite correlation between the achievement potential of the student and the social, cultural and economic background of the parent. . . . [T]he character of a student body in a given school reflects to a very high degree the character of the people in the neighborhood."[20] Another white teacher cited "the chaos [black children] live in . . . no stability whatsoever—no family, no home, no one to talk with them. . . . You can't talk with them about the future—say about jobs—because they won't know what you're talking about." A third teacher, however, revealed some of the resentment that sometimes lurked beneath the surface of race-neutral pronouncements about the culture of poverty: "I hate these kids. They're impossible. How did they get this way?"[21]

In 1964, the UFT attempted to attack the culture of poverty with an ambitious, multimillion-dollar program of compensatory education called More Effective Schools, or MES. MES provided saturation-level services to selected ghetto schools, including reduced class sizes, two and sometimes three teachers per class, reading specialists, and extended class hours.[22] Costing approximately six hundred dollars extra per student, MES was expensive and labor-intensive; UFT collective bargaining sessions with the city Board of Education during the 1960s frequently broke down over the teachers' demands for funds for it.[23] MES was dear to the hearts of both UFT leaders and rank and file, and not solely because of the increased hiring levels it required. MES would do what the Coleman Report said was necessary to improve the academic performance of poor children. It would remove these "educational cripples," as one supporter put it, from the world of their parents, exchanging the culture of poverty for a structured setting more conducive to the learning process.[24] MES's stated goal was to bring minority schools up to the level of those in white middle-class areas of the city, both by raising reading scores and by expanding the cultural horizons of lower-class black pupils. The UFT fought relentlessly for MES during the course of the program's twelve-year existence, in the face of Board of Education recalcitrance, black community criticism, municipal budget cuts, and questions regarding its cost-effectiveness.[25] It was, indeed, one of the UFT's motivations for initially supporting the decentralization experiment at Ocean Hill–Brownsville itself. The single-mindedness with which the UFT supported MES testified to the hold of the culture of poverty idea on its members. For them, the culture of poverty theory both explained low black achievement and offered a solution: change black children by improving their culture.

The third element of white teacher, and white majority, culture in New York City in the mid-1960s revolved around understandings of cultural pluralism. White teachers, primarily Jews and Catholics, had been the major New York City beneficiaries of the national wave of cultural pluralism that came out of the World War II years. Serving as a perfect entree for second-generation ethnics into what still was, as late as the 1950s, a Protestant-dominated mainstream culture, this brand of cultural pluralism defined expressions of ethnic identity, within common boundaries, as the essence of "Americanism" itself.[26] It thus replaced the older idea of the "melting pot" with a more flexible and accommodating one: ethnicity did not need to disappear, but merely bow in the direction of broad cultural unity. By the mid-1960s, with Jews and Catholics in control of the New York City school system, a "moderate" brand of cultural pluralism had come to dominate both its and the city's culture. This pluralism recognized ethnic distinctiveness, but discouraged overenthusiastic expressions of particularism, and emphasized that despite group affiliations, standards of individual merit continued to apply. It sought to recognize the contributions of various ethnic and racial groups to a "common" culture with a Western, European-based core. And it attempted to dilute racial and ethnic conflict by encouraging multiple affiliations, based on economic, professional, or avocational interests.

This "moderate" approach to cultural pluralism may have been expressed best in 1963 by Glazer and Moynihan in *Beyond the Melting Pot*. "There are," they wrote, "many groups. They differ in wealth, power, occupation, values, but in effect an open society prevails for individuals and groups. . . . [E]ach group participates sufficiently in the goods and values and social life of a common society so that all can accept the common society as good and fair. . . . Groups and individuals participate in a common society. Individual choice, not law or rigid custom, determines the degree to which any individual participates, if at all, in the life of an ethnic group, and assimilation and acculturation proceed at a rate determined in large measure by individuals."[27]

Board of Education policy and curriculum statements during the 1960s reflected this approach to pluralism. "[T]he goals of cultural pluralism and humanism are the stated goals of the New York City public schools," it announced at the beginning of the decade.[28] "How can we find the common characteristics of a group?" asked a Board of Education curriculum guide in 1966. "Why should we judge the individual rather than the group? . . . In spite of differences, how are Americans alike?" New York City, it confidently stated, "is the outstanding example of cultural pluralism in our country."[29]

The UFT's approach was similar. Its original proposal for MES in 1964 had called for curricula "to reflect contributions of various groups to our common culture."[30] By this time, the union was focusing its attention on the teaching of black history in the New York City public schools. The UFT leadership prided itself on its sensitivity to the issue of racist and stereotyped portrayals of blacks in secondary school textbooks. Many such texts continued to rely on the interpretive frameworks of the pro-southern Phillips and Dunning schools of history, when they discussed black history at all. (In 1963, only three textbooks on the Board of Education approved list covered black history in any detail.)[31] The union attempted to rectify this situation through its Committee on African-American History, founded in the fall of 1966. The objective of the committee, whose work was personally supervised by Albert Shanker, was to help "children learn the contributions made by all ethnic groups to our pluralistic society."[32] For the UFT, this meant treating the history of black Americans as it had that of white immigrant groups—as component parts of a Western-oriented whole. The purpose of studying the history of Africa, according to the committee, was "to learn about the contributions of past African civilizations to Western civilizations."[33] "Many Negroes, past and present, have made worthwhile contributions to America and the world," stated a union-approved Negro History Week exhibit. "Many Negroes are good citizens."[34]

The UFT sought to portray "pluralist" black leaders like Martin Luther King and Frederick Douglass as role models for students. "Respond to hate with _____ is the philosophy of Martin Luther King," asked a question from a UFT-prepared black history workbook in 1967.[35] Frederick Douglass, a third-grade class was told during a UFT-endorsed Negro History Week commemoration, was "eager to get an education and studied every book he could find." King, according to the same materials, "taught peace and love" and "believed in freedom and dignity for all men."[36] This UFT-endorsed "moderate" pluralism would be exemplified during the Ocean Hill–Brownsville crisis itself by a social studies lesson given at JHS 271 by a white teacher, R. J. Papaleo—one that was disrupted by African-American Teachers Association leader Leslie Campbell. The plan for the lesson asked: "How is America divided on the question of civil rights?" It divided a hypothetical "American Highway" into three lanes—two narrow ones for left- and right-wing "extremists," and a wide "center lane." Discussion questions included "What happens to America when either the right or left lane becomes more crowded?," and "Why is the key to peace and happiness found in observing moderation in things?"[37]

In general, the UFT endorsed a pluralism that sought to acknowledge the "contributions" of all groups to a cultural mainstream, deemphasized differences by implying that group identities were subordinate to shared attributes and attitudes, and placed the history of blacks in America within the same interpretive framework as that of white immigrant groups. It was a pluralism confident in its ability to tolerate and absorb virtually all interests and groups within a common cultural matrix.

The culture of the white majority of the UFT in the 1960s was, to a large degree, a reflection of that of the white middle class in New York City as a whole. Both were built around conceptions of individualism, marketplace competition, and objective merit, a critical view of lower-class black cultural expressions, and a moderate pluralism featuring a cautious endorsement of group distinctiveness bounded by a common cultural framework. It was a white middle-class culture for a predominantly white middle-class city. In the years after 1964, however, its assumptions would be challenged by other actors, mostly black, to whom this culture did not speak. They would lay the groundwork for a cultural debate that would carry through the Ocean Hill–Brownsville controversy and into the 1970s.

The implications of the culture of poverty theory in the New York public school system were not lost on black intellectuals and educational activists in the city. As early as 1963, Kenneth Clark was taking the culture of poverty, and the related concept of cultural deprivation, to task. There were no "culturally deprived" children, he wrote, only "children who are being denied their rights as human beings . . . deliberately and chronically victimized by the larger society in general, and by educational institutions, specifically." Black lower-class children, he argued, would learn effectively "if they are respected" by "middle-class and middle-class-aspiring teachers."[38] By the following year, Clark was in a position to act on his beliefs, with the beginning of the national War on Poverty and its endorsement of the principle of community action as an organizational tool. Community action, based on the "opportunity theory" of sociologists Lloyd Ohlin and Richard Cloward, rejected the idea of a "culture of poverty." Opportunity theory advocates argued instead that the poor, through participation and empowerment, could change their local institutions, thereby obviating the necessity of adjustment to these institutions that the culture of poverty theory stressed.[39] They proposed, in effect, to alter the structure of incentives and rewards that governed political and economic relations in America, establishing a new set of national marketplace rules. Thus, in the words of opportunity theory proponents, "poverty is less the result of individual pathology than structural barriers, of institutions that were involved in the lives, yet unresponsive to the needs of the poor. The psychological problems associated with poverty are the result of the failure of these institutions. Thus, while the poor were told anyone who worked hard could succeed, they nonetheless came out of a school system that failed to educate them to hold skills and professional jobs. . . . Deviant and delinquent behavior could then be explained as the inability of the poor to achieve culturally acceptable goals by the use of legitimate means and existing institutions."[40]

Clark applied these ideas to New York City in his work with HARYOU on *Youth in the Ghetto,* and his 1965 book on Harlem, *Dark Ghetto: Dilemmas of Social Power.* Cultural deprivation, he argued in the latter, was a "cult," an "alibi" for white teachers: "[Black] children, by and large, do not learn because they are not being taught effectively and they are not being taught because those who are charged with the responsibility of teaching them do not believe that they can learn, do not expect that they can learn, and do not act toward them in ways which help them to learn. . . . Stimulation and teaching based upon positive expectation seem to play an even more important role in a child's performance in school than does the community environment from which he comes."[41] Clark thus attempted to shift the focus of the debate over black student achievement levels from the child and the culture of his community to the teacher and the institutional structure of the school system. If white teachers showed respect for the cultural idiom of their black pupils, made instruction relevant to their lives outside the classroom, and, most importantly, evidenced confidence in their ability to learn, Clark argued, black students would respond as well as middle-class white ones. Clark, however, conceded that ghetto culture was unhealthy, even pathological, albeit explainable as a reaction to white racism. Other black intellectuals and activists would go further than Clark and argue that the lower-class black culture that discomforted Clark and was rejected by white educators was in fact legitimate and worthy of respect on its own terms.

One of the first to do so in New York was Preston Wilcox. During the 1966 attempt by Harlem parents to have a black principal appointed at Intermediate School 201, Wilcox issued a call for a "community-centered school," modeled on the work of Leonard Covello, the principal of the predominantly Italian-American Benjamin Franklin High School in East Harlem during the 1930s and 1940s. Covello, a disciple of John Dewey, insisted that the school "deal with the child in connection with his social background and in relation to all forms, disruptive as well as constructive, that contribute to his education." Echoing Covello, Wilcox proposed that the community-centered school "be sympathetically responsive to the customs and values of the community it serves." The principal of such a school would use the culture of his black lower-class student population as a positive value, not as something to be dismissed as a sign of "cultural deprivation." "Instead of being committed to the elimination in his pupils of all he feels is repulsive in their backgrounds and values," Wilcox wrote, "the principal would be committed to utilizing these values as a resource for education." "The operating philosophy of the existing [school] system," he argued, "is too often manifested in a conscious or unconscious belittling of the values and lifestyles of much of its clientele."[42]

The community-centered school Wilcox envisioned would be something more than a weak reflection of more privileged schools. It would have different values and reward different types of behaviors. "Instead of approval being attached almost exclusively to matters of comportment and dress," he suggested, "rewards may come to be derived from fulfilling one's obligations to his peers and community. We must find a better balance between scholarship and citizenship."[43] Wilcox thus attempted to distinguish between what he saw as the mores of the middle class ("comportment," "dress," "scholarship") and those of the ghetto ("obligation to peers and community," "citizenship"). He argued that the communal ties that bound black lower-class neighborhoods were as important and as worthy of respect as the individuated, behavior-oriented values that characterized white middle-class areas. Black lower-class culture was neither "impoverished" nor "deprived." On the contrary, it was the foundation of a regenerated black community in the city. Wilcox wished to reconfigure New York's public education system to reward attributes that whites, in his view, had either undervalued or cast aside altogether. His critique of that system offered a set of values he associated with the black community as an alternate currency, which could be employed to obtain benefits in the same way that whites used examination scores and advanced degrees.

Other black educational activists soon took up this argument, continuing to insist that the culture of black lower-class youngsters was as legitimate as that of the white middle class. One of their main forums was *Freedomways,* which had been founded in 1961 as a journal of independent black cultural expression by Shirley Graham—the wife of W. E. B. DuBois—and historian John Henrik Clarke. In its pages, educational administrator Edward Weaver criticized compensatory education programs such as MES for seeking to change the culture of the poor black child. Compensatory education, and the culture of poverty theory upon which it was based, argued Weaver, was

> a condescending approach to the culture of the black people with no effort to structure dignity for [their] life-style, linguistic habits and behavior, but rather designed to produce white middle-class conventional behaviors. . . . [It] educates the black ghetto child so that he will become a black "Anglo-Saxon." It postulates that a black "Anglo-Saxon" can or should escape from the ghetto. . . . Its obsession that black ghetto children must be held to the same standards as white middle-class children is based on the dogma that the black ghetto child must look forward to that tenuous future when, as a black "Anglo-Saxon," he will leave the dependent environment for the white world. [Compensatory education] proposes that the black ghetto child become a super-child, lifting himself through reading and language skills to a nobler and greater world of the future.[44]

Another *Freedomways* contributor, Doxey Wilkerson, a professor at the Yeshiva University School of Social Work, wrote that educational theories based on the culture of poverty meant that white teachers were "again off the hook." The cultural deprivation idea, he maintained, was "bankrupt": "When provided with learning experiences appropriate to their developmental needs, [black] children, despite their impoverished backgrounds, do learn effectively. Their academic failures must be attributed in large measure to inappropriate learning experiences." Citing a study by educational sociologists Robert Rosenthal and Lenore Jacobson that found student achievement levels to be directly related to teacher expectations, he argued that "much of the academic retardation so prevalent among Negro children is a function of negative attitudes and inept practices among the professionals who run the schools."[45]

Others in the city's black community echoed this theme. "There are those," editorialized the newsletter of the Brownsville Community Council, the community action organization in Ocean Hill–Brownsville, "who have said that our children are unable to relate to the values of our society. We see now, however, it is the teacher who cannot relate to our values."[46] A parent-activist at IS 201 articulated the black community's reaction to the culture of poverty and cultural deprivation theories: "I don't want to be told my daughter can't learn because she comes from a fatherless home or because she had corn flakes for breakfast instead of eggs."[47] A math teacher at Ocean Hill–Brownsville's JHS 271 was equally blunt. "Students can't learn," he said, "until they feel good about themselves."[48]

Political scientist Charles Hamilton, writing in *Freedomways,* fully developed the black critique of the culture of poverty and cultural deprivation theories. Hamilton moved beyond criticism of compensatory education and defense of the culture of the black lower class and questioned the "legitimacy" of the white-dominated educational structure itself. He attacked the Coleman Report's reliance on reading scores as the measure of student achievement, asking rhetorically whether black pupils "in the process of preparing to achieve high scores on 'standardized tests' [were] being induced to try to emulate the culture of another ethnic or racial group." Black parents, he noted, were "becoming as concerned about the normative values received by their children as they are about the technical skills acquired. It is not sufficient simply to know how not to split infinitives." Even successful black students, he argued, were "permanently crippled, psychologically, while at the same time measuring up to criteria others have decided are the major determinants for 'achievement.'" He called for the replacement of a white middle-class educational structure based "solely on the acquisition of verbal skills" by one based on black "normative values," which he defined as "color consciousness, not color-blindness, group cohesion, not individualism [and] respect for Afro-American culture, not assumption of white, western cultural superiority." "And," he wrote, "I see this as a formal, overt, public process." White educators, he concluded, were attempting to "impose a consensus on black people who insist on the illegitimacy of that consensus."[49]

Black intellectuals and activists, then, were developing a critique of the culture of poverty theory even as whites embraced it. This critique was built around the proposition that poor black children were, in the words of a Preston Wilcox *Freedomways* article, "culturally different, not culturally deprived," and that the values of the lower-class black community, as CORE's Floyd McKissick argued in the *New York Amsterdam News,* embodied "the actual and factual soul of black people."[50] Another closely related critique challenged the competitive individualism and materialism of the city's middle class. It attempted, moreover, to specifically associate "middle-class" values with those of the white community in New York, melding them into a single, indivisible term that was often employed as an epithet. By the onset of the Ocean Hill–Brownsville dispute, "white middle-class" had become a powerful and frequently used term of negative reference for black intellectuals and activists in the city.

As had been the case with the culture of poverty issue, one of the first blows against the values of the white middle class was struck by Kenneth Clark. In *Dark Ghetto,* Clark described a white middle-class world that, apart from the damage it did in the ghetto, was itself "sick." Rebellion against such a world by poor blacks, Clark argued, was in fact "the evidence of health."[51] He also harshly criticized the practice of tracking pupils, under which, he argued, white middle-class teachers used "a powerful arsenal of half-truths, prejudices and rationalizations" against black children, who were "being systematically humiliated, categorized, classified [and] relegated to groups in terms of slow learners . . ."[52] By the mid-1960s, through his work with HARYOU, Clark had become convinced that community action, in general, and community control of education, in particular, were the means by which lower-class blacks could "cure" their white middle-class-imposed pathology. The culture of community action, in his view, was the antidote for the rampant individualism and competition of white schools and white society.

Charles Hamilton and Stokely Carmichael, in their 1967 book *Black Power,* also argued that the black community should disassociate itself from the white middle class. White values, they argued, were "based on material aggrandizement, not the expansion of humanity," and "supported cloistered little closed societies." They dismissed the idea of individual "merit" as "fit[ting] the white middle-class mold." Again, their prescription for the excesses of white middle-class individualism and materialism lay in "an attitude of brotherly, communal responsibility among all black people for one another."[53]

Harold Cruse, in *The Crisis of the Negro Intellectual,* also published in 1967, took aim at the black middle class, which he viewed as a weak imitator of its white counterpart. It had, he argued, passively accepted the cultural cues of the "commercially deprived white middle class," and blundered down the same blind alleys. "Caught up in the maze and vagaries of American materialistic values and the middle-class ethos," he wrote, the black middle class was "just as trapped by the system as the poor." Cruse called for "a new black middle class organized on the principle of cooperative economic ownership and technical administration," which "would teach the Negro masses the techniques of ethnic group survival under capitalism—group economics, group cultural self-education—in short, cooperative self-help on every level of human experience and need in industrial society . . ."[54]

By the late 1960s, then, many black intellectuals had identified certain cultural traits with the middle class, and linked them specifically to whites. They had, moreover, begun to define a black oppositional culture built around values they associated with the black poor, which, in their view, the white middle class had rejected or ignored. And they had begun to create a cultural atmosphere which sharply circumscribed the ability of blacks to adopt the attributes associated with the white middle class and still retain their racial bona fides.

These intellectuals shared platforms, picket lines, and the pages of publications such as the *New York Amsterdam News, Freedomways,* and *Liberator* with black educational activists in New York City. They clearly influenced the latter's critique of the culture of white UFT teachers. To these activists, the white teachers were living embodiments of what Clark, Hamilton, and Cruse had described in more theoretical terms. Reverend Milton Galamison, perhaps the most visible pro–community control spokesman in the city, argued that the "merit" system so dear to the hearts of the white teachers was morally bankrupt. For them, he wrote, education was simply "rote memorization for sterile examinations, a necessary procedure for making money." In white teacher culture, he argued, "passing an examination is more important than learning [and acquiring] the qualifications to demand a huge salary are more important than the development of the mind and spirit." It was a culture in which "pushing and shoving and competing . . . defeat the very ends for which education is designed."[55]

David Spencer, who, as the chairman of a neighborhood committee that would later become the local school board of the IS 201 district in Harlem, had worked alongside Preston Wilcox in 1966 during the attempt to have a black principal appointed at that school, questioned the motivations of the white teachers he had observed. He described a number of different "types" of white teachers, all united by a desire for material gain at the expense of black schoolchildren: "the divorcee who has children to support, and that's her reason for staying in teaching; the trousseau teacher, who is planning on getting married and took the job so she could afford to get married and settle down; and the mortgage teacher, who has a home mortgage to pay for and this is his reason for teaching." Spencer, moreover, rejected the culture of the classroom itself, one that, in his view, was imposed on black pupils by white teachers obsessed with identifying and nurturing the "best" students at the expense of the others: "I'm tired of teachers who say, 'I've got two or three pupils here who are tops. Look what I have done.' What I see when I look is that there's twenty four more who ain't doing nothing. When you show me fifteen or seventeen that you've done something with, then I'm happy. . . . They need the push, not the kid with grades of ninety or ninety-five."[56]

Black educational activists in Ocean Hill–Brownsville described white teachers as "bourgeois people" with a "9 to 3 . . . then go home" culture.[57] "All teachers have so far accomplished," charged black Ocean Hill–Brownsville teacher Ronald McFadden, "is a more efficient way to teach kids what it takes to make a dollar in America."[58] A *New York Amsterdam News* correspondent wrote that white-dominated education "stresses vocation rather than intellectual education." "The emphasis on marks," he complained, "is ridiculous."[59] "We say the philosophical outlook of the West is destructive of the human spirit," editorialized the *Liberator.* "We say we don't want to go whitey's way."[60] Rhody McCoy chaired a conference of black New York City school officials which unanimously resolved that "white middle-class values are harmful to black schoolchildren."[61]

White community control supporters took a similar stance. Mario Fantini of the Ford Foundation charged that whites "strive to create middle-class schools in the slums," schools that were "not the best of all possible educational worlds" because they failed to "stimulate intellectual competition with self—working to realize one's potential to the fullest—rather than competition with others."[62] And Robert Fox, a white activist Catholic priest in Harlem, viewed community control in black neighborhoods as a force that would "catalyze America" and begged his fellow whites not to "seduce [blacks] into our value system."[63]

Thus, beginning in the mid-1960s, black intellectuals in New York, aided by a small but influential group of sympathetic whites, sought to link a series of attributes—competition, individualism, and materialism—specifically to the white middle class. In the context of the New York City public education system and the fight for community control, black activists and their white allies associated these same attributes, which they viewed as shallow and fraudulent, with white UFT teachers. They mounted this challenge, moreover, at a time when the white teachers had come to believe that these attributes were legitimate and fair, offering the examples of their own professional careers as proof. As with the issue of black lower-class culture and the culture of poverty idea, blacks and whites in New York City were again on a collision course.

The third and final prong of the challenge to "white" culture mounted by black intellectuals and activists attacked the "moderate" version of pluralism which held sway in New York during the mid-1960s, and to which white UFT teachers in particular were especially dedicated. The challenge was built around a "radicalized" version of pluralism that dismissed attempts to blunt expressions of racial and ethnic identity as themselves ethnocentric. "Radical" pluralism placed such identities squarely and openly at the center of any argument over distribution of resources in the city. It argued that "humanist," moderate pluralism was itself exclusionary and restrictive. It objected to what the challengers considered a white, Western, and European-dominated civic culture. And it asked for an "opening up" of that culture to include new possibilities, including the idea that the city was not made up of "contributors" to a coherent whole, but of a series of communities sufficient unto themselves. If, as one supporter of this radical version of pluralism put it, "all could find justice somewhere, in one community or another," and "people can 'find' themselves, not in themselves, but in their communities," then the premises of moderate pluralism, which stressed individual identities within group affiliations, lost their explanatory power.[64]

Harold Cruse and Charles Hamilton again set the general theoretical parameters of this radical pluralist challenge. Both argued, in effect, that it was proper for blacks to use group identity as a form of currency in the race for the rewards offered by American society. Cruse's vision of civic culture revolved around "a struggle for democracy among ethnic groups," which would receive formal recognition from the government and in civil society. The black poor, he argued, were ill served by calls from the black middle class—itself in thrall to whites—"that [they] must give up [their] ethnicity and become human, universal, full-fledged American." To Cruse, the idea of "humanism" in America was a myth; the nation was not the cultural empty vessel it purported to be, but instead a stronghold of "European cultural and spiritual values" which rewarded groups, not unaffiliated "human beings." White middle-class culture, which argued that society rewarded "meritorious" individuals on a color-blind basis, was fraudulent and hypocritical. The ultimate goal of Cruse's brand of pluralism was amending the Constitution itself to grant formalized legal status to racial and ethnic groups, "mirroring the basic group reality of America."[65]

Charles Hamilton echoed Cruse's focus on group difference as the fundamental governing principle of American society. It was, he argued, "too late" for moderate pluralism's "private and informal" recognition of group identity in distributing resources.[66] "America asked [blacks] to fight for opportunity as individuals," he wrote, along with Stokely Carmichael in *Black Power*, while "what we have needed most is opportunity for the whole group." Blacks, they continued, need not "apologize for the existence of this form of group power, for we have been oppressed as a group, not as individuals. We will not find our way out of that oppression until both we and America accept the need for Negro Americans, as well as for Jews, Italians, Poles and white Anglo-Saxon Protestants, among others, to have and wield group power."[67]

Once again, this critique influenced black New York City educators and activists. Preston Wilcox urged blacks to develop an alternative system of values that, unlike those of whites, would "emphasize that which is private and ethnic as against that which is public and culture-blind," and which would redefine the public education market to reward resources found in the black community. "The descendants of Africa," he argued, "are coming to see their destinies as being directly tied to their ability to articulate and implement . . . a black national consensus as it relates to the individual, the family, the community, institutions, and self-governing, self-developing, self-connecting strategies and modus operandi."[68]

Other activists sought to redefine white-influenced presentations of black history in the New York City public schools. United Bronx Parents, a pro–community control group, criticized the emphasis placed by white educators on Western cultural themes and "approved" black historical figures. It demanded that the curriculum balance discussions of ancient Greece and Rome with those of the African Ashanti culture, and the American, French, and Russian Revolutions with Marcus Garvey, Malcolm X, and Stokely Carmichael. In a *Freedomways* article, James Campbell, an assistant principal in the New York City public schools, asserted that "[w]e need to know the relationship of our labor to this land and its development. It was not a 'contribution' as many curriculum guides are beginning to teach."[69] Keith Baird, the director of African-American education in the Ocean Hill–Brownsville school district, designed a black history curriculum that would offer an alternative to standard texts "written from a European point of view," and to "white schools reflecting white interests, a white self-concept and white culture." "We aren't concerned with putting one culture over another," he argued, "but with supplying the missing pages of black culture."[70] Baird's curriculum included African language, history, and even, through the use of the African number game Owari, mathematics.[71] The Ocean Hill–Brownsville district's curriculum advisory committee demanded "a curriculum based on the glory and greatness of the African-American culture, history, and experience that will be the well-spring from which all areas will flow, [and] counter the total focus in today's curriculum on the European Anglo-Saxon experience."[72]

The United Federation of Parents and Teachers, a pro–community control activist group, used an analogy based on the Arab-Israeli conflict to make a point about white portrayals of black historical figures in the New York public schools. What, it asked, if all textbooks on Israeli history were written by Arabs, "very, very moderate Arabs, but still Arabs?" What if they "dealt almost exclusively with Arabs and their successes," and praised "not the Jewish Freedom Fighters but rather those who accommodated to dominant Arab power?"[73] This, the organization argued, was equivalent to what black students and educators faced in the New York public school system. Milton Galamison may have expressed the frustrations of critics of the white pluralist approach to black history most succinctly. "For years," he observed, "Americans have sat in the theatre and applauded in all the wrong places, accepting the villains as the heroes and the heroes as the villains."[74]

Symbolic of the differences between the two brands of pluralism, and a harbinger of conflicts to come, was the Racism in Education Conference held in Washington, in December 1966, and sponsored by the UFT's national parent, the American Federation of Teachers. The UFT, which was the prime mover behind the conference, had expected it to provide a platform for discussion of the need to add more black history material to public school curricula. Instead, a contingent of New York–based black educators, writers, and activists turned it into a platform from which to attack the legitimacy of the white teachers' version of pluralism.

Actor Ossie Davis set the tone when he began the conference by listing some of the sixty negative synonyms for "black" that appeared in his thesaurus. "The English language," he said, "is my enemy." Davis asserted that blacks were "the last ethnic minority to use communal strength," and that they could "achieve equal opportunity only by concerted action of the group." Black scholar John Henrik Clarke then argued that whites were incapable of teaching black history properly, drawing reproaches from unsettled white teachers in the audience. Black teacher William Kelly supported Clarke's contention that whites were incapable of teaching black history because of their refusal to face up to the "genocide" committed by whites against blacks and Indians. He called for an "honest American history" that would acknowledge a white "killing" culture. Another black educator proclaimed his moral superiority to the whites in the audience: "I've been living around you all my life, but I've never lived with you and as a result I've been able to develop something you've lost." He went on to echo Harold Cruse's call for the black intellectual to eschew "universalities" and the false humanism of white pluralism for a distinct black cultural outlook and body of work. The session ended in acrimony, with a black teacher cutting off a white who asked how "to learn how to do our jobs better," with "you probably aren't doing your job at all now," as whites in the audience groaned.[75]

White teachers left the Racism in Education Conference in confusion and anger. The UFT's house organ, the *United Teacher,* reported that the black educators' pronouncements were "upsetting" to the white teachers, who "didn't understand this type of reaction and protest," and "rejected it out of hand." Some white teachers went so far as to resign from the union over the conference. One such teacher wrote:

> To indict the English language as the carrier of racism is arrant nonsense. . . .
> [Should] we teach the history of Liberia in the 1830s, or the current history
> of the 37 new African states as case studies of civil liberties, economic opportunity, and belief in the rights of minorities? It is obvious that traditions of
> democracy and equality, albeit not yet realized, have their origins and widest
> development in the Western societies, particularly the English and American,

that [black educators] are so ready to have the Negro cut himself off from. . . .
It would appear as if history teachers at this conference attended the teacher
training institutions of Hitler's Germany. . . . Simply substitute the words "white
man" for "Jew" and the books are ready for reprint.[76]

The reaction of the white media that covered the conference was also negative.
"Started from a desire to correct the frequently grossly inaccurate treatment of
Negroes in history books," observed the *Long Island Press,* "the conference mean-
dered through revival-type sessions ('Tell 'em, brother') to angry back-to-Africa
speeches and general confusion."[77]

The Racism in Education Conference was one of the first overt confrontations
between the moderate pluralism of the white UFT teachers and an emerging radical pluralist critique based in the community of New York black educators, writers,
and activists. The conference unsettled the white teachers in attendance, because
they had constructed their version of pluralism around a presumption of a consensus that clearly did not exist. White teachers had assumed that the addition
of black history books to already existing public school curricula would address
the concerns of black educators and "solve" any cultural inequities that existed.
They were wrong. Black educators, viewing "humanism" as a cover for white particularism, and ambivalent about the need for a cultural consensus of any kind,
were demanding a change in perspective that the moderate pluralism of the white
teachers, almost by definition, could not accommodate.

Thus, even before the events of the Ocean Hill–Brownsville crisis began to un-
fold, conflicting "white" and "black" cultural approaches had developed side by
side in New York City. The former was built around conceptions of individualism; competition; "objective," examination-based measures of achievement and
reward; black lower-class cultural weakness; and moderate, "common denomi-
nator" pluralism. The latter emphasized mutuality and cooperation; the cultural
legitimacy of the black poor; the use of the cultural resources of the black community as a form of currency in the local and national marketplaces; and a pluralism
based on community and group distinctiveness. Troubling questions, which en-
twined race and class, had been placed on the civic agenda: Were lower-class black
children "culturally deprived"? Were the ideas of "individualism" and "merit"
myths in city life? Were "middle-class" values necessarily "white" ones? Was it
possible to be both "black" and "middle-class"? And was a pluralism that sought
to dilute the force of racial and ethnic particularism through expressions of broad
cultural unity merely a perpetuation of white dominance and black marginalization? By the end of 1966, as black and white educators, intellectuals, and activists
offered strikingly different answers to these questions, this volatile mix lacked only

a spark, a specific set of circumstances to animate it and give it momentum. Over the next two years, events at Ocean Hill–Brownsville would provide this spark, pitting the two New Yorks against each other, and forcing virtually every citizen of the city to choose sides. In so doing, they would transform Rhody McCoy and Fred Nauman, who in 1966 did not even know each other, into symbolic adversaries for a divided city.

4

THE OCEAN HILL–BROWNSVILLE

COMMUNITY CONTROL EXPERIMENT

The Ocean Hill–Brownsville community control experiment had its genesis, perhaps fittingly, in a display of Board of Education bureaucratic arrogance: it would not permit a woman to speak at one of its meetings because her name was not on the proper list. On December 19, 1966, the Board held one of its periodic public hearings at its 110 Livingston Street headquarters. These meetings, one of the Board's rare bows in the direction of positive public relations, were tightly choreographed. Representatives of established organizations with ties to New York's educational bureaucracy spoke first. On this afternoon, these included the United Parents Association, the "official" parent liaison group in the city school system; the Public Education Association, the longtime voice of the city's upper middle-class reform constituency in educational policy; and the Citizens Committee for Children, another predominantly upper middle-class group with ties to the reform wing of the city's Democratic party and to the UFT. The Board of Education relegated EQUAL, HARYOU-ACT, the Harlem Parents Committee, CORE, and other prominent civil rights and community action organizations, as usual, to the end of its program.

Near the end of the afternoon's schedule, Lillian Wagner, a black single mother from Ocean Hill–Brownsville, approached the podium and asked to be heard.

Checking the speakers' list before him, Board Vice President Alfred Giardino ruled her out of order. Only those who had submitted their names in advance could speak, and Mrs. Wagner had not done so. Giardino raised his gavel to continue the session. He was interrupted, however, by the audience, led by Ellen Lurie of EQUAL: "Let her speak, we pay the taxes!" Impassive, Giardino repeated that Mrs. Wagner was out of order. As the chants of "Let her speak!" grew louder, Mrs. Wagner shouted: "The voice of the people is with me. I don't want my child to grow up in the same ghetto as I did." At this, Lloyd Garrison, the president of the Board of Education, and a descendant of the legendary nineteenth-century abolitionist, announced he was adjourning the hearing because of the disruption. He and his colleagues exited the room through doors located directly behind their desks.

But Lurie and her supporters would not let the moment pass. Scrambling over the barrier separating the spectators' gallery from the now-empty row of desks, they sat down in the red-cushioned swivel chairs and refused to leave. "We are staying here," said one protester, "because the Board of Education would not listen to us. They showed they are not responsible to the parents. They held a public hearing, but they really don't want to hear." From his chambers, Garrison held to procedural niceties. He sent word that it was "impossible" to continue the hearing if the speakers appeared out of turn. But neither would he order the protesters removed immediately. He would wait them out.

It was now early evening. The protesters, some twenty to thirty men and women from EQUAL, CORE, HARYOU-ACT, United Bronx Parents, and the Brownsville Community Council, sent for Milton Galamison. They had decided to form themselves as the "People's Board of Education," and they wanted to elect him "president"; he arrived to assume his "duties" around 11:00 P.M. The People's Board, after electing Lillian Wagner "Superintendent of Schools," began taking testimony from members of the audience on conditions in the city's black-majority schools. It passed a resolution calling for community control of public education in New York. "We have attempted hearings before every conceivable public body," it charged in a statement released to the press waiting outside the chamber. "We have studied, analyzed and reacted to voluminous reports; we have made recommendation after recommendation. None of our efforts have made any appreciable difference in the education of our children. No one has listened to what we have to say." "We are infuriated," one protester told a reporter. "We have been infuriated," another broke in, "for a long time."

The sit-in lasted through the night and into the next day. When Board of Education President Garrison appeared that morning and tried to get Galamison to leave his desk, the latter, no doubt with ironic pleasure, told him he was "out of order."

Garrison once again retreated, but he was running out of patience. After another fruitless day of waiting, he finally gave the order for the police to move in. Galamison, Lurie, and ten others were carried out of the Board of Education chambers and arrested, as their supporters stood outside 110 Livingston Street with signs reading "Will Jail Help My Child To Read?"[1]

They had, however, made their point, both to the Board of Education and the city at large: without community control of education in black neighborhoods, there would be no peace in New York. And the protesters themselves would come to see the shared experience of the "People's Board of Education" sit-in as a landmark not only in the battle for community control, but in a larger struggle for their vision of political and cultural "equality" in the city. Another, less expansive vision, embodied by the UFT and its supporters, would stand in their way.

As the "People's Board of Education" drama unfolded, the Ocean Hill–Brownsville neighborhood was emerging as a hotbed of pro–community control sentiment. This development also owed much to the workings of an awkward Board of Education bureaucracy. The central Board had combined Ocean Hill–Brownsville and the predominantly white and middle-class East Flatbush section of Brooklyn into one district, Number 17, as part of its largely ineffectual attempt to promote racial balance in the public schools. East Flatbush residents, however, commandeered all the seats on the district's local school board, denying representation to Ocean Hill–Brownsville. In early 1967, exasperated Ocean Hill–Brownsville parents and activists began a boycott of the local board and formed their own "Independent School Board No. 17," a localized model of the "People's Board of Education" of the previous December that contained some of the same personnel, including Galamison.

Although the "Independent School Board No. 17" had no official legal standing, it received initial support from an unlikely source, in view of subsequent events— the UFT. Union leaders favored an alliance with the Independent Board for two interrelated reasons. First, they wished to curry favor with black parents by joining their demand that 110 Livingston Street pay more attention to the Ocean Hill–Brownsville community. And second, to the UFT, "attention" meant services— more teachers, more specialists, more equipment—in a word, "more." "More," of course, would mean additional employment opportunities for UFT members. And the More Effective Schools, or MES, program for poor neighborhoods was particularly promising in this regard. MES-designated schools received an infusion of labor-intensive educational services that required more hiring—two and sometimes three teachers per class, remedial reading and mathematics specialists, guidance counselors, and program coordinators. The desire of union leaders for MES designations for as many Ocean Hill–Brownsville schools as possible, in fact, provided the single best explanation for the UFT's support of the initial stages of the community control movement in the district.

Albert Shanker dispatched Sandra Feldman, his most trusted field representative and later president of the UFT, to Ocean Hill early in 1967 to help the Independent Board and local residents pry "more" from the central Board of Education. In February of that year, Feldman organized a demonstration at PS 144 with local Ocean Hill–Brownsville parents, seeking its designation as an MES school. They also demanded the removal of 144's unpopular principal, whose bureaucratic instransigence was well known, and who was notorious for his customary response — "I get my orders from downtown" — to any suggestions that smacked of innovation or change. The protesters obtained the transfer of the principal, and, while rebuffed in their campaign for MES designation, were able to force the Board of Education to promise upgraded services at the school, including additional reading teachers and guidance counselors.[2] The UFT, encouraged by this qualified victory in its quest for "more," continued to work informally with the Independent Board in Ocean Hill–Brownsville during the winter and spring of 1967.

But the union leadership may have misapprehended the goals of the Independent Board and the parents and activists of Ocean Hill–Brownsville with whom they sought to ally around the demand for "more." Ocean Hill–Brownsville residents, by 1967, were moving beyond this idea, and beginning to question the legitimacy of the city's public education system itself. For the UFT, both leadership and rank and file, this legitimacy was an article of faith; they believed in money, not redistributive change, as an instrument of reform. In 1967, most UFT teachers felt that residents of neighborhoods such as Ocean Hill–Brownsville shared their belief that more services and facilities would cure what ailed the New York City public schools. But, even as they marched with the UFT at PS 144, Ocean Hill–Brownsville parents were showing signs that their understanding of "school reform" was very different from that of the union.

Their increasingly ambivalent reactions were best illustrated by Elaine Rooke, the president of the Parent-Teacher Association at Ocean Hill–Brownsville's flagship school, Junior High School 271. In May 1968, Rooke would sit on the local school board that voted to fire Fred Nauman, but in 1966, she was a supporter of 271's white principal, Jack Bloomfield, and his staff of mostly white UFT teachers. Bloomfield had arrived at the school in 1964. His tenure had been relatively successful, if measured by the traditional standards of reading and mathematics scores, which improved substantially between 1964 and 1967, although they still ranked below the city average.[3] He also attracted additional educational services and resources to the school. Bloomfield sought to link JHS 271 and Ocean Hill–Brownsville community residents through an "Ocean Hill Community Council," on which Rooke sat. The council, while not an activist group, did provide a forum for discussion and air-clearing. Apparently, Rooke was satisfied with this arrangement, and with Bloomfield, in 1966. In June of that year, she presented him with a certificate commending him for his work, and wrote in the school magazine: "The teachers of the school have certainly shown [students] how much they feel they are special. . . . We have worked closely and harmoniously toward keeping [JHS 271] among the top schools that New York City has ever had."[4] Yet, only a year later, Rooke left the Ocean Hill Community Council for a different community group with a much more socially transformative agenda, the Brownsville Community Corporation. This group, the officially designated War on Poverty agency in Ocean Hill–Brownsville, sought to use community action as a means of resource redistribution in the neighborhood. It viewed white educators as part of the problem, not the solution.

By 1967, Rooke was accusing white teachers in the district of having "bad attitudes." "They don't live in the neighborhood," she complained, "and they rush out of the school and the neighborhood before three o'clock."[5] Two newcomers to Ocean Hill–Brownsville, who became acquainted with Rooke through the Brownsville Community Corporation, played a major role in her change of heart. C. Herbert Oliver, who as the chairman of the Ocean Hill–Brownsville local school board would help draft Fred Nauman's termination letter, was a minister who had arrived in 1965 to head the Westminster Bethany United Presbyterian Church. Oliver came from Birmingham, where he had been active in the Southern Christian Leadership Conference. Oliver was skeptical of the abilities and motives of white educators in the Ocean Hill–Brownsville schools, for personal as well as philosophical reasons. His son, a student in the Ocean Hill schools, was performing poorly in most subjects, and failing math. Since the boy had made the honor roll in Birmingham, where he had been taught by black teachers, Oliver concluded that the fault lay with indifferent white educators who did not believe his son was as capable as white students.[6] He believed there was no point in adding "more" services and programs to an already dysfunctional educational structure as long as white teacher attitudes remained the same.

Rooke's other major influence was also a man of the cloth. The Reverend John Powis, a white worker-priest, had come to live and organize in Ocean Hill–Brownsville in the mid-1960s. He quickly made his Our Lady of Presentation Church into a clearinghouse for local community control activists. In 1968, he, like Oliver, would sit on the local school board that sought to oust Fred Nauman.

Powis's political philosophy was closer to anarchism than anything else. He viewed the public education system as the racist bulwark of a "sick society."[7] His institutionalized definition of "racism" damned white teachers as a group, regardless of their personal attitudes. With advisers such as Oliver and Powis, it is hardly surprising that Elaine Rooke's opinions about the public schools in Ocean Hill–Brownsville shifted drastically between 1965 and 1967.

While the UFT leadership sought to attribute Rooke's change of heart solely to the influence of "irresponsible extremists," her motivations were much more complex. Rooke, and many Ocean Hill–Brownsville parents like her, saw their children caught up in a cycle of failure in the neighborhood schools. Reading and mathematics scores had indeed risen under Bloomfield, but they still lagged far behind those in white middle-class areas of the city. It was also true that the UFT had succeeded in attracting more money, services, and programs to the district. The community's schools, however, seemed to be training their children for blue-collar and unskilled jobs that no longer existed, since the unemployment rate in Ocean Hill–Brownsville was 22 percent, and even higher among those under twenty-five years of age.[8]

And the white teachers themselves, while rarely employing overtly racist language, were, at best, condescending and patronizing toward black children. Rooke thought the white teachers were different — very different — from their pupils and their parents. They dressed differently, spoke differently, lived differently. They seemed to need different things. They wanted to get ahead, of course, as most people did, but with a hard, aggressive edge that Rooke wasn't used to. She had heard them talking to each other at school when she headed the PTA. Everything seemed to be about job announcements and tests and promotions, and often, down payments on houses in nice neighborhoods she couldn't afford, or vacation trips to places she knew she'd never see. And when the white teachers spoke about their students, they usually talked about their failures, large and small. The teachers seemed to think that the way they lived was better than the way she and her children lived, as if their lives were some sort of an example for her to emulate. But Rooke was not sure whether, for all their material success, the white teachers were the examples she wanted her children to follow. Of course, she hoped they would have financial security, but neither did she want her children to be the white teachers. Yet this is what the white teachers seemed to want. And the way things were in Ocean Hill–Brownsville, this couldn't happen even if she wanted it to.

By 1967, then, Elaine Rooke, and many Ocean Hill–Brownsville parents like her, viewed the UFT and its white teachers with growing suspicion and anger.

Sandra Feldman and other UFT leaders argued that "more" programs and services would help their children, but the people they really appeared to benefit were the teachers themselves, with "more" jobs, money, and material comforts. The union said it wanted a parent-teacher alliance, but only on its own terms. It assumed that what was good for the UFT was also good for black parents. UFT leaders did not appear fully to comprehend the depth of despair felt by parents such as Elaine Rooke. And they certainly could not understand why Rooke would blame white teachers for problems whose origins lay far beyond their classrooms. There was, of course, much justification for their feelings of bewilderment on this score. But white teachers, in Ocean Hill–Brownsville and elsewhere in New York, may not have understood the extent to which they had become symbols for parents like Elaine Rooke, symbols of an economic, social, and educational system that marginalized her and her children. It was this emotion that had led one of Rooke's friends to tell a white Ocean Hill–Brownsville teacher: "You ruined my life—you're not going to ruin my children's too."[9]

Exaggerated as these sentiments may have been, they spoke volumes as to the perceptual chasm separating white teachers and black parents in neighborhoods like Ocean Hill–Brownsville by 1967. White teachers viewed the educational system as one that, while flawed, had helped them, and would help anyone wishing to work hard. Black parents saw the system as a failure. Each generalized from their own experiences and projected them onto the other. As a result, by the spring of 1967, Sandra Feldman and Jack Bloomfield would be no match for C. Herbert Oliver and John Powis in the battle for the allegiance of Elaine Rooke and other Ocean Hill–Brownsville parents. It was obvious to them that white control of black schools had led nowhere. It was time, as one parent would put it, "to make our own rules for our own schools"—time, in other words, for community control.[10]

John Lindsay's thoughts at this time were proceeding along similar lines. He also had a more prosaic problem to solve. He needed to find a way to pry more funding for New York City's public schools out of the State Legislature in Albany, a body dominated by "upstaters" traditionally lukewarm to the city's financial needs.[11] In the spring of 1967, Lindsay asked the legislature to consider the five boroughs of the city as separate entities for school funding purposes, an accounting maneuver that would significantly increase the total allocated to the city as a whole. The legislature responded by asking the mayor to decentralize the city's public educational system down to the borough level, in order to make the arrangement more than just a paper transaction.

This was the go-ahead signal that Lindsay was hoping for when he made his

2. Ocean Hill–Brownsville local school board member Elaine Rooke attempting to block the return of Fred Nauman and other white educators to Junior High School 271, May 1968. NYT Pictures/*The New York Times*

borough-wide funding proposal. He announced his intention to go the State Legislature one better: he would decentralize the schools below the boroughs, all the way down to the community level. He appointed a task force headed by Ford Foundation president McGeorge Bundy to study the issue and report back to him with a plan through which each of the city's communities would control its own schools. In the meantime, he prodded the central Board of Education to begin experimenting with various forms of community control. In April 1967, the Board announced its intention to do just that, issuing a policy statement inviting localities to apply for authorization to implement community control plans. The Board also announced that it would permit funding for such plans to be solicited from outside sources, including private sources, a departure from its traditional policy.[12]

The central Board's guidelines for such plans were relatively cautious. They continued the central assignment of teaching and administrative personnel, and competitive, examination-based hiring procedures. In an effort to facilitate the recruitment of minority faculty, they permitted local school boards to petition the Superintendent of Schools to waive formal hiring requirements "if exceptional circumstances exist," and request that he make teacher assignments based on "due consideration of the differences in needs as reflected in the pupil population of districts." The guidelines also permitted local control of curriculum, but only within the "framework" set by the central Board of Education and the State Department of Education. In general, the Board of Education sought to make local school boards, which had heretofore been virtually irrelevant, into limited partners, but not co-managers, in the business of running the public school system.[13]

On their face, the Board's guidelines appeared to promise little more than some administrative reshuffling, a fine-tuning to make the educational system more responsive to its constituents. This, at least, is what Schools Superintendent Bernard Donovan and Alfred Giardino, the new president of the Board of Education, believed. Neither, however, took into account the intensity of the passions swirling through neighborhoods like Ocean Hill–Brownsville.

Ocean Hill–Brownsville was a logical candidate to serve as one of the Board of Education's sites for "experimentation" in community control of education. By the spring of 1967, C. Herbert Oliver and John Powis lived in the neighborhood, and Milton Galamison, the city's best-known civil rights activist and a community control supporter, preached nearby. Lillian Wagner, whose demand to be heard by the Board of Education had sparked the "People's Board of Education" demonstration in December 1966, was an Ocean Hill–Brownsville resident, as were other "People's Board" veterans. And in "Independent School Board No. 17," the neighborhood already had an informally functioning "experiment" in community control.

It was also logical for the Ford Foundation to be interested in Ocean Hill–Brownsville. The foundation's director, McGeorge Bundy, a community control supporter, was already serving as chairman of the Lindsay-appointed panel studying the issue, and his chief educational policy adviser, Mario Fantini, was actively searching for possible projects to fund. Ford and Ocean Hill–Brownsville were brought together by members of the staff of the Institute for Community Studies at Queens College (ICS), a group of New Left–influenced academics attracted by the link between community control and the principles of participatory democracy. ICS's head, Marilyn Gittell, a professor of sociology at Queens College, would co-author a book on community control of education with Fantini.[14] And both Gittell and Fantini were personally acquainted with Powis and aware of his work in the Ocean Hill–Brownsville community. Thus, a number of personalities and forces converged in support of the community control impulse at Ocean Hill–Brownsville in the spring of 1967.

Community control also made a great deal of sense to Ocean Hill–Brownsville residents, because it spoke to their basic concerns. In addition to the hope of improved educational opportunities for their children, it offered the possibility of changing the rules governing the public education market in the city to make more jobs and political power available to them. Community control's premise that outside bureaucrats had failed meant employment possibilities for local residents, who could work as paraprofessionals and teacher's assistants in the Ocean Hill–Brownsville schools. In addition, the end of the central Board of Education's stranglehold on awarding contracts for school construction and maintenance might provide local men with a long-awaited opportunity to break the near-monopoly held by whites in these areas; in 1968, the Board of Education had awarded two-thirds of the contracts for these services to just two white-owned firms, each with virtually no black employees.[15]

Community control also promised to end the political marginalization of the average Ocean Hill–Brownsville citizen, by creating an alternative route to empowerment. This route to political influence, ironically, did not involve traditional currencies of power. The architects of the community action apparatus wished it to be independent from the established political structure in areas such as Ocean Hill–Brownsville, because they considered that structure to have failed. While local residents voted for representatives to "community corporations," these elections were in practice marked by low levels of voter participation. There were no primaries or endorsement battles that served to eliminate "outsiders." Consequently, one did not need a broad popular base to be elected, only some name recognition in the neighborhood, which could mean simply being seen "around." The democratic features of this new currency were obvious. They did, on the other hand, tend to empower individuals who did not have broad-based electoral support, and were not skilled in the politician's art of compromise. Community action thus had the potential to create "leaders" who purported to speak for the "community," but who in fact represented narrow constituencies.[16]

In 1967, little of this seemed to matter, but by the time of the city's fiscal crisis in the mid-1970s, community control's seductive promise of political power without the requirement of an electoral base would play New York's black population false, since only the mass electoral muscle that community control implicitly discouraged could stave off budget cuts and service reductions that impacted black citizens disproportionately. With power on community boards but not at the polls, where blacks represented close to a quarter of the city's population but only about 15 percent of its voters, black leaders were unable to prevent these cuts.[17] They would learn the hard lesson that "community," if not translated into a political organization plausibly able to threaten retribution at the ballot box, offered only imperfect protection against shifts in the city's political winds.

In the spring of 1967, however, all this lay in the future. Ocean Hill–Brownsville citizens saw community control as a chance to change the rules of an unfair market, and end decades of economic and political marginalization. They, and the educational activists who supported community control, were joined at this early stage by the UFT. The union supported Ocean Hill–Brownsville as a site for a community control experiment in the spring of 1967, although its motives presaged the disagreements that were to come.

Albert Shanker was encouraged by Sandra Feldman's limited success in joining with parents to obtain "more" services at Ocean Hill–Brownsville's PS 144, and hoped that the union and the community could now unite in a campaign to make all of the district's schools MES. To Shanker, in fact, the idea of "community control" meant, essentially, MES. Shanker was also uncomfortable with the very term "community control," which he rarely used in public. He preferred "decentralization," a more limited arrangement under which local boards would "consult" the union and the central Board of Education as they decided the essential questions of school governance. As a co-manager of the public education system in New York, the UFT had a vested interest in preserving the apparatus of centralized control that the Board of Education had created. Shanker's version of "decentralization" thus had no room for local control of spending, personnel, and curriculum. Shanker believed that his brand of decentralization offered a significant advance over past practice, and he was right. Since 1898, local school boards had been little more than rubber stamps. But "decentralization" according to Albert Shanker, and "community control" according to John Powis, C. Herbert Oliver, and Elaine Rooke, were very different things.

Swayed largely by the UFT's recommendation, Schools Superintendent Bernard Donovan chose Ocean Hill–Brownsville as one of the Board of Education's experimental community control districts in May 1967. Donovan proposed a procedure and timetable that bespoke the central Board of Education's bureaucratic caution. He called for the formation of a "planning council," composed of Ocean Hill–Brownsville residents, teachers, and school administrators. The planning council would prepare a detailed blueprint for community control; this would govern methods of electing local board members and delineate the powers of the board. The blueprint would then be submitted to Donovan for his approval in the fall of 1967.[18] This was typical Board of Education practice: a leisurely planning process, followed by an extended high-echelon review.

UFT teachers in Ocean Hill–Brownsville, including Fred Nauman, began meeting with community leaders to formulate this blueprint. The UFT also envisioned a leisurely process, especially with the summer recess approaching, and one, moreover, that it would control. Accordingly, the union produced what was essentially a plan to formulate a plan. Its "Plan for an Experimental School District in District 17," which Sandra Feldman sent to the Board of Education, contained Donovan's "planning council" idea, as well as modest proposals for local input into personnel, curricular, and financial matters. The Ocean Hill–Brownsville local school board, whenever it was installed, would prepare a list of candidates for the position of "Unit Administrator" to serve as the nominal head of the district's schools, but Donovan would make the final selection. While the plan did not define the unit administrator's powers with specificity, Feldman clearly envisioned roughly the same limited, consultative responsibilities as exercised by the administrators of the city's other, nonexperimental school districts, who were known as "district superintendents." The plan also provided for a continuation of the competitive examination system, although it did express the hope, in a bow to local sensibilities, that teachers chosen in this manner would maintain sympathetic relations with the Ocean Hill–Brownsville community. Most importantly to the UFT leadership, the plan asked that all eight schools in Ocean Hill–Brownsville be designated MES schools. This amounted to a demand for the expansion of the teaching force in the area by some 25 percent, a typical expression of the union's philosophy of "more."[19]

As the UFT charted its course, however, other actors were proceeding with their own, different plans for community control in Ocean Hill–Brownsville. In June and July, they emerged to confront the union. The Ford Foundation was eager to provide funding to the nascent Ocean Hill–Brownsville experiment. The foundation's education liaison, Mario Fantini, worked with Powis and the ICS's Marilyn Gittell to execute an end run around both the union and the Board of Education, taking most of the Ocean Hill–Brownsville community with them. Without consulting Shanker or Donovan, Fantini announced a Ford Foundation grant of forty-four thousand dollars to the Ocean Hill experimental project in late June. Fantini deliberately routed the grant funds through Marilyn Gittell's ICS and Powis's Our Lady of Presentation Church. Fantini also announced that the Ocean Hill–Brownsville local board, when it came into existence, would have the power to hire and fire school personnel independent of the central Board of Education, another circumvention of Shanker and Donovan.[20] Donovan protested ineffectually, telling Fantini on June 30 that he was moving too "definitively" for his tastes.[21] But Donovan did not, either at this time or during the critical summer months that followed, put his foot down and order that the process of setting up the Ocean Hill–Brownsville experimental district be slowed or modified to fit his agenda. Instead, Donovan implicitly accepted the different direction the project was taking.[22] Donovan's reticence can be explained in part by his reluctance to be perceived as an obstacle to the aspirations of the Ocean Hill–Brownsville community. He was especially wary of accusations of racism, as Powis, who had observed his behavior during the IS 201 controversy in 1966, was well aware. Powis, Rhody McCoy, and the community control supporters would use this sensitivity for their own purposes as the Ocean Hill–Brownsville controversy developed.

The UFT teachers who served on the Ocean Hill–Brownsville "Planning Council" did not head off Powis and Fantini's alternative plans for the project for a simpler reason: they were not around. The Spring 1967 semester ended on June 30, and the UFT representatives duly packed their belongings and turned their attention to the traditional summer activities of New York public school teachers— second jobs, graduate courses, and summer camps. Their contacts with the Ocean Hill–Brownsville neighborhood during the summer were sporadic, because they expected that the "planning" for the community control experiment would resume in earnest in the fall. But they miscalculated: by then events had moved past them.

At the beginning of July, Fantini, Gittell, and Powis agreed that by September the Ocean Hill–Brownsville community control experiment would have an elected board, a unit administrator, and a plan of operation. All would be as independent of the UFT and the central Board of Education as possible. Powis turned his attention first to the matter of the unit administrator. He introduced Rhody McCoy to the planning council, at a meeting attended neither by the UFT representatives nor by any official from Donovan's office.[23]

McCoy was an eighteen-year veteran of the New York City public schools. A native of the city, he had begun his career in the system after graduating from

3. Ocean Hill–Brownsville Unit Administrator Rhody McCoy (right) outside Junior High School 271. NYT Pictures/*The New York Times*.

Howard University. He was a quiet, deliberate man, not prone to displays of emotion. Many of his professional acquaintances believed him to be apolitical. Only close friends know of his interest in, and admiration for, Malcolm X, whose Harlem meetings he attended in the early 1960s. By the summer of 1967, McCoy was the acting principal of a "special service" school for emotionally disturbed children on Manhattan's West Side. He had refused to take the examination required for permanent appointment, on principle. McCoy believed that it rewarded rote knowledge unrelated to the skills actually required by the job. He was thus not on any Board of Examiners eligibility list when Powis nominated him for unit administrator.[24] For this reason, the UFT teachers on the planning council, when they heard of his nomination, opposed him, and proposed Junior High School 271 principal Jack Bloomfield instead. Incensed, Powis and the rest of the council, at a meeting to which the teachers had not been invited, selected McCoy.[25]

To them, McCoy's lack of "paper" credentials was a point in his favor, not a reason to reject him. McCoy was known as one of the rare public school administrators whose leadership style combined compassion and firmness. He liked black children, and had not given up on their capacity to learn, even under the trying conditions of a "special service" school which housed "difficult" children. He believed in the black community and in community control. These qualities, above all others, recommended him to Powis and his allies on the Ocean Hill–Brownsville planning council.

McCoy moved quickly to align himself with the parent members of the planning council, all of whom were women on some form of public assistance. He authorized payments to them from the Ford Foundation grant as "consultants" in the upcoming election for representatives on the permanent Ocean Hill–Brownsville local board. McCoy continued these payments to the parent members of the permanent board when it was elected, assuring himself of ongoing support from the most influential parents in the Ocean Hill–Brownsville district.[26]

With McCoy installed as unit administrator, the planning council began drafting its own community control plan for Ocean Hill–Brownsville. Once again, the UFT representatives were largely excluded from this process. Powis, Fantini, and the newly appointed McCoy set out to produce a document that was very different from the previous UFT-approved version. They intended, in fact, to construct a community control structure completely separate from the union and school bureaucracy, seizing the moment in a preemptive strike Donovan and Shanker would have no choice but to accept.

On July 29, after four weeks of concentrated effort, the planning council, minus the UFT members, produced its plan for community control in the Ocean Hill–Brownsville schools. Its preface, written by McCoy, began by describing the marginalized life of the typical Ocean Hill–Brownsville resident, although it could also have described much of the rest of black New York in 1967. "There are people here," McCoy wrote, "who feel themselves out of sight of other people, groping in the dark. The city takes no notice of them. In the midst of a crowd, at church or in the marketplace, these people are about as obscure as they would be if locked somewhere in a cellar. It is not that they are censured or reproached; they are simply not seen — the invisible people. To be wholly overlooked and to know it is intolerable." "Men are capable of putting an end to what they find is intolerable without resort to politics," McCoy warned. "The ending of oppression and the beginning of a new day has often become a reality only after people have resorted to violent means." The Ocean Hill–Brownsville community control experiment, he concluded, "represents the last threads of the community's faith in the school system's purposes and abilities."[27]

The community control plan went on to claim sweeping powers for the Ocean Hill–Brownsville local board, which it envisioned replacing the central Board of Education in the district's schools. The local board would control hiring, curriculum, and finances. It would have the right to continue to solicit funds from sources outside the central Board, a privilege denied other school districts in the city, and one that would give it the potential to use Ford Foundation support to eventually become independent of the entire public school system. And, in a deliberate slap at the UFT, the plan made no provision for MES in any of the district's schools.[28]

The election for positions on the Ocean Hill–Brownsville local board took place on August 3 and 4, almost immediately after the release of the Powis-McCoy community control plan, and once again without the active participation of the UFT or the official sanction of the central Board of Education. The neighborhood parents whom McCoy had designated as paid "election consultants" ran as candidates themselves, and went door-to-door soliciting votes. Polls were also open at the neighborhood schools. Eleven hundred residents participated, representing about 22 percent of the parents in Ocean Hill–Brownsville, and approximately 10 percent of the area's registered voters. This turnout, while relatively light, did approximate the average rate for legislative races in the district.[29]

Seven parents, all of whom were already serving as McCoy-appointed "election consultants," emerged victorious, including Elaine Rooke. They, in turn, chose five community representatives to join them on the local board. Notable among these were Powis, Assemblyman Samuel Wright, and the Reverend C. Herbert Oliver, who was elected the board's chairman. The local board completed its roster by selecting Professor Stephen Lockwood of Brooklyn College, a community control activist with ties to Powis and Fantini.[30]

From the start, the parent members of the local board held the balance of power. They came from similar backgrounds: most were black, poor, and female. All had been active in the Ocean Hill–Brownsville schools, and many, like Elaine Rooke, had served as Parent-Teacher Association officers. They shared Oliver's disillusionment with white teachers. The parents were also driven by a desire for a measure of respect from them. The parent representatives were all too aware of their lack of educational credentials; most had not finished high school. When white teachers in Ocean Hill–Brownsville questioned their decisions on the local board, the parents believed they were really questioning their qualifications to decide educational policy. The UFT leadership invariably justified its criticism of the Ocean Hill local board by asking whether "nonprofessionals"—a veiled reference to the parent representatives—could properly play such an important role in the schools. "The terrible thing for most opponents of community control," wrote McCoy, mockingly describing this attitude, "is that the thrust for control is being made by people who 'aren't equipped' to exercise it. They're backward. There are no Ph.D.'s or college presidents among them. They're just 'folks' and what on earth do they know about schools?"[31] White teachers who criticized the parents on the local board may well have believed they were debating policy issues, and meant nothing personal. What the parents actually heard, however, was an attack on their legitimacy, and, indirectly, their lives. Like Oliver and McCoy, their day of reckoning with the white teachers of Ocean Hill–Brownsville would come on May 9, 1968.

The newly elected Ocean Hill–Brownsville local board's first order of business was the appointment of principals for the schools in the district that had vacancies. Ordinarily, the board would have had nothing to decide, since principals were centrally appointed by Superintendent Donovan from a list according to examination scores. For elementary school principals, the superintendent was bound by the "rule of three" to select one of the three top scorers. By 1967, the system had become so rigid that in practice, the superintendent invariably chose the applicant with the highest grade.[32] Selection of junior and senior high school principals was governed by a "qualifying list" system, under which the superintendent could elevate any candidate attaining a designated minimum examination grade, although, once again, in practice those with the highest scores were usually chosen first.

McCoy and the Ocean Hill–Brownsville local board, however, viewed the principal selection issue as the first real test of their authority, and were determined to assert their prerogatives. They also wished to make a point about the racial distribution of principalships in the public school system. Only 1 percent of the principals in New York were black in 1967, and the existing eligibility lists were composed almost entirely of whites.[33] Accordingly, McCoy informed Donovan that he wished to fill Ocean Hill–Brownsville's vacancies with principals who were not on

any Board of Examiners list. Their only qualification would be New York State certification, which consisted of basic college education courses and did not involve
passing an examination.[34]

Donovan was uncomfortable with the idea, but he did not wish to risk a confrontation. He placed the matter on the desk of his superior, State Education
Commissioner James Allen, whose sympathies for community control were well
known, and asked whether the examination requirements for appointing principals could be waived. Allen replied that while they could not, he would nonetheless attempt to find a way to give the local board what it wanted. He contacted
Howard Kalodner, a Columbia University law professor who was also sympathetic
to community control, and asked him to find an alternative legal route. Kalodner complied by creating an entirely new category, that of "demonstration" school
principal. Requirements for this new position, as Kalodner outlined them, would
consist of New York State certification, plus rapport with the community that the
principal would serve. Demonstration principal appointments could be made immediately on an acting basis by the Ocean Hill–Brownsville local board, without
any examination requirement. Kalodner's guidelines called for a flexible examination, to be developed at an unspecified future time, that would emphasize community relations rather than administrative arcana. Kalodner and Allen assured
McCoy that whenever such an examination was developed, he would have the
major voice in determining its form.[35]

For the time being, however, there would be no examination, and in late August, McCoy and the local board set out to make their choices. They chose Louis
Fuentes, a reading consultant, who would be only the second permanent principal of Puerto Rican ancestry in the city system, to head PS 155. Ralph Rogers, a
black assistant principal, was tapped to head PS 144. Irving Gerber, a white who
had expressed interest in working in a community-controlled district, and who
was the only one of the local board's choices to be on an eligibility list, would lead
PS 87.

The final principal chosen was Herman Ferguson, a black teacher active in the
militant Revolutionary Action Movement, then under indictment for conspiring
to murder civil rights leaders Roy Wilkins and Whitney Young. Ferguson's appointment was too much even for the accommodating Donovan, who immediately
suspended him pending the outcome of his trial. He did, however, permit Ferguson to serve as a paid adviser to one of the other districts experimenting with
community control, IS 201 in Harlem, until his case was finally decided.[36]

When the UFT representatives on the planning council returned for the fall
semester, McCoy announced that he expected them to ratify the actions taken by
the local board during the summer, including those relating to principal selection.

The UFT members immediately disassociated themselves from the local board, complaining that they had been frozen out of decision making and that they were the victims of racial harassment. From that point forward, the UFT would have no representation on the Ocean Hill–Brownsville local board.[37]

Both UFT leaders and McCoy agreed that the events of the summer of 1967 in Ocean Hill–Brownsville permanently defined their relationship. They agreed on little else about them, however. Fred Nauman, the union chapter chairman at Junior High School 271, saw them as illustrating the unreasonableness of the local board members:

> The teachers who were selected to help in the planning (of the community control experiment) quickly found that their job was not a simple one. Suggestions on their part were taken as attempts to destroy the plan, although that was not their intent at all. It became apparent to them that they were not invited to all of the local board's sessions. Portions of the plan were presented to them as already approved. Rhody McCoy, who had been selected as acting Unit Administrator for the summer without any consultation with the teachers, informed them that items that could not be agreed on would be decided by the local board. The (community control) proposal was rewritten during the summer, largely without the knowledge or presence of the teachers.[38]

McCoy's interpretation of the summer's events was quite different. He emphasized the intransigence of the UFT. The teachers' objections to the principals the local board had selected, McCoy argued, "emanated from their determination to see that no militants or black power advocates were selected. This, to us, was an attempt to exclude a vital segment of the community and to deny the exercise of free choice. . . . Every attempt was made to eliminate [community control]. . . . Racism was rampant. [Local board] members were involved in answering UFT charges. They spent innumerable hours interpreting the program to the community and attempting to maintain solidarity and support. They practiced self-restraint and reason throughout."[39] The disagreements of the summer of 1967 would set the tone for the succeeding winter, fall, and spring: one set of circumstances, two sets of interpretations.

The UFT did more than disassociate itself from the Ocean Hill–Brownsville local board to protest the demonstration principal idea. It joined a lawsuit brought by the organization representing the city's principals, the Council of Supervisory Associations (CSA), challenging the validity of the new category, as well as the appointment of McCoy as unit administrator, under the state Education Law and the state and federal constitutions.[40] The UFT's action was unprecedented. Never before had teachers reached across class lines to ally with their nominal superiors in a legal proceeding. While some UFT leaders questioned the union's action on this basis, the majority, led by Shanker, argued successfully that, as during the IS 201 controversy the year before, the merit principle, and the idea of "equality" itself, were at stake. McCoy had stated during the summer that his eventual goal was an all-black teaching staff in Ocean Hill–Brownsville, and Shanker viewed the "off-list" principals issue as merely the opening salvo in a battle that would eventually involve his teachers.[41] Shanker also knew that the "merit" hiring issue was an emotional, visceral one to his rank and file, and felt he had to take a stand, if only to keep abreast of them. A union election loomed in June 1968.[42]

The CSA lawsuit began what would become a year-and-a-half-long odyssey through the New York State court system. In March 1968, a trial court ruled that the demonstration principal idea violated the portion of the State Education Law mandating that all appointments to pedagogical positions be governed by substantive written examinations, as well as the antidiscrimination provisions of the state constitution. The court upheld McCoy's appointment, however, ruling that the unit administrator position was a new category that could be filled without an examination on a temporary, experimental basis.[43] An intermediate appeals court upheld the invalidation of the demonstration principals in November 1968, a major victory for the UFT, which was then in the midst of its third citywide teachers strike aimed at obtaining the reinstatement of Fred Nauman and the other union teachers terminated by the Ocean Hill–Brownsville local board. Shanker refused to settle that strike until he received assurance that the demonstration principals would be removed pending a further appeal.[44] In January 1969, after the strike had ended, the state's highest court reversed the lower courts and upheld the demonstration principal appointments, although on narrow grounds, permitting them only as limited experiments and mandating the preparation of written examinations for the category in the future.[45] Despite losing its immediate battle, the UFT had made its point. It would fight for its view of "equality" and "merit" in the city's public education market, a view that was intimately bound up with the civil service examination system. But by supporting the demonstration principal concept, McCoy and the local board had made their point as well. They would fight as tenaciously as the UFT for their own, different understandings of these words.

The citywide teachers strike of September 1967 further poisoned relations between the union and the Ocean Hill–Brownsville local board. This strike, unlike the one that would come a year later, did not arise out of events specific to Ocean Hill–Brownsville. Nevertheless, many in that community, including McCoy and the members of the local board, interpreted it as directed at them. In its negotiations for a new contract with the Board of Education in the spring and summer of 1967, the UFT demanded wage increases, an expansion of funding for MES programs, and, most controversially, a "disruptive child" provision permitting teachers to unilaterally remove seriously misbehaving pupils from their classrooms and schools. The union struck all of the city's schools in September over these issues.[46]

While the 1967 strike, which lasted two weeks, affected all of New York, black communities, and especially Ocean Hill–Brownsville, viewed it as a racial affront—an attempt to withhold educational services from black schoolchildren. In Ocean Hill–Brownsville, McCoy and the local board kept the schools open throughout the strike. Members of the ATA helped staff the classrooms on a skeleton basis.[47] Emblematic of the perceptual gulf between the local board and the UFT was the latter's offer, made through Nauman, of a quid pro quo—in the form of MES designation for all Ocean Hill schools—exchange for the local board's support of the strike. The board, which viewed MES as little more than a jobs boondoggle for the UFT, dismissed the offer out of hand, as the union leadership should have known it would. The local board then launched a campaign to punish the striking UFT teachers in Ocean Hill–Brownsville. It notified the draft boards of strikers, asking that their deferments be revoked. It also encouraged community residents who worked in the Ocean Hill–Brownsville schools as monitors and teachers aides to harass the teachers upon their return to work.[48]

The 1967 strike produced an alliance between the local board, the ATA, and Mayor Lindsay, who, as Shanker's opponent at the bargaining table, had reasons of his own to oppose the union. After the strike ended, with the UFT winning substantial wage increases but failing to obtain expansion of MES or the disruptive child provision, Lindsay thanked the president of the ATA, JHS 271 assistant principal Albert Vann, for his "instant response to the teachers' strike," and for his role in keeping the Ocean Hill–Brownsville schools open. The mayor praised Vann's actions as reflecting "the finest traditions of service to the city."[49] The UFT, of course, had another term for what Vann had done: strikebreaking. The incident exacerbated a deteriorating relationship between it, on one side, and the mayor and the black community, on the other.

The release of McGeorge Bundy's report on decentralization for the entire city in early November hardened these divisions. Lindsay had stacked the deck when he appointed the commission to study the subject. Four of its five members were strong community control supporters. The commission, whose research staff was headed by Mario Fantini, gave Lindsay what he wanted—a strong endorsement of the idea of community control for the city's public schools.

The report, officially entitled "Reconnection for Learning: A Community School

System for New York City—Report of the Mayor's Advisory Panel on Decentralization of the New York City Schools," but informally referred to as the "Bundy Report," called for the city to be divided into thirty to sixty independent school districts. Each would possess almost unfettered power to hire, fire, and grant tenure to teachers and administrative personnel. The report called for the elimination of all examination requirements for hiring and promotion in the city school system, and, echoing the Ocean Hill–Brownsville local board, the substitution of New York State certification as a minimum floor for applicants. This, it argued, would "liberate the recruitment and promotional system from restrictions that have outlived their purpose and strengthen and broaden the concept of merit. No city can afford to hobble itself with a recruitment and selection process that discourages talented people from entering the system." While acknowledging that "broadening" the merit system by eliminating examinations would cause a degree of personal hardship among passed-over teachers, the report contended that defenders of the status quo "confuse past values with present needs." The report also recommended that localities be given full authority to determine the content of curriculum in their districts, and control over all spending, including school contracting, maintenance, and finance.[50]

Reaction to the Bundy Report divided along roughly the same lines as did reaction to the September teachers' strike. Most of the city media, which had opposed the strike, applauded the report. "If this proposal is radical," editorialized the *Times,* "it is because the situation is desperate. Something new and revolutionary is needed."[51] The *Post* called it "a thoughtful, provocative alternative to the intolerable status quo."[52] And the *New York Amsterdam News* praised the report's rejection of the idea "that only middle-class Caucasians have the right to set standards for themselves and the rest of society." The UFT's opposition to the elimination of examination requirements, the newspaper charged, showed "contempt for the ghetto. We cannot sympathize with the cry for 'orderly promotional procedures based on qualifications and experience' when the Board of Examiners has licensed only three Afro-Americans and no Puerto Ricans in a school system in which they make up over half the pupil population."[53] McCoy, the Ocean Hill–Brownsville local board, and the African-American Teachers Association also praised the report, as did corporate leaders, academics, educational activists from EQUAL and United Bronx Parents, and Manhattan-based political figures, including, in an ironic prelude to his later career as the city's first neoconservative mayor, Edward Koch. Lindsay made the Bundy Report, with minor modifications, the basis for the decentralization law he submitted to the State Legislature in Albany.

But the UFT reacted furiously, and launched a frontal assault on both the bill and the Bundy Report. In December, it released its own decentralization plan, contained in a union-issued "Statement on Decentralization," that harshly criticized the report. The "Statement on Decentralization" echoed the UFT-sponsored decentralization plan for Ocean Hill–Brownsville, calling for limited consultative powers for local boards in matters of curriculum and finances, with final authority resting with the central Board of Education. Educational personnel would continue to be centrally assigned from ranked lists, although the UFT was willing to accept the elimination of Board of Examiners tests and their replacement by the more widely used National Teachers Examination. The UFT plan also featured a smaller number of larger school districts than the Bundy Report—about fifteen—ostensibly to facilitate school integration, which the union continued to support rhetorically.[54]

The UFT's "Statement on Decentralization" also attacked the Bundy Report on philosophical grounds. "The history of local community participation in American cities," it argued, "has been a sad one," as New York's failed experiment with the ward system of school governance in the nineteenth century proved. Now, in a repetition of the mistakes of the past, "teachers will be hired and fired not on the basis of educational competence, but on the basis of race, political conformity to parochial community prejudices, and favoritism." The Bundy Report's call for "community standards" in hiring, charged the UFT, "is a proven failure. This is precisely the method used in school districts across the country which reward submissiveness and conformity. The UFT cannot accept the introduction of this system in New York. The present system of licensing must be changed, but not by abandoning educational standards altogether."[55]

The UFT also questioned the Bundy Report's assumption that "laymen without professional experience" could make decisions on educational policy, as well as the report's apparent faith that without a central assignment system, teachers would voluntarily choose to work in black-majority schools.[56] Since the number of teachers wishing to transfer out of such schools exceeded those desiring to transfer in, the union predicted an exacerbation of the already serious shortage of experienced teachers in ghetto schools.

Viewed side by side, the Bundy Report and the UFT "Statement on Decentralization" encapsulated the growing perceptual chasm between supporters of local control and the union over understandings of "equality" and definitions of "community." Both sides were confronting a series of unsettling conundrums. The UFT had always prided itself on being a "populist" organization. Broad-based worker democracy was part of its heritage. Yet its "Statement on Decentralization" showed the union leadership to be profoundly suspicious of "the people," in both black and white "communities." Supporters of community control, on the other hand, as the Bundy Report illustrated, also celebrated the idea of a "people's democracy" in theory, but applied it primarily to black neighborhoods, unable or unwilling to come to grips with its implications for more conservative whites. Moreover, the UFT had always regarded the competitive test system, where, ostensibly, nothing but ability in the examination room mattered, as the embodiment of "equality" in a democratic society. Many of its members had spent their professional lives fighting for such a "fair chance." But how could a system that produced such racially skewed ratios of success be described as an "equal" one? UFT leaders and rank-and-filers had no satisfactory answer to this uncomfortable question. And, conversely, supporters of the Bundy Report's call for elimination of the use of all competitive examinations in the New York City public school system evinced a literal egalitarianism that nonetheless begged questions of racial and ethnic favoritism in the distribution of societal rewards. Both sides plunged stubbornly ahead—ironies, contradictions, and all.

In Ocean Hill–Brownsville, the UFT and the local board continued to feud. The 1967–68 academic year had already gotten off to a tumultuous start with the UFT strike in September. In its angry aftermath, dozens of white Ocean Hill–Brownsville teachers demanded to transfer out of the district. Shanker, who did not wish at this point to be held responsible for the community control experiment's demise, asked them to remain, invoking, somewhat incongruously, the example of "the kids at Little Rock" who had integrated that city's public schools a decade earlier.[57] Shanker was able to prevent a mass exodus of union teachers from the Ocean Hill–Brownsville schools, but did negotiate an upward modification of the citywide rule that limited transfers to 5 percent of a school's teacher population in any one year. In Ocean Hill–Brownsville, 10 percent per semester would now have this option.[58] While placating the teachers, the compromise infuriated McCoy and the local board, who viewed it as emblematic of white teacher disrespect for the Ocean Hill–Brownsville community control experiment.

On the heels of this came the request of all of the district's assistant principals, who were not subject to teacher transfer quotas, to leave Ocean Hill–Brownsville. After Donovan reluctantly granted the transfers, McCoy demanded that the new assistant principals be chosen without examination requirements, in the manner of the demonstration elementary school principals. Donovan, however, bowing to CSA and UFT pressure, chose them in rank order from the Board of Examiners list; all were white.[59] Meanwhile, McCoy complained about his inability to obtain supplies from the central Board of Education, a problem common to most district superintendents, but one which took on a racial tinge under the charged circumstances. McCoy viewed his seven-week wait for office space and telephone service at the start of the 1967–68 school year in similar, racially conspiratorial terms.

McCoy's anger at the UFT, and at white unionized teachers in Ocean Hill–

Brownsville generally, was often directed at Fred Nauman, the UFT's chapter chairman at Junior High School 271, and Shanker's informal point man in the Ocean Hill–Brownsville district. Nauman, like McCoy, was a child of poverty who had used the city's public education system as a route to a better material life, but the similarities ended there. He had been born in Germany, and had come to America in the late 1930s as a small boy with his parents, fleeing Nazi persecution. A product of the New York public schools and Brooklyn College, he became a science teacher after graduation, and quietly worked his way up the ranks, serving as a guidance counselor, department chair, and, for a brief period, assistant principal. He joined the UFT's small predecessor union, the Teachers Guild, in the 1950s, and was one of the charter members of the infant UFT in 1960.[60]

Nauman had benefited personally from the Board of Examiners system. In fact, his career up to 1968 had been a classic example of what one study of advancement in the New York City public education system had considered significant enough to grace with an acronym: "GASing," or "Getting the Attention of Superiors."[61] GASing was the route to upward mobility for teachers in the city schools, and Nauman had used it well. By 1968, with his UFT chapter chairmanship factored in, he was the most influential white teacher in Ocean Hill–Brownsville. Nauman had faith in the New York public schools as a functioning, working system, in a way that McCoy did not. The "system" had certainly worked for him. Thanks to it, he, and others like him, had a measure of financial security and social status their parents could only have dreamed of.

Nauman credited much of this success to the labor movement. Unlike McCoy, who viewed education unions as obstructionist and often racist, Nauman believed fervently in their power for good. "Dignity" was an important word to Nauman. Teachers had been denied dignity in New York for too long, until the UFT did something about it. Thanks to the UFT, teachers were no longer subject to the whims of administrators, principals, and, for that matter, local school boards. The union had forced the central Board of Education to raise salaries, improve benefits, and perhaps most important, to treat teachers as professionals, with the control over work conditions that this status entailed. Now, Nauman believed, everything the union had fought for and won was in danger, thanks to McCoy and the local board. If they had their way, teachers would lose control over their lives in the workplace. The UFT had stood up to the central Board of Education in the past, and it would stand up to Rhody McCoy here. Union teachers would not lose their dignity.[62]

Nauman and McCoy differed in another crucial respect. If McCoy was a quiet admirer of Malcolm X, Nauman's hero was Martin Luther King. To Nauman, King, a longtime UFT ally, represented the essential link between labor and civil rights that lay at the heart of the politics of liberalism in New York City after World War II. Nauman revered King for what he symbolized to him: a color-blind democracy of merit in which men were judged, in King's well-known words, "not by the color of their skin but by the content of their character." This often-repeated 1963 phrase captured the essence of what Nauman understood "equality" to mean. He, and thousands of other liberal white UFT teachers in New York City, became fixated on this phrase—and the vision of King it encapsulated—even as King himself edged away from it in the last years of his life, toward an acceptance of the use of racial preferences in the name of "equality." Nauman's understanding of King, then, may have been flawed and unrealistic. But it was heartfelt nonetheless, and he viewed McCoy, with his talk of an all-black teaching staff in Ocean Hill–Brownsville, as the very antithesis of his hero and his dream.[63]

Fred Nauman and Rhody McCoy, then, had both philosophical and practical reasons to distrust each other. Their different understandings of the meaning of labor rights, civil rights, and "equality" spilled out into the day-to-day operations of the Ocean Hill–Brownsville community control experiment, magnifying what might otherwise have been containable disagreements into a series of unmanageable crises.

By early 1968, conditions in the Ocean Hill–Brownsville schools, especially Junior High School 271, had reached new levels of chaos and acrimony. In February, William Harris, a black assistant principal, succeeded Bloomfield as principal. Also that month, Leslie Campbell, a social studies teacher who was one of the ATA's leaders, was transferred into 271. There, he joined Albert Vann to make the school home to that organization's two most important figures. Campbell made his classroom a center for the study of Afro-American history from a Marxist and nationalist perspective. He used the lives of Nat Turner, Denmark Vesey, Frederick Douglass, and Malcolm X to illustrate the need for a "revolution" in the modern-day black community, and did not shrink from discussing the possibility of violent forms of self-defense. Campbell also encouraged a flowering of black cultural forms among his students, including African art and dance, Afro-American novels and poetry, and contemporary soul music. This elicited expressions of horror from many of his white colleagues, one of whom derisively described Campbell's students as "uncontrollably twitching to that James Brown selection [he] played for them."[64] Campbell welcomed their discomfort, making no secret of his contempt for them.

Campbell, with Vann's approval, also encouraged the physical separation of black and white teachers at JHS 271 in cafeterias, lounges, and other common public spaces.[65] The school was now divided almost entirely along racial lines, with Nauman and most of the white union teachers and administrators arrayed against the black teachers, led by Vann and Campbell. White teacher absenteeism ran rampant, and acts of student vandalism occurred on almost a daily basis, including an incident in which a student threw a desk out of a third-story window.[66]

An epidemic of unexplained fires also plagued the district as a whole, and one such occurrence further poisoned relations between white teachers and the Ocean Hill–Brownsville community. In April, a fire occurred at PS 178, at about 2:00 P.M., and teachers and students evacuated into the street. They were still waiting there at 3:00 P.M., the end of the school day. Some ten teachers then left their classes standing outside the school and went home, causing panic among the unsupervised students. McCoy was outraged, accusing the teachers, all of whom were white, of abandoning the children. He charged that the incident symbolized their lack of commitment to black students. A telegram sent to Donovan after the incident by a local activist group, Project Method, went further: "We openly declare war. Recognized or not, this community will begin to act. Assistant principals and teachers will be fired this week. No hearing. . . . We declare our independence and will act as we desire."[67] Through retelling on the streets of Ocean Hill–Brownsville, what became known as the "fire incident" took on exaggerated proportions, with the number of white teachers abandoning their classes increasing as the story was repeated. It became a symbol of the Ocean Hill–Brownsville community's perception of white teachers.

The news of the assassination of Martin Luther King on April 4 pushed the district further toward the edge. The day after King's death, students at JHS 271, urged on by Campbell, rampaged through the halls, assaulting white teachers, setting off fire alarms, and vandalizing classrooms. At an impromptu memorial ceremony in the school auditorium, Campbell told the students to "stop fighting among yourselves. You save your money and finally get enough to buy a leather jacket and your brother steals it. You've got to get your minds together. You know who to steal from. If you steal, steal from those who have it. Stop fighting among yourselves."[68] The next day, a white assistant principal, in a letter to Donovan, spilled out his anger and frustration: "You must spend many a sleepless night trying to figure out what it is that makes people so difficult to deal with when all you want to do is help. The worst part is they won't even believe you and they keep on accusing you of things that never entered your head. This is the only letter I'm sending to anyone. I was going to send one to Rhody McCoy but I don't believe I will. He would probably say it's untrue or that I'm prejudiced. Well, I'm not prejudiced, I'm desperate."[69]

As the Ocean Hill–Brownsville schools themselves careened out of control, the issue of the powers of the local board, never resolved, burst to the surface. For

4. African-American Teachers Association leader Leslie Campbell telling student boycotters at Junior High School 271 not to go to a "white power school," May 15, 1968. ©Bettmann/CORBIS

months, McCoy had sidestepped Donovan's request for help in developing a written examination for the demonstration principal position. In April, McCoy and the local board dropped all pretense, and informed Donovan that "we will accept no other principals except those chosen by us and will not permit them to be subject to any new examination."[70] They also demanded that all other administrative positions in the Ocean Hill–Brownsville schools be exempted from examination requirements. After the Board of Education balked, the local board announced a boycott of the Ocean Hill–Brownsville schools for April 10. When UFT teachers came to work that day, they found no one to teach; every student in the district supported the boycott. After two days, the local board ended the boycott, and the students returned, with no change in either side's position, and the Board of Education warily awaiting the local board's next move.[71]

Albert Shanker, however, could see what that next move would be: the local board would try to fire a UFT teacher on its own initiative. Everything that the board had said and done over the past months pointed in this direction. Shanker had already moved to capture the procedural high ground on the issue. In January, a black student at Junior High School 258 in Brooklyn accused his white teacher, George Fucillo, of striking him, a charge Fucillo denied. Black community leaders demanded that Fucillo be removed from the school, and 258's principal asked Fucillo to accept a transfer to a school outside the district. Shanker contacted the teacher, however, and told him to refuse to go anywhere without a hearing. Shanker then had the UFT's Delegate Assembly adopt a resolution threatening to boycott the schools of any district in which a teacher was involuntarily transferred without a formal hearing.[72] Shanker hoped this resolution would make McCoy and the local board think twice before dealing with Fred Nauman or any UFT teacher in Ocean Hill–Brownsville in such a manner, and, if they went ahead anyway, stake out an unassailable legal position on the issue of hearings for involuntarily transferred teachers.

But, in reality, it was not entirely clear under the relevant law—in this case, the bylaws of the New York City Board of Education and the latest UFT/Board of Education collective bargaining agreement—whether hearings actually were required before a teacher could be transferred against his will. The rules governing teacher termination, in contrast, were clear. The collective bargaining agreement contained an array of due process protections, including hearings, internal reviews, and court appeals. But the agreement did not mention transfers, as distinguished from outright terminations, and the Board of Education bylaws stated only that the superintendent of schools could transfer a teacher outside a district, without specifically mandating hearings.[73]

In practice, the question rarely came up, because most teachers usually agreed "voluntarily" to interdistrict transfers arranged by their principals or district supervisors. This, in fact, was how ineffective teachers who "washed out" of white middle-class schools found their way to ghetto districts. Faced with the unwelcome alternative of a formal "unsatisfactory" rating entered on their record by a principal or department chair, they usually agreed to transfer out without a hearing.[74] Often, the UFT itself helped with this process, quietly pressuring the teacher to go along. In a few "hard" cases, usually involving severe personality clashes between a supervisor and a teacher, the union stood aside while the superintendent of schools made the transfer himself.

But the Fucillo case and the looming Nauman imbroglio presented different problems. Both teachers had good records, and neither wanted to transfer. Fucillo had not been, and Nauman would not be, offered a hearing. While they may have deserved them under basic principles of equity, the actual documents governing the issue said nothing about them. Shanker knew this, and intended to use the UFT resolution as Nauman's first line of defense. He also knew, however, that the issue would be much less complicated, and much more favorable to the UFT in the court of public opinion, if he could argue that Nauman was terminated, and not merely transferred, by the Ocean Hill–Brownsville local board.[75] Much would depend on the language the local board employed when it finally acted. Shanker hoped the board would use the word "terminate," and not "transfer"; this would make his job much easier.

In the meantime, Shanker and the UFT continued the legislative fight over community control in Albany. The union had codified its objections to the Bundy Report, offering its own decentralization bill providing for continued centralized control of public school personnel, curriculum, and finances; a small number of large school districts; and limited consultative powers for local boards. Bundy, Lindsay and the State Board of Regents, led by its most prominent member, Kenneth Clark, had coalesced around a more expansive bill based on the Bundy Report that vested thirty local school boards around the city with almost complete control over personnel, finances, and curriculum. The UFT lobbied against this bill in March and April, calling in all available political chips, and even offering support to machine Democrats—usually considered off-limits by the liberal union—in exchange for assistance in blocking the Lindsay/ Bundy/Regents bill.[76] By late April, however, it appeared likely that this bill would pass, since most upstate Republicans, who held the balance of power in the legislature, seemed inclined to give New York City the same powers that their own local constituencies exercised in school governance. Lindsay, a fellow Republican, was doing some hard lobbying of his own, channeling his efforts through a group he had recently formed for this purpose, the Citizens Committee for Decentralization of the Public Schools.

The Citizens Committee was composed of representatives of the two major elements of the pro–community control coalition — business and civic elites, and the
black poor. It included RCA president Robert Sarnoff, Thomas Watson of IBM,
former Harvard University president James Conant, Columbia Teachers College
president John Fischer, Milton Galamison, Isaiah Robinson of the Harlem Parents
Committee, and the East Harlem Tenant Council's Edward Ortiz. The assertion by
a Lindsay education aide that the group was "broadly representative" indicated
the limitations of its perspective, and fueled Shanker's growing suspicions regarding an alliance of rich and poor against his teachers.[77] Shanker would have felt
justified had he been present at an April 26 meeting at the offices of the Carnegie Corporation between members of the New York Urban Coalition's Education
Task Force, the Citizens Committee for Decentralization of the Public Schools, and
the Ocean Hill–Brownsville local board. John Powis, speaking for the local board,
announced that "we're firing" a group of UFT teachers hostile to the idea of community control. John Simon of the Taconic Foundation, a member of the Citizens
Committee, replied that he had no objection to this action, but suggested that
the board prefer formal charges and hold hearings before dismissing the teachers.
Powis refused: "No — every time you bring charges, you lose." Neither Simon nor
any of the others pressed the issue, and the meeting broke up with the matter decided. The local board would dismiss UFT teachers of its own choosing in Ocean
Hill–Brownsville.[78] Although the parties present did not realize it, they had given
Albert Shanker what he had hoped for — a "termination," rather than a "transfer."

Only the formalities of choosing the teachers to be terminated and drafting
the appropriate letters remained. The Ocean Hill–Brownsville local board met for
these purposes on May 7. Some names, like Fred Nauman, were obvious. Others
were UFT chapter chairs in other Ocean Hill–Brownsville schools. Still others,
while not union leaders, had been overheard complaining about the hiring of the
demonstration school principals or community control generally in Ocean Hill–
Brownsville. A handful appeared to have been chosen almost at random, including
a black teacher, whose last name had apparently been confused by the local board
with that of a white, and who was later dropped from the termination list after
he identified himself. Seven assistant principals, all civil service list hires who had
arrived in the district that year over McCoy's protests, completed the list. There
were nineteen altogether, twelve teachers and seven supervisors, all white except
for the one black teacher included by mistake.[79]

During the meeting, one board member raised the question of hearings and due
process, asking whether the terminations would pass legal scrutiny without them.
Another suggested that the board's action might hurt the chances of the Lindsay/
Bundy/Regents decentralization bill then pending in the State Legislature. Neither

argument convinced Powis, Oliver, or the local board majority. Clara Marshall, the chair of the board's personnel committee, dismissed the due process point, arguing that "the people in the street considered the [due process] laws written to protect the white monied power structure of this city." White teachers, she charged, were racists and incompetents "who sought protection from the civil service list." As a sop, the board voted to offer the terminated teachers and supervisors the opportunity to meet with it for informational purposes only, without the accoutrements of a formal hearing.[80] The final text of the letter produced by the board informed each recipient that "the Governing Board of the Ocean Hill–Brownsville Demonstration School District has voted to end your employment in the schools of this District," and that "this termination of employment is to take effect immediately." The educators were ordered to report Friday morning to Personnel, 110 Livingston Street, Brooklyn, for reassignment.[81]

The board then notified McCoy that it wished to "terminate the services" of the nineteen teachers and supervisors, and instructed him to deliver copies of the letter to each.[82] McCoy had the letters typed, copied, and signed the next day. They were waiting for Fred Nauman and the others when they reported for work the following morning, Thursday, May 9, 1968.

5

THE STRIKES

Albert Shanker was not surprised by Fred Nauman's telephone call from Ocean Hill–Brownsville that morning. The letter's language satisfied the union president: it contained the essential word "termination." Shanker asked Sandra Feldman to meet with Nauman and the other teachers who had received the letter in the afternoon to plan strategy.[1]

Rhody McCoy was also expecting a telephone call that morning, but of a less friendly variety. He knew that Bernard Donovan would be on the line the minute he found out about the letters, and that the schools superintendent would not be a happy man, to say the least. Sure enough, Donovan called at mid-morning. There were procedures for terminating teachers, explicit procedures, he said, and McCoy had not followed them. Puffing calmly on his pipe, McCoy replied that the local board had not intended to fire the teachers, they just wanted them out of the Ocean Hill–Brownsville schools. Where they went next was not the local board's concern. Donovan asked why McCoy had not requested informally that he transfer the teachers—he would have done so without publicity. McCoy had no answer. Later, he would claim that he had, indeed, written Donovan with the names of teachers he wanted transferred. "Where are his carbons?" snapped the exasperated superintendent, knowing that none existed. Donovan ended his conversation with McCoy by telling him to prefer formal charges against the teachers he wished to be rid of. McCoy was noncommittal, except to reiterate that however outsiders wished to define what the local board had done, the teachers would never work in Ocean Hill–Brownsville again. He calmly bid the superintendent a good day, and hung up.[2]

In the early afternoon, Sandra Feldman met with the teachers at an Ocean Hill–Brownsville luncheonette. She told them that this was an important case, a test case, and that the union wanted to fight the local board on the issue of due process rights for teachers. She asked the teachers if they were willing to fight too. All said yes. In that case, said Feldman, ignore McCoy and the local board and go back to your schools and your jobs.[3]

But Feldman, and Shanker, knew it would not be that simple, and they were right. By May 14, the Ocean Hill–Brownsville community and the ATA had had time to organize in support of McCoy and the local board. On that morning, the teachers and administrators who had received letters found a wall of neighborhood residents and black teachers barring their path into JHS 271.[4]

Lindsay had sent police to the school, along with two of his close aides, Sidney Davidoff and Barry Gottehrer, whom he employed as troubleshooters in tense ghetto confrontations. Davidoff and Gottehrer customarily mediated between community residents and the police to defuse racial violence. Lindsay, who had just completed his work on the Kerner Commission, had dedicated his administration to avoiding a major riot in New York City. He walked the streets of Harlem and Bedford-Stuyvesant in shirtsleeves on hot summer evenings at the first hint of trouble, to show residents he cared. He met unapologetically with black spokesmen that his political rivals branded as "militants," men whom his predecessor, Robert Wagner, would not have sat in the same room with. He ordered his police not to wear helmets or carry nightsticks in black neighborhoods, to avoid "the appearance of a conquering army."[5] And he had succeeded; almost alone among major American cities after 1965, New York had not suffered a large-scale civil disturbance.

Gottehrer and Davidoff executed Lindsay's antiviolence strategy. They went wherever the trouble was, and on the morning of May 14, there was clearly trouble at JHS 271. Led by Nauman, the UFT teachers lined up outside the main entrance of the schools, separated by the police from Oliver, Powis, Vann, Campbell, and other local board and ATA members who blocked the doorway. As epithets flew back and forth between the two sides, Davidoff and Gottehrer sized up the situation and conferred with the mayor over the police radio. They decided it was too dangerous to have the police force the teachers into the school. They told Nauman and the others they would not teach that day.[6]

Shanker was furious. He told a reporter that Lindsay was "a profile in weakness."[7] To Shanker, this incident symbolized the mayor's attitude toward both the Ocean Hill controversy and race relations generally in New York City. Would Lindsay have given in so easily if a white mob had blocked a school doorway to a group of blacks? Shanker thought he knew the answer. Lindsay seemed to think that because of racism in America, he had to say "yes" to blacks even when, as here, they were in the wrong. Well, Albert Shanker did not operate that way. He had heard Marilyn Gittell of the Institute for Community Studies say that in the area of race relations, the literal facts surrounding an event did not matter so much as the larger truths of white racism and black oppression, and that, accordingly, she would base her judgments on those broader, metaphorical "facts."[8] But Shanker did not place much stock in metaphors. His mind went doggedly, stubbornly, straight ahead. He was comfortable with literal facts, those that went from "point A" to "point B." And the solution to the problem at JHS 271, in his mind, was simple and logical. Fred Nauman and his colleagues had a right to teach in the school. The mayor had the obligation to make certain this occurred. And anyone who said otherwise was wrong, even if they happened to be black. Shanker had been at the March on Washington, at Selma, and in Memphis to honor Martin Luther King's memory just a month before, but he would have no trouble doing at Ocean Hill–Brownsville what Lindsay and Gittell apparently could not do. He would tell Rhody McCoy he was wrong. An aide had floated a compromise plan before him that day. Under it, the teachers could come back, but they would be assigned vaguely defined "professional duties," which might or might not include actual teaching. The aide suggested mildly that this might offer a face-saving way out for everyone. Shanker cut him off: "Fuck you. I want those teachers in the classrooms now."[9]

Donovan too wanted the teachers in the classrooms, albeit with less outward passion. His orderly bureaucrat's mind also needed to place what McCoy and the local board had done into a recognizable administrative framework. Accordingly, he wrote McCoy on May 14, demanding that he press formal charges against the teachers and administrators. Initially, McCoy balked, claiming that since he was merely "transferring" them to central Board of Education headquarters, formal charges—and hearings—were not required. In any event, he claimed, the Ocean Hill–Brownsville community had the right to choose teachers for its children without interference from outsiders. But Donovan continued to hammer away over the next two weeks, and finally induced McCoy to press charges. This activated

5. Standoff between supporters of the Ocean Hill–Brownsville local school board and UFT teachers at Junior High School 271, May 1968. United Federation of Teachers Collection, UFT Photo Collection, Robert F. Wagner Labor Archives, New York University.

6. UFT President Albert Shanker speaks to demonstrators supporting Fred Nauman and his union colleagues, May 23, 1968. United Federation of Teachers Collection, UFT Photo Collection, Robert F. Wagner Labor Archives, New York University.

the requirement for hearings under the Board of Education bylaws and the UFT contract, however one wished to define the letters Nauman and the others had received.

In agreeing to bring charges, McCoy may have been driven more by the rising tide of his anger than anything else. He considered the refusal of the teachers and administrators to obey his order of "transfer" to be insubordinate, and said so. Once he had accused Nauman and his colleagues of insubordination, hearings seemed a logical next step. Another incident, in which McCoy summoned the nineteen teachers and administrators to his office, to have only a handful show up, had also fueled his pique.[10]

In addition, McCoy felt pressure from his allies in the community control movement to bring formal charges. He had assured Fantini, Gittell, and the members of the Citizens Committee for the Decentralization of the Public Schools, among others, that there was plenty of evidence against the teachers and administrators he wished to be rid of. Taking him at his word, they argued that by publicly unmasking incompetent teachers, the hearings would make the case for community control all the more compelling. Finally, Donovan offered McCoy the opportunity to have his charges heard by a black judge, retired Civil Court Judge

Francis E. Rivers. On May 27, still averring that "not one of these teachers will be allowed to teach anywhere in this city—the black community will see to that," McCoy agreed to formal hearings before Judge Rivers, and began drawing up charges.[11]

McCoy's decision to participate in hearings would prove to be a grave tactical misstep. It gave Albert Shanker all the ammunition he needed for his due process arguments in the corning months. If, as McCoy claimed, the local board had sought to transfer, not terminate, Nauman and the others on May 9—and it was, at best, unclear whether the Board of Education by-laws required hearings for transfers—then agreeing to appear before Judge Rivers gave the opposite impression. It bolstered Shanker's assertion that, however McCoy wished to justify himself, his intent was punitive. In the future, whenever supporters of the local board claimed that it had merely sought routine transfers, Shanker would employ the best rejoinder in any debate—his opponent's own words and actions. McCoy had ceded the procedural high ground on the terminations-versus-transfers question, and simplified a potentially complicated issue into a clear, easily digestible one for the public Shanker hoped to reach. Now he would not have to cite arcane provisions from collective bargaining agreements and Board of Education bylaws. He could instead talk about due process protections for employees whose jobs were in jeopardy, something every New Yorker who worked for a living could understand. McCoy had given Shanker what he wanted.

McCoy blundered by agreeing to hearings before Judge Rivers for yet another reason, one that he had not seen fit to share with his supporters in the community control movement. The evidence against most of the teachers and administrators was sketchy. Virtually all of it related to expressions of hostility to the idea of community control rather to actual job performance. Most of the teachers, in fact, had satisfactory employment records. Even William Harris, JHS 271's principal, conceded that Fred Nauman, for example, was a good teacher. McCoy's charges against Nauman alleged merely that he had "expressed opposition" to the community control project and "contributed to the growing hostility" between black and white teachers.[12]

When McCoy's charges did touch upon matters of professional competence, they were frequently exaggerated and inaccurate, and, sometimes, outright fabrications. In one instance, McCoy sought to buttress his charge that a teacher, Paul Satlow, could not control his class, by alleging that his students threw chairs around their classroom. The incident could never have occurred, however, since the chairs in Satlow's room were bolted to the floor. Other allegations of use of profane language and corporal punishment rested on uncorroborated hearsay. Still others, such as "failure to decorate the classroom properly" and "excessive use of the blackboard," were trivial.[13] All in all, most of the evidence offered by McCoy involved the sorts of infringements on freedom of expression least likely to impress a judge.

Why, then, with so much to lose, did McCoy agree to hearings that he claimed were unnecessary? While Donovan's pressure and the momentum of his own anger played a major role in his turnabout, McCoy may have agreed to this bureaucratic procedure, paradoxically, because of his own antibureaucratic personality. Procedural niceties meant little to him; in this sense, he was the polar opposite of Donovan and Shanker. One of the things that drew McCoy to the Ocean Hill–Brownsville community control experiment in the first place was its romantic, antirationalist quality. It is possible, then, that McCoy agreed to hearings because of his contempt for them, his feeling that in the final analysis they did not really matter. However Judge Rivers ruled, McCoy believed, the Ocean Hill–Brownsville community alone would decide the ultimate fate of the teachers. So McCoy went through with what he considered to be a meaningless charade, but what the UFT viewed as a definitive airing of the issues. After hearing the evidence presented by both sides, Judge Rivers took the case under advisement, promising a decision before the 1968–69 school year opened in September.

Meanwhile, Ocean Hill–Brownsville had become even more tense. After a number of abortive attempts by the teachers to enter JHS 271, Shanker had prevailed upon a reluctant Lindsay to approve the deployment of police escorts for them. Surrounded by a jeering crowd, the teachers and their protectors pushed their way into the school, only to have the local board close all of the Ocean Hill schools in protest.

When they reopened, it was the UFT's turn to act dramatically. Almost all of the approximately 350 union teachers in Ocean Hill–Brownsville walked out in support of Nauman and his colleagues on May 22.[14] They would remain out for the duration of the school year. McCoy, accusing them of "leaving our children," began searching for nonunion replacements on university campuses.[15] These politically left-leaning, pro–community control "amateurs"—or, as the UFT called them, "scabs"—would man the Ocean Hill–Brownsville schools throughout the tumultuous fall of 1968. The local board proclaimed that the 350 union sympathy strikers, like the original group of disputed teachers led by Nauman, would never return: "We decide who will teach our children—no Donovan, no Shanker, no Lindsay, no 500 cops—we decide!" If a confrontation was inevitable, argued Marilyn Gittell, "it might as well come now."[16]

The termination letters had also served to doom the Lindsay/Bundy/Regents decentralization bill pending in the State Legislature in Albany. The legislature, skittish in the wake of the disturbances at Ocean Hill–Brownsville, and influenced by a wave of UFT lobbying, delayed the entire question of decentralization for one year in a bill sponsored by Republican State Senator John Marchi. The so-called Marchi Law postponed a final resolution of the issue until the 1969 legislative session, and in the interim, allowed the central Board of Education to delegate powers of its choosing to local school boards in the city. It also expanded the Board of Education by four new members, to be appointed directly by Lindsay.

The Marchi Law, while an immediate victory for the UFT, which would have accepted almost any alternative to the Regents/Lindsay/Clark bill, presented the union with a number of potential minefields in the longer term. It permitted the central Board of Education to delegate its powers, including personnel powers, giving local boards throughout the city the ability to do what the Ocean Hill–Brownsville board had done to Fred Nauman. The new law also allowed Lindsay to name four new members to the Board of Education, now expanded in number from nine to thirteen. Since, in addition, three of the more conservative board members were scheduled to leave in the early fall, Lindsay would name a majority of the body that would determine the rules for the upcoming 1968–69 school year—the worst of possible outcomes for Shanker and the UFT leadership.

The mayor had reacted to the terminations, in Shanker's view, with a singular lack of moral outrage. Lindsay had deplored the local board's action in ritual language, but made no secret of his true sympathies. The UFT, he said, lacked "understanding of the causes of the deep community frustrations" that led to the letters of May 9.[17] Had the Board of Education given the local board the powers it deserved, Lindsay argued, "this would not have happened."[18] The mayor also put pressure on the recipients of the letters to quietly accept transfers into another district. In late May, the six administrators, who were members of the Council of Supervisory Associations and not the UFT, agreed, along with two nontenured substitute teachers. The ten UFT teachers who remained would press their challenge to McCoy and the local board for the duration of the controversy.

Lindsay's appointees to the newly expanded Board of Education confirmed Shanker's fears. The mayor selected Milton Galamison along with three other strong community control supporters, making this veteran of the community control struggle an "insider" with one stroke of the pen. A few weeks later, Lindsay would name three more Board of Education members, most notably John Doar. Doar, whose Ivy League background and bearing resembled Lindsay's, had played a major role in the admission of James Meredith to the University of Mississippi in 1962 as assistant attorney general for civil rights. In the mid-1960s, he came to New York to direct the Bedford-Stuyvesant Restoration Corporation, an early community action experiment in the black neighborhood adjacent to Ocean Hill–Brownsville. Earlier in 1968, Doar had enraged Shanker when, referring to the

7. New York City Board of Education President John Doar. United Federation of Teachers Archives, UFT Photo Collection, Robert F. Wagner Labor Archives, New York University.

looming crisis in Ocean Hill–Brownsville, he had told an interviewer: "Union concepts of security and seniority were formulated in the period of struggle between company and union. Now the struggle is between the Negroes and the unions. It is our position that a basic conflict exists between labor union concepts and civil rights concepts. Something has to give."[19] Together, Doar and Galamison, who by October would be named, respectively, president and vice president of the Board of Education, symbolized the alliance of city elites and poor blacks that Shanker feared most.

But the UFT did not lack for allies of its own. Shanker, while identifying himself with the left wing of the American labor movement, had been carefully building bridges to powerful mainstream leaders for years, including AFL-CIO president George Meany, and, closer to home, Harry Van Arsdale, the president of the influential New York Central Labor Council. The council brought together the heads of virtually all unions in New York City, public and private, but was dominated by the mandarins of the conservative craft and construction unions, notably Van Arsdale himself, a crusty electrician. Shanker, one of the most liberal members of the council's slate of officers, had nurtured alliances with, and performed political favors for, these leaders. He had not, for example, publicly criticized the War in Vietnam, despite his own personal misgivings and the opposition of the majority of his rank and file, because Meany and Van Arsdale supported it. Now, facing the most important battle in his union's history, Shanker prepared to call in his IOUs. In the coming months he would ask for, and receive, crucial political and financial support from the mainstream wing of organized labor in New York City.

The UFT also had markers out to the city's old-line liberal and socialist intellectuals and activists, including A. Philip Randolph and Bayard Rustin, whose Randolph Institute, a labor research and lobbying center, survived on UFT financial support. Shanker, Feldman, and other UFT leaders who had come of age in the democratic socialist movement of the 1950s and early 1960s maintained close relations with Michael Harrington, the movement's leader in 1968; there were many instances of institutional cross-pollenization between the UFT and Harrington's League for Industrial Democracy. Shanker was also on friendly terms with public intellectuals identified with various shades of the Left, including old-line socialist Irving Howe, moderate liberal Nathan Glazer, and emerging neoconservative Norman Podhoretz, whose *Commentary* magazine was one of the first of the journals of ideas to champion the UFT's cause after the termination of Nauman and his colleagues.

The most significant source of support for the UFT, however, came from the white population of the city. Shanker attempted to cast the controversy in race-neutral terms whenever he could, as when he reminded the readers of a union flyer that "due process—which protects the worker against arbitrary discharge—has no color and no race." He also sought to present the controversy as a traditional labor dispute between employer and employee, arguing that while "the local board of Ocean Hill–Brownsville doesn't think of itself as 'bosses' against whom its employees need the protection of a union contract, they are . . ."[20] But the Ocean Hill–Brownsville local board did not "employ" the teachers—this, after all, was the union's point in fighting the terminations—and the principals, who resembled "the bosses" much more closely, supported the UFT. Much as Shanker sought to elide the issue, white New Yorkers flocked to the union's side after the May 9 letters less because Fred Nauman was a union man than because his antagonists were primarily black.

This support went well beyond union members, and, for that matter, well beyond the teachers and their families. The developing crisis was changing the social and political landscape of the city, ending the rivalry between Jews and white Catholics that had defined civic life in New York for decades. This rivalry affected mayoral elections, patterns of neighborhood formation, business development, levels of city services, intellectual life, leisure, and even newspaper readership. The rationalist, cosmopolitan "Jewish" ethos, and the more traditionalist "Catholic" ethos described by Nathan Glazer and Daniel Patrick Moynihan in the 1963 edition of *Beyond the Melting Pot* found expression in disagreements over state aid to parochial schools and "regular" versus "reform" wars for control of the Democratic party.[21] These, argued Glazer and Moynihan in 1963, were only the most recent manifestations of an ancient civic rivalry that showed few signs of abating.

Yet by the summer of 1968, only five years after the publication of *Beyond the Melting Pot,* the long history of ethnoreligious animosity between Jews and white Catholics in New York was giving way to the shared imperatives of racial identity. The major shift occurred in the city's outer boroughs. Here, living in close proximity, the two groups found many areas of race-related common ground. Both feared the influx of black students into their neighborhoods and schools, as the massive outpouring of support for PAT in the early 1960s proved. Both were disturbed by the rise in welfare costs in the city, which more than doubled during the first Lindsay administration, a result of welfare rights activism and new, more generous city policies.[22] And both feared the city's skyrocketing violent crime rate, which had increased every year since 1960.[23] Measured against these concerns, questions of parochial school funding and Tammany "machine" control of the Democratic party appeared comparatively trivial. In 1966, for the first time in any city observer's recent memory, outer-borough Jews had joined their Catholic neighbors on a major political issue, rejecting Lindsay's proposal for a civilian review board to investigate allegations of police misconduct. Analysts who had expected outer-borough Jews to vote with their more traditional black and white Protestant allies, as well as with their Manhattan coreligionists, now began describing a race-and-crime-based political and social realignment in the city.[24]

By the summer of 1968, middle-income outer-borough Jews and Catholics, riding a tide of racial anger, represented the UFT's core constituency. Their support for the union, as evidenced in polls, was the highest in the city, by a wide margin.[25] Taken together, Jews and white Catholics made up almost two-thirds of New York's population in 1968.[26] "Jewish" and "Catholic" world views notwithstanding, they would be Albert Shanker's most important weapon in his battle against Rhody McCoy.

The spring semester in Ocean Hill–Brownsville ended with the 350 boycotting UFT teachers still out. McCoy, after reiterating that none of them would ever work in his schools again, stepped up his efforts to replace them. Donovan, oscillating between anger at McCoy over the termination letters and sympathy for his need to staff his schools, agreed to waive formal licensing requirements for the teachers McCoy recruited from college campuses. By summer's end, this process was complete, and some 350 mostly white recruits, short on experience but long on enthusiasm for community control, prepared to begin the fall 1968 semester in the Ocean Hill–Brownsville schools. Donovan, no doubt, could foresee the chaos that would accompany the return of the boycotting UFT teachers to their positions in these same schools. Desperately rushing from brushfire to brushfire, however, the beleaguered superintendent did not have the luxury of advance planning. He would, by necessity, cross that bridge when he came to it.

Two events in late summer made a citywide teachers strike almost inevitable. On August 17, the Board of Education, led by its four new Lindsay appointees, fulfilled its mandate under the Marchi Law by announcing its decentralization plan for the 1968–69 school year. The plan permitted local school boards to hire teachers directly, without reference to Board of Examiners lists, and to transfer teachers out of their districts involuntarily, as long as another district was willing to accept them. Shanker immediately denounced the plan as "a violation of the collective bargaining agreement between the UFT and the Board of Education."[27]

The other major development was more to Shanker's liking. On August 26, Judge Rivers released his decision on the legality of the local board's letters to Fred Nauman and his colleagues. In sweeping language, he ruled that all the teachers were entitled to return to their jobs. Rivers held that McCoy's charges of incompetence were unfounded, and that those relating to criticism of community control were protected by constitutional free speech guarantees. The Fourteenth Amendment's admonition against taking property without due process of law, Rivers concluded, required hearings, when, as here, the right to continued employment was at issue.[28]

Shanker, then, had gotten what he said he wanted. Rivers had ruled that the letters did in fact amount to attempted terminations, and that Nauman and his colleagues had been deprived of due process. But in a sense, the union president may have received more from the decision than he needed. Rivers's decision left little room for compromise, with the beginning of the 1968–69 school year set for September 9, only two weeks away. Shanker, having won all the cases, would now be unable to reach an accommodation with McCoy on some of the individual teachers without losing face with his membership. Neither could McCoy, whom Rivers had left with no room to maneuver, comply with the ruling without giving the appearance of abject surrender.

The reaction of the members of the Ocean Hill–Brownsville local board to the Rivers decision was predictable: they ignored it. Their supporters were equally defiant, and urged them to stand fast.[29] As the days ticked down to September 9, each side prepared to do just that. The Rivers decision, legally correct though it may have been, had left both Shanker and McCoy with nowhere to go.

On Friday, September 6, three days before the scheduled opening of the New York public schools, Lindsay and Donovan convened a marathon negotiating session aimed at preventing a citywide teachers strike. The UFT and local board representatives, closeted in separate wings of City Hall, never spoke directly to each other. On Sunday, the local board presented Lindsay with a prepared statement. "We will no longer act as a buffer between this community and the establishment," it read. "This community will control its schools and who teaches in them. We do not want the teachers to return to this district. Since the legal machinery of this sick society is forcing these teachers on us under threat of closing our schools and dissolving our district, the Board of Education should return to our district any of the teachers who wish to return. Our original decision remains as before. We refuse to sell out. If the Board of Education and the Superintendent of Schools forces them to return to a community which does not want them, so be it."[30]

Lindsay, grasping at straws in search of a settlement, took the language "the Board of Education should return to our district any of the teachers who wish to return" out of context, and announced that the dispute was settled, since the local board "will not seek to prevent" the reinstatement of the UFT teachers. An angry Oliver, speaking for the local board on the steps of City Hall, disputed the mayor, accusing him of "saying something that was in his mind, not in ours." Hearing this, Shanker walked out of City Hall, and drove to midtown, where the union's Delegate Assembly was waiting for him. He asked for, and received, their authorization to conduct an immediate strike vote by the membership at large. By 12,021 to 1,716, they voted to strike all of the city's public schools the next day, Monday, September 9.[31]

Fifty-four thousand of New York's fifty-seven thousand public school teachers went out that day. In a show of sympathy for the teachers that was unprecedented in their sometimes stormy relationship, most of the city's principals closed their schools. The custodians union also honored the strike, making it difficult to obtain basic services in the small number of schools that did open. UFT-ers picketed the Ocean Hill–Brownsville schools, which were open and operating with replacement and ATA teachers. Standing in front of JHS 271, Nauman compared his position to that of James Meredith at the University of Mississippi, a veiled slap at John Doar, Lindsay's choice for a seat on the Board of Education, who had opposed the use of police force on the union teacher's behalf.[32]

Shanker, responding to Lindsay's charge that the strike was racially motivated, claimed that it was about due process protections for teachers of all races, a public position he maintained throughout the crisis: "This is a strike to protect black teachers against white racists in white communities and white teachers against black racists in black communities." If a white school board attempted to fire a black teacher, he promised, "then we will be back here again fighting his battle."[33]

Many of the black members of Shanker's own union, however, disagreed with this characterization. Led by Assistant Treasurer Richard Parrish, the UFT's highest-ranking black officer, they used the occasion of the strike to form the UFT Black Caucus, and announced their "unequivocal support" of the Ocean Hill–Brownsville local board.[34] Parrish's group sought to combine union loyalty—most of its members honored the strike—with support for community control, in a tenuous balance that typified the dilemma of other black unionists, and which threatened to come crashing down at any time.

The UFT strike lasted two days before ending in a settlement that the Ocean Hill–Brownsville local board had no part in negotiating, and which presaged future trouble. Lindsay and Donovan agreed to order all UFT teachers in Ocean Hill–Brownsville back to their jobs. This included Nauman and his nine test case colleagues, along with the sympathy boycotters from the spring, now reduced from 350 to approximately 200 by attrition. The parties also agreed that all cases of involuntary teacher transfer would be settled by binding impartial arbitration, and not, as the regulations released by the Board of Education on August 17 had provided, by local boards. Before the teachers went back to work, Shanker obtained membership authorization to call a second strike if the settlement terms were violated. Shanker, Lindsay, and Donovan now waited to see what the Ocean Hill–Brownsville local board would do.

They did not have to wait long. Early in the morning of Wednesday, September 11, the day the teachers returned to work, Sandra Feldman visited Rhody McCoy's office to discuss—she thought—procedures for giving the UFT-ers classroom assignments in the Ocean Hill–Brownsville schools. She found him on the telephone, cryptically telling a succession of callers that the "arrangements" they had agreed upon the night before were to be put into effect that morning. He refused to explain himself further to Feldman. When the returning UFT teachers reported for work, they were told to go to the auditorium of one of the Ocean Hill–Brownsville schools, IS 55, for an "orientation session." As they arrived, approximately fifty community residents, most from the Brooklyn branch of CORE, surrounded them, brandishing sticks and bandoliers of bullets. While the men cursed the teachers, threw the bullets at them, and threatened to "carry you out in pine boxes," McCoy entered the room, and quietly observed the scene, offering no assistance to the terrified educators. After a few minutes, he told them to report back to their respective schools. When they did so, however, they were refused teaching assignments. At JHS 271, students attacked Nauman and other UFT teachers. Principal Harris herded them into a locked classroom for their safety. Police rescued them later in the afternoon. That night, the UFT's Executive Board, exercising the option given to it by the membership at the conclusion of the first strike, voted to send the teachers out again.[35]

The second strike lasted another two weeks, until late September. Shanker, Lindsay, Donovan, and Doar now agreed that the UFT teachers in Ocean Hill–Brownsville had the right to reinstatement. They differed, however, over the proper strategies to achieve this objective. Shanker viewed the matter as one of simple contract enforcement. He had settled the first strike on Lindsay's promise that Nauman and the others would return to their jobs. The mayor, he felt, had stood by impotently while the Ocean Hill–Brownsville community wrecked that agreement. Now, he wanted guarantees before the teachers would go back. He wanted Lindsay to force the local board to agree to reinstatement, backed, if necessary, by police stationed in the Ocean Hill–Brownsville schools themselves.

To Lindsay and Doar, however, this smacked of heavy-handedness, and more than a hint of racism. Both believed that municipal unions had too much power in city life. Lindsay had been at odds with them from the day he took office in January 1966, when he faced a strike by the city's transit workers union. Lindsay had approached that strike as he would all the others that marked his first term: as affronts to the public weal, and, especially, to the city's black community. When he took office, Lindsay promised that the days of cozy, lucrative deals with labor leaders brokered personally by his predecessor, Robert Wagner, were over. But while Lindsay did end the last-minute backroom deals that were a Wagner trademark, his more confrontational style resulted in long municipal worker strikes that ended up costing the city even more money in settlements. Lindsay never forgave the city unions for besting him at the bargaining table. To him, public employee union leaders were little more than narrow-minded, self-interested potentates— and Shanker, insistent, unbending, and relentless, was the worst example of the type. He was the only municipal labor leader Lindsay would not invite into his

8. Schools Superintendent Bernard Donovan during negotiations to end the second city-wide teachers' strike, September 24, 1968. NYT Pictures/*The New York Times*.

personal living quarters at Gracie Mansion, the mayor's official residence, during negotiations.[36]

Shanker, for his part, viewed Lindsay as epitomizing a "type" as well: the sanctimonious upper-crust moralist, with an added whiff of genteel anti-Semitism. The mayor, complained Shanker, "makes himself out to be acting on high ethical standards, while the teachers act only in self-interest." "What you have," Shanker said on another occasion, with Lindsay in mind, "is people on the upper economic level who are willing to make any change that does not affect their own position. And so it is the middle-class interests that are narrow and selfish and the civil service teacher who must be sacrificed. I'm not sure that is a WASP attitude. I think it's only human. But what if you said give twenty percent of Time, Inc. or U.S. Steel to the blacks? Who would be narrow then?"[37] Lindsay and Shanker's communication difficulties during the Ocean Hill–Brownsville crisis, then, were as much culture- and class-based as they were political, and the rushed circumstances of the dispute left neither man the luxury of walking a mile in the other's shoes.

Doar's personal relations with Shanker were less hostile, but the Board of Education president also believed the UFT leader's straight-ahead approach to the problem of returning the UFT teachers to the Ocean Hill–Brownsville schools was counterproductive. The defining moment of Doar's career had been helping to enroll James Meredith at the University of Mississippi, and he believed the same tactics he employed in the South would work in Brooklyn. He spelled those tactics out in a televised debate with Shanker: "The way to [get compliance] is to continue to move forward and show restraint, show patience, but be firm, move forward, keep persuading, keep negotiating, keep appealing to the best in people. And that is the best way to serve your teachers."[38]

Doar felt he could convince McCoy and the members of the local board to voluntarily accept the return of the teachers through patient negotiation that permitted as much face-saving as possible. Doar, of course, may have been drawing quite different conclusions from the Meredith integration crisis than were warranted by the actual facts of the episode. It had ended, after all, with a display of decisive federal action, as Shanker was quick to point out. But to Doar, who was as devoted as Lindsay to the idea of community control in Ocean Hill–Brownsville, obtaining Fred Nauman's reinstatement at the point of a sword, as Shanker appeared to demand, was self-defeating. It would, essentially, kill the promising Ocean Hill–Brownsville experiment for the sake of a labor leader's pride —in Doar's view, a singularly uneven exchange.

This, then, was the problem as the second strike began. Lindsay and Doar's philosophical commitment to community control in Ocean Hill–Brownsville forced them to accept behavior that was difficult to defend, as when Lindsay told

9. Albert Shanker arriving at a pro-strike rally in City Hall Park, September 16, 1968. NYT Pictures/*The New York Times*.

an incredulous crowd at a parents meeting during the second strike that the local board had "more or less" complied with his directive to give the UFT teachers assignments in the Ocean Hill–Brownsville schools, or when Doar defended a fellow Board of Education member who had picketed UFT headquarters with a menorah mounted upon a coffin as a "fine, fine Christian woman."[39] Neither Lindsay nor Doar believed that telling a teacher he would be "carried out in a pine box" constituted acceptable behavior, whatever Shanker may have thought. They were trapped, however, by their allegiance to community control, and this, combined with their suspicion of overweening union power and abhorrence of racism, led them to resist coercive measures against McCoy and the local board.

Shanker was trapped as well. He had made the reinstatement of the disputed teachers his union's defining issue. "You or a member of your family may be employed on jobs protected by union contracts or civil service regulations," he had written in a UFT advertisement. "How would you react if you could be fired without any charges or any procedures to hear your objections? I think you will agree that a union is worth nothing if it fails to defend the rights of its members to their jobs and to a fair procedure for dismissal."[40] But having phrased the issue in this all-or-nothing manner, he was forced to minimize the clear racial implications of his calls for the use of hundreds of police to force white teachers on an unwilling black community.

And McCoy, Oliver, and the Ocean Hill–Brownsville local board, in their own way, were also trapped. They had articulated the issue of the return of the UFT teachers in stark terms of racial authenticity, branding black leaders who sought compromise—Samuel Wright, Whitney Young, even the pro–community control Kenneth Clark—as traitors and Uncle Toms. It is doubtful that McCoy, for example, honestly felt that the mere fact of Fred Nauman's presence in JHS 271 would by itself wreck education in that school, or that the practice of terrorizing white teachers offered any long-term solution to the problems of educating black children in New York City. Yet having allowed the question of Nauman's continued presence in Ocean Hill–Brownsville to become a test of "authentic" black identity, McCoy, like the other principals to the controversy, had little choice but to act as he did. As the second citywide teachers' strike began, then, Lindsay, Doar, Shanker, and McCoy were all prisoners of their ideologies, their constituencies, their fears, and the facts they had helped create.

Negotiations to end the second strike soon took on a repetitious quality, with Shanker demanding that Lindsay and Doar force the local board to take back the teachers, and the mayor and the Board of Education president refusing to do so. Finally, after a brief suspension of the local board did nothing to shake its resolve, and some muscle-flexing by the union in the form of fifteen thousand white pro-

UFT demonstrators at City Hall—at least four times the size of the largest Ocean Hill rally—the parties reached an uneasy settlement on September 29. The Board of Education agreed to guarantee classroom teaching assignments for the returning UFT-ers, and to station observers in the schools to report incidents of noncompliance. The union teachers would be paired in teams with the replacement teachers. Doar, continuing to advocate "voluntary compliance," opposed the settlement as too harsh toward the Ocean Hill–Brownsville local board, but was overruled by Lindsay. On Monday, September 30, the teachers once again went back to work.[41]

The settlement began to unravel almost immediately. Nauman and the other UFT-ers received no teaching assignments on Monday and Tuesday. Donovan shut JHS 271 on Wednesday after community residents, including local board members, invaded the school and engaged in altercations with observers and teachers. On Thursday and Friday, with 271 once again open, Principal Harris, on orders from the local board, assigned most UFT teachers to lunchroom, hall, and bathroom duty, or to empty classrooms. The replacement teachers shunned the UFT-ers. Over that weekend, the local board instructed McCoy to remove all UFT teachers from the Ocean Hill–Brownsville schools. When McCoy and the principals announced their intention to obey this order, Donovan suspended them, along with the local board. On Wednesday, October 9, he also closed JHS 271 after clashes between UFT and replacement teachers. But that Friday, at Doar's urging, Donovan did an about-face. Claiming that the Ocean Hill–Brownsville principals had now promised him that they would give the UFT-ers teaching assignments, he reinstated them, and ordered 271 reopened for the following Monday.

JHS 271 did, indeed, reopen that day, but without UFT teachers. Instead, they were once again outside the school carrying picket signs. Shanker, enraged at what he considered Donovan's duplicity, had obtained yet another strike vote from his membership over the weekend.[42] For the third time in a month, the city's teachers were on strike.

6

LIKE STRANGERS

The Third Strike and Beyond

The third Ocean Hill–Brownsville strike was the most bitter of all. It drew in the rest of the city. The strike divided the city in two important respects. First, by pulling blacks and Jews apart, and bringing Jews and white Catholics together, it reconfigured New York's social landscape in sharp, defining shades of black and white. Second, it brought long-simmering class resentments to the surface, arraying poor blacks and corporate, government, media, and intellectual elites against the teachers and their allies in the city's white middle-class population.

Shanker raised the stakes in this final, five-week drama. He demanded the permanent removal of McCoy and the local board, and the termination of the Ocean Hill–Brownsville experiment. This, in turn, brought virtually the city's entire black community in on the side of Ocean Hill–Brownsville—even moderates like the Urban League's Whitney Young, who had previously been skeptical of community control—on grounds of racial loyalty. The city's white middle-class population, traumatized by images of disorder and violence emanating from Ocean Hill–Brownsville, closed ranks behind the UFT, ending decades of ethnic, religious, and political animosity as they did so. Jewish teachers, who had long regarded Irish policemen as goons, now looked to them for protection on picket lines from angry blacks. A reporter for the *Nation* looked on in amazement as these erstwhile enemies chatted cordially outside one Ocean Hill–Brownsville school, separated from black counterpickets by police sawhorses. The policemen, he observed, were half-smiling, half-smirking, at "the birth of an ally."[1]

As the Jewish-Catholic alliance gestated, relations between blacks and Jews deteriorated. The Ocean Hill–Brownsville crisis brought out the unrealistic expectations each had for the other. Anti-Semitic material circulated in Ocean Hill–Brownsville and in the city's other black neighborhoods during the strike, some of it quoting approvingly from the *Protocols of the Elders of Zion*. Vann, Campbell, and other ATA members also issued anti-Jewish statements, which linked the UFT to alleged acts of "mental genocide" against black schoolchildren.[2] The most notorious example of anti-Semitic animus came in the form of an unsigned letter placed in the mailboxes of UFT teachers at JHS 271:

> If African American History and Culture is to be taught to our Black Children it Must be Done By African Americans who Identify With And Who Understand The Problem. It is Impossible For The Middle East Murderers of Colored People to Possibly Bring To This Important Task The Insight, The Concern, The Exposing Of The Truth That is a *Must* If The Years Of Brainwashing And Self-Hatred That Has Been Taught To Our Black Children By Those Bloodsucking Exploiters and Murderers Is To Be Over Come. The Idea Behind This Program Is Beautiful, But When The Money Changers Heard About It, They Took Over, As Is Their Custom In The Black Community, If African American History and Culture Is Important To Our Children To Raise Their Esteem Of Themselves, They Are The Only Persons Who Can Do The Job Are African-American Brothers And Sisters, And Not the So-Called Liberal Jewish Friend. We Know From His Tricky, Deceitful Maneuvers That He is Really Our Enemy and *He* is Responsible For The Serious Educational Retardation Of Our Black Children. We Call On All Concerned Black Teachers, Parents, And Friends to Write To The Board of Education, To the Mayor, To The State Commissioner of Education To Protest The Take Over Of This Crucial Program By People Who Are Unfit By Tradition And By Inclination To Do Even An Adequate Job.

The letter was never linked to any person officially connected to the Ocean Hill–Brownsville experiment, and the district's replacement teachers, approximately 40 percent of whom were themselves Jewish, issued a statement disavowing anti-Semitism. Shanker reprinted five hundred thousand copies of the letter and distributed them throughout the city; their effect on the Jewish community was shattering.[3]

Jewish leaders who expected their black counterparts to issue specific denunciations of such material during the strike were bitterly disappointed when they were rebuffed.[4] But, as Floyd McKissick of CORE explained, "if a black leader is to be responsive to the needs of his people, he cannot be a Jewish leader, he must be a black leader. By definition, this means that the interests he represents will sometimes be in conflict with other groups, sometimes Jewish groups."[5] McCoy was more blunt: "We have more things to be concerned about than making anti-Semitism a priority."[6]

Black leaders, however, were equally unrealistic in their expectations that Jews forego their own interests during the strikes. "The real Jews," wrote one such leader, Preston Wilcox, "are out on the street helping us. The others . . . are rejecting their own heritage."[7] The ATA's Albert Vann argued that Fred Nauman and the other Jewish teachers who received the May 9 letters were obligated as "responsible" Jews to support the Ocean Hill–Brownsville local board, despite its attempts to remove them from the district's schools.[8]

Behind the unfulfilled expectations and demands of both groups during the Ocean Hill–Brownsville strikes, however, lay an uncomfortable truth. New York's outer-borough Jews, after decades of ambivalence, now viewed themselves as "white," with more in common with Irish and Italian Catholics than with blacks. When black writer James Baldwin, a supporter of the Ocean Hill–Brownsville local board, later wrote that "it is cowardly and a betrayal of whatever it means to be a Jew, to act as a white man," he captured the essence of what was driving Jews and blacks apart during the Ocean Hill–Brownsville crisis.[9]

Black intellectuals like Baldwin, Harold Cruse, and Julius Lester had long complained of Jewish ambivalence—an ambivalence of convenience, in their view—toward white identity. These criticisms peaked during the Ocean Hill–Brownsville crisis. Black supporters of the local board responded to allegations of anti-Semitism by arguing that they harbored no special animus toward Jews. They opposed the UFT teachers, they maintained, not because they were Jewish but because they were white, and acting "white." As a writer in *Liberator* put it, "the Jew should not be singled out for any particular righteousness or duplicity. For ultimately, in the American context, he is a white man, no more, no less."[10] During the Ocean Hill–Brownsville crisis, black resentment at what they considered the unfair privileges of Jewish racial ambivalence—identifying as white or as a besieged minority, depending on the circumstances—finally burst to the surface. By attempting to fire Fred Nauman and his UFT colleagues, McCoy and the local board forced a choice. And, in October and November 1968, the Jews of New York's outer boroughs made their choice. Pushed by a black community that regarded them as "whites, no more, no less," and pulled by the promise of a race-based coalition with white Catholics, they used the Ocean Hill–Brownsville crisis to complete their journey to unambiguous white identity, the last group of Caucasians in New York to do so.

A poll conducted by Louis Harris & Associates in the immediate aftermath of the strikes confirmed this new configuration. Harris found that Ocean Hill–Brownsville produced "a new coalition of Jews and white Catholics, . . . not simply in the city's politics but in the behavior of individuals in their daily lives. The basis for this coalition was essentially negative: fear and an active aversion to the thrust of the blacks." Harris's data showed the attitudes of the city's black and Jewish-Catholic populations to be reverse-mirror images of each other. Jews favored the UFT in the dispute 63 to 8 percent, white Catholics by 48 to 9 percent. Blacks supported McCoy and the Ocean Hill local board 50 to 14 percent. By 66 to 12 percent, Jews believed that blacks preached anti-Semitism during the dispute; white Catholics agreed by 40 to 20 percent. Blacks, by 40 to 23 percent, dismissed anti-Semitism as an issue. And, in a clear break with past patterns of belief, Jews now saw blacks, not white Catholics, as the main source of anti-Semitism in the city, by a margin of almost 2 to 1. "Seven out of ten Jews, Italians and Irish in New York City," Harris concluded, "have clearly joined common cause." In contrast, Harris observed that "it is almost as if blacks and whites are living in different worlds instead of the same city."[11]

The third UFT strike also turned the city into a cauldron of class anger. The union, Lindsay said disdainfully, lacked "moral authority" in city life. The *Post's* Jimmy Breslin termed Shanker "the worst public person I have seen in my time in the city of New York," and compared him to Joseph McCarthy. "There are maybe six people you will meet in your life," he added, "who are as good as John Doar."[12] Whitney Young described the union's white middle-class supporters as "affluent peasants." "You're more likely to find prejudice," he argued, "among lower- and middle-class whites who've just made it—who are a generation away from WPA and welfare—people with middle-class incomes but not undergirded by civilized views, by aesthetic, cultural and educational experiences."[13]

Shanker responded by attacking "an alliance of civic groups, the newspapers and the Ford Foundation." "Listen to the radio, read our 'free' press, watch your TV screens," wrote one UFT rank-and-filer. "They are all against us."[14] UFT-ers picketed the offices of the hostile *New York Times,* and began a boycott of Ford products. Shanker demanded an end to the Ford Foundation's tax-exempt status and attacked "people on poverty payrolls" for "using public offices, public funds and daytime hours to engage in strikebreaking activities."[15] UFT pickets taunted the child of a prominent businessman and community control supporter, who had been sent by his father to an Ocean Hill–Brownsville school in a show of solidarity, with cries of "WASP! WASP!" Expressions of UFT anger sometimes bordered on farce. A female teacher picketed the Ford Foundation offices wearing a girdle outside her dress, carrying a sign reading "This Is My Ford Foundation."[16]

The contrasting events of one day during the third strike, October 15, provide a snapshot of class divisions in the city. On that day, the United Presbyterian and Episcopal churches announced their support for the Ocean Hill–Brownsville local board, with the latter accompanying its endorsement with a four-hundred-dollar donation. The Protestant Council of New York City added its backing, attacking the UFT as "intransigent," and stating that "the people in Ocean Hill–Brownsville must be supported by all the people in New York City. This experiment must have a chance. We must return the schools to the people. It's as simple as that." John Robertson, a high-ranking administrator at the New York University School of Education, warned that "we cannot treat the Ocean Hill–Brownsville school district as a colony run by a colonial government and demand submission as the price for education. . . . We in the white establishment seem bent on crushing the spirit of the people who can save our schools." The New York branch of the American Civil Liberties Union, which four days earlier had issued a report classifying community control as a protected civil liberty and supporting the local board, defended itself against harsh UFT criticism. And the *New York Times,* in an editorial, called the strike "an illegal, inexcusable play for power by a militant special interest group," that had "destroyed an entire school system."[17]

That same day, the New York Central Labor Council reiterated its "full support" for the UFT; the Council of Supervisory Associations voted to back the third strike, as it had the two others; and the National Maritime Union sent sound trucks through the streets of Manhattan denouncing the Ocean Hill–Brownsville local board as strikebreakers. Shanker charged that Lindsay, McGeorge Bundy, and other civic and business leaders were seeking to form "a big-name committee" to force an unfavorable settlement on the union.[18]

And, that night, in what his aide Barry Gottehrer later called "the low point in his mayoralty," Lindsay was booed off the stage of the East Midwood Jewish Center in Brooklyn by a crowd of 1500 as he tried to address the congregation. When the rabbi sought to quiet the crowd by asking "is this the exemplification of the Jewish faith?" the hecklers answered, "Yes! Yes!" Five thousand UFT supporters stood outside the synagogue, chanting "Lindsay must go!" The mayor was forced to leave by way of the fire escape. As he drove away, the crowd surged around his car, pounding on the hood, kicking the doors, and throwing trash at it.[19]

Two days later, at a City Hall rally attended by some forty thousand, virtually all white, UFT supporters—the largest such rally veteran political reporters had ever seen—demonstrators cursed and baited Breslin, Murray Kempton, and others in

10. Albert Shanker and John Doar (left) at a televised debate moderated by WNBC's Gabe Pressman during the third teachers' strike. United Federation of Teachers Collection, UFT Photo Collection, Robert F. Wagner Labor Archives, New York University.

11. Mayor John Lindsay is heckled by a pro-UFT crowd at the East Midwood Jewish Center in Brooklyn, October 15, 1968. Vincent Riehl, *New York Daily News.*

the hostile media. Kempton had recently written a column accusing union teachers of avarice and indifference to black school children. He attacked Shanker as a "goon" bent on "breaking the Ocean Hill local board and making certain that no other community body raises its head to suggest that a teacher or supervisor do an honest day's work again." He also had described Nauman, back at work after the second strike, as "not teaching, of course, but gathering grievances." Enraged UFT-ers at the rally set upon him, spitting and kicking.[20]

Another striking teacher chose a somewhat more peaceable venue to answer Kempton's charges. Writing in the *Village Voice,* in an article pointedly entitled "Why Teachers Strike: A Lesson for Liberals," UFT-er Patrick Harnett expressed

12. UFT demonstration in City Hall Park, October 17, 1968. United Federation of Teachers Archives, UFT Photo Collection, Robert F. Wagner Labor Archives, New York University.

the fear of an alliance between "Park Avenue" and the black poor that haunted the teachers during the strike:

> I believe that people like John Lindsay and John Doar, who are products of an upper middle-class milieu, together with intellectuals like Nat Hentoff (of the *Village Voice*) and James Wechsler (of the *Post*) find it genuinely difficult to deal open-mindedly with a teacher group who represent, in the main, a lower middle-class ethos. . . . The sympathies of white liberals and intellectuals are with the truly oppressed in our society—black people. They know that black people, in their struggle to gain the place and dignity of human beings in our society, find that their most immediate and rabid enemy is the lower and lower-middle economic class of whites.
>
> There is a reason for this, however, not always recognized for what it is. It is the white person from this economic group whose life is most immediately and actually affected by the struggle of blacks for social justice. This person's job, his home, his neighborhood—often his physical safety and well-being—are directly affected by the social waves created by an out class struggling desperately to get in. His life is affected in ways which the white liberal minister living on Park Avenue or the white liberal intellectual living in his Connecticut Shangra-La [sic], can have no experience.
>
> The upper middle-class person and the intellectual are therefore really outside the conflict of black insurgency—safely removed and able to abstract the situation. What they often abstract is a group of grasping white bigots denying the black person his basic rights for no other reason than they are intrinsically racist. Everyone knows that the less affluent class of whites are the most "bigoted," this thinking goes. Everyone knows that the slave-owning Southern gentleman was less bigoted than the non-slaveowning white.[21]

Harnett's imputation of a link between the average white southerner and the middle-class white teachers of New York, which would have been almost unimaginable only a few years before, during the southern phase of the civil rights movement, now elicited few disavowals from the strikers. Indeed, some white teachers were now talking publicly about voting for George Wallace, whose presidential campaign was then in full swing. Although this support never materialized, it was clear by the third Ocean Hill–Brownsville strike that the emergence of an angry, self-conscious white middle class had called into question many of the accepted truths about the structure of class relations in the city.[22]

New York's population could no longer be divided neatly into groups of "bosses" and "workers," as so many in the city's left-wing activist and intellectual communities sought to do. No one who had seen forty thousand vociferous white UFT supporters in front of City Hall on October 17 could argue seriously that they and the city's poor black population were "natural" allies. And no one who had observed the scene outside the East Midwood Jewish Center on October 15, as Lindsay fled from a debris-throwing white mob, could claim that the city's white middle class was "in the pockets" of "the rich." Ocean Hill–Brownsville clarified the changes in New York's class structure that had taken place over the past quarter-century. It established the city's white middle class as an independent force, with a distinct voice of its own and interests that were different from both the city's poor and Manhattan elites. The crisis crystallized its language of fear. It made white middle-class New Yorkers sufficiently afraid to engage in acts of public violence—acts they had heretofore associated almost exclusively with the black poor—in order to defend their culture, and their New York.

Ocean Hill–Brownsville also symbolized the expansion of the idea of "class" itself in city life beyond conceptions of pure economics. The teachers hated John Lindsay, John Doar, and McGeorge Bundy not so much because they were well-to-do, but because they had influence, knowledge, and access to power. They also sensed, moreover, that Lindsay and the others disdained them as much for their values—their doggedness in pursuit of upward mobility, their materialism, their cultural insularity—as anything else. This sense of siege, of attack on both fronts by those who rejected them for the way they lived and acted—Shanker, after all, was not good enough to step into Lindsay's living room, and his teachers, to Young, were nothing more than "affluent peasants"—turned groups of normally quiescent, respectable, men and women into a cursing, screaming, trash-throwing mob during the third Ocean Hill–Brownsville strike.

It is ironic that, in a decade known more for civil disorders in black neighborhoods, a series of white middle-class "civil disorders" not only ended the Ocean Hill–Brownsville controversy, but changed the political, economic, and social landscape of the city for years to come. But, this is essentially what occurred in October 1968. While these white middle-class upheavals, to be sure, did not produce the loss of life and property damage associated with those in urban ghettos, they were similarly effective as expressions of discontent. Ocean Hill–Brownsville's third strike unleashed white middle-class rage as an ongoing impulse in the political and cultural life of the city. Whether it played out, as here, in raw, public fury, or more quietly and subtly, as in the case of white acquiescence in municipal social service cuts during the 1970s, city leaders ignored this impulse at their peril. As much as Lindsay may have believed in the redistributive potential of community control in the city's public education system, as much as he may have believed that conditions in black neighborhoods were traceable to the racism of the white middle class, and as much as he may have believed that the values of the white middle class were shallow and vulgar, he could not afford to ignore two-thirds of the city's population.[23] When civil servants with master's degrees and mortgages became angry enough to take to the streets, Lindsay knew not only that the UFT had beaten him at Ocean Hill–Brownsville, but that his brand of racial politics had failed as well.

Lindsay had hoped to use the power of New York's civic and professional elites to secure racial justice for the city's poor black population. He had also hoped to attract enough of its white middle class to make this endeavor successful. Now, with much of that middle class calling, sometimes literally, for his head, he knew that his plan had not worked. Henceforth, white middle class New Yorkers would determine the direction of racial politics in the city, and if Lindsay wished to survive as a politician, he would have to adjust his own, more expansive vision to theirs. By late October, with the third Ocean Hill–Brownsville strike in full fury, Lindsay knew that, as difficult as it was to swallow, he would have to give Albert Shanker what he wanted.

Even so, the strike dragged on until mid-November. In late October, Lindsay offered to personally guarantee the safe return of the UFT teachers, to immediately suspend any individual who interfered, and to allow the union to decide if any Ocean Hill–Brownsville school should be closed in the event of violence or harassment. Shanker's distrust of the mayor was so intense at this point that he rejected this offer to virtually cede managerial powers over the Ocean Hill schools. Shanker continued to hold out for the permanent removal of McCoy and the local board, and the termination of the Ocean Hill–Brownsville experiment. But Doar, tugging at the mayor's other sleeve, continued to insist that this would constitute a cave-in to the city's unions and a betrayal of the black community. The strike ground on.[24]

During the first week of November, both Shanker and Lindsay began grandstanding, each seeking to exploit their respective strengths. Lindsay proposed submitting the dispute to an arbitration panel composed of prominent citizens. Shanker, wary at this point of any initiative involving "prominent citizens," almost predictably countered with an offer to conduct a binding citywide referendum, which the mayor and Doar, just as predictably, rejected.[25]

Shanker then sought to ratchet up the pressure on the local board by calling for a special session of the State Legislature to address the entire question of community control. This enraged black leaders, such as Whitney Young and Kenneth Clark, who had heretofore been at least on speaking terms with the UFT, because Shanker had promised he would never do this. A special session of the legislature with the schools in chaos could only bode ill for community control, as Shanker well knew. Moderate black leaders interpreted Shanker's demand as a gratuitous slap at the black community, and moved closer to the McCoy/local board camp. Young, whom many in the Ocean Hill–Brownsville community had previously derided as an "Uncle Tom," was especially vociferous. He pulled out of back-channel negotiations aimed at settling the strike, blasting Shanker for fomenting "racial strife." Blacks, Young said, "have a historic, intuitive sense" of bias, and implied that he was now getting that sense from Shanker. Shanker in turn accused Young himself of bias: "It is unfortunate that Mr. Young does not believe that teachers, too, should enjoy civil rights. His failure to denounce racism and anti-Semitism, his failure to denounce violence, will do much to impair his effectiveness as a civil rights leader and will lend encouragement to backlash forces in the white community."[26]

This bitter exchange was the breaking point for the black members of Van Arsdale's Central Labor Council, who had become increasingly restive during the strikes. Three major Central Labor Council unions had a black membership of at least 30 percent—Local 1199 of the Drug and Hospital Workers, District Council 37, AFSCME, and District Council 65 of the Retail, Wholesale and Department Store Union. When the third strike began, the leaders of these three unions had sponsored a resolution in the Central Labor Council supporting both due process rights for teachers and the idea of community control. Shanker had used his influence with Van Arsdale to prevent the resolution from even reaching a vote. By November 13, New York's black unionists had had enough. Fifty of them staged a sit-in at Van Arsdale's office demanding he end, or at least temper, his support of the UFT, for whom he had raised over a hundred thousand dollars during the strikes. Leslie Roberts of District Council 65 threatened that "if we have to split the labor movement and go our own way, we will," sentiments echoed by Thomas Mitchell, vice president of Local 1199: "Those of us who are black and Puerto Rican will set up our own labor movement." Another black unionist told a reporter he considered himself a black man first and a union man second.[27]

Conspicuously absent from the sit-in were the only prominent black labor leaders to support the UFT during the Ocean Hill–Brownsville dispute, democratic socialists Bayard Rustin and A. Philip Randolph. Both were clearly influenced by their institutional ties to the union, which, through sponsorship of the Randolph Institute, essentially employed them, but there was more to it than that. Randolph and Rustin had dedicated their careers to the cause of interracial social democracy. Randolph, the longtime head of the Brotherhood of Sleeping Car Porters and a founder of the influential Negro American Labor Council, and Rustin, the inspiration behind the 1963 March on Washington, believed that civil rights and labor rights were mutually reinforcing principles. The Ocean Hill–Brownsville controversy, however, put those beliefs to a severe test, and forced the two leaders to make a choice.

Randolph and Rustin chose the UFT. In September, they placed an advertisement in the three major New York City newspapers, which they induced twenty black labor officials to co-sign. The advertisement stated that the Ocean Hill–Brownsville dispute was essentially about class, not race, and that its "real issue" was "the right of every worker to be judged on his merits, not his color." "If due process is not won in Ocean Hill–Brownsville," it argued, "what could prevent white community groups in Queens from firing black teachers? Injustice must not be camouflaged by appeals to racial solidarity."[28]

But by the third Ocean Hill–Brownsville strike, the pull of racial solidarity had become too great for other black labor leaders to resist. On October 16, fifty-four leading black unionists, including most of the signers of the Randolph/Rustin advertisement, wrote to Lindsay in support of community control.[29] Randolph and Rustin, argued one such leader, were asking the impossible by demanding that "the black union member support the teachers against his black brothers in the ghetto [and] repudiate the black man's right to demand equality of opportunity if it conflicts with the alleged right of a predominantly white group. This position is unrealistic. It matters not whether we see it [that] way. The black people of New York see it that way."[30] The UFT, charged another, was "burning whatever remaining bridges it has to the Negro community." And by the time black Central Labor Council members sat in at Van Arsdale's office in November, Randolph and Rustin stood virtually alone, written off as race traitors by their erstwhile colleagues. "People like A. Philip Randolph and Bayard Rustin do not speak for us," said Leslie Roberts. "[They have] sold out. Whatever you have done in the past, you have destroyed."[31]

Randolph and Rustin never regained their stature among black unionists, or in New York's black community as a whole. The contradictions between class and race that had lurked beneath their vision of social democracy throughout their careers burst to the surface at Ocean Hill–Brownsville, and they were no more successful in resolving them than were the black unionists who sat in at Van Arsdale's office. Their defeat symbolized the failure, for both men, of a lifelong struggle to unite the races under the banner of economic democracy. New York, as Ocean Hill–Brownsville had shown so dramatically, was not so much a city of bosses and workers as it was one of blacks and whites.

By November, the third strike had, in the words of one observer, "become nihilist." White UFT supporters screamed "nigger scab" at a black teacher in Ocean

13. Albert Shanker with UFT supporter Bayard Rustin. United Federation of Teachers Collection, UFT Photo Collection, Robert F. Wagner Labor Archives, New York University.

Hill–Brownsville, "nigger lover" at a white replacement teacher, and called a local board ally a "cannibal."[32] The word "genocide" now appeared in the public statements of local board members on almost a daily basis, in a clear attempt to inflame Jewish sensibilities. Shanker's words of choice were "extremists" and "mobs." Even Whitney Young, whose relationship with Shanker had been poisoned by the latter's call for a special session of the State Legislature, appeared to lose control, asking rhetorically, "it's a pity, isn't it, that there are only two thousand blacks you can get killed on Ocean Hill."[33]

With the entire city ready to snap, State Education Commissioner James Allen realized he had to enter negotiations directly and somehow end the strike. In early November, he began laying the groundwork for a settlement. Shanker distrusted Allen, a longtime community control supporter who had sponsored the demonstration school principal idea that so vexed the UFT membership. But he believed that Allen was more likely to use the power at his disposal to ensure that Ocean Hill–Brownsville complied with the settlement terms that would be agreed on than Lindsay, who, in his view, had reneged twice before. And he preferred Allen's pragmatism to what he saw as Doar's sanctimony. Allen, as Shanker knew, harbored national ambitions—he later served as United States Commissioner of Education in the Nixon administration—and the strikes were damaging his reputation. Shanker also knew that while most of his constituency still backed the strike, his ranks were beginning to thin: 15 to 20 percent of the teachers were now crossing picket lines.[34]

Allen began sketching out a plan that would give the UFT most, but not all, of what it wanted. Nauman and all other UFT teachers would return to their schools, with written teaching assignments distributed in advance. To enforce this, the Ocean Hill–Brownsville school district would be removed from the jurisdiction of the Board of Education and placed under the control of an Allen-appointed state trustee. And to protect UFT teachers in Ocean Hill–Brownsville and around the rest of the city from reprisals, a three-man supervisory committee would be empowered to conduct hearings and mete out punishment, including suspensions, dismissals, and school closings. Shanker would have veto power over the composition of this committee. Echoing the agreement that ended the first strike in September, involuntary transfers of teachers would be made contractual grievance matters, with impartial hearings, appeals, and other due process protections, although Allen had to twist Doar's arm to get him to agree to this clause.

Allen, however, insisted that McCoy be allowed to continue as unit administrator of the Ocean Hill–Brownsville experimental project, provided he obeyed the orders of the state trustee. And, the Ocean Hill–Brownsville community control experiment itself would continue, albeit with the local board under suspension. Once the district returned to normal operations, the trustee would step aside and reinstate the board.[35]

As the parties haggled, the negotiations received a push from an unexpected source. The demonstration principal issue had hung over the controversy ever since a state court had held them illegal in March 1968. The principals had retained their jobs while the Board of Education appealed this ruling, standard procedure in such circumstances. Donovan had suspended them in October for refusing to give Nauman and the UFT-ers teaching assignments, then reinstated them, thereby provoking the third strike. Now Shanker insisted that the demonstration principals be removed from the Ocean Hill–Brownsville schools, not only because he did not trust them to give Nauman and the others teaching assignments when they returned, but because he considered their appointments a violation of the merit principle. Allen and Doar dug in their heels, and negotiations appeared to be breaking down over the issue, when, on November 14, the Appellate Division, New York's intermediate appeals court, surprised everyone by releasing its decision: the demonstration principal appointments were indeed illegal, and the lower court ruling invalidating them was affirmed.[36]

The Board of Education vowed once again to appeal, this time to the state's highest court, the New York Court of Appeals, which normally would have allowed the principals to retain their positions in the interim. But now Shanker dug in his heels. Appeal or no appeal, he wanted them out, or the entire settlement was off. After thirty-seven lost school days, millions in municipal financial losses, and with both blacks and whites in the streets, Lindsay could take no more. He asked Allen to give in on the demonstration principal issue and settle. At 10 A.M. on Sunday, November 17, Shanker, Lindsay, Allen, Doar, and Donovan shook hands warily across a Gracie Mansion conference table.[37]

Oliver and Powis, representing the Ocean Hill–Brownsville local board as nonparticipating "observers," had walked out hours before, when the parameters of the settlement became clear to them. "Hey, baby, now we burn down Brooklyn," Powis had barked as he left.[38] Despite his customary apocalyptic rhetoric, he had reason to be angry. Throughout the Ocean Hill–Brownsville dispute, Shanker, Lindsay, Donovan, and the other negotiators had talked about, and sometimes around, the local board, but they had rarely talked to them as equals. When the mayor or superintendent made promises to Shanker, they made them on behalf of the local board, not in conjunction with them. In the end, even the city officials who supported the idea of community control in theory, like Lindsay, hesitated to allow the local board an independent voice at the bargaining table. While Lindsay was legally correct in this position—in late November, a federal judge, ruling on

14. Albert Shanker and John Lindsay, flanked by Council of Supervisory Associations President Walter Degnan and State Education Commissioner James Allen (holding document), announcing the settlement of the third and final teachers' strike on the steps of Gracie Mansion, November 17, 1968. W. Sauro/*The New York Times.*

the local board's challenge to its suspension, held that the board was merely "an unofficial body of citizen advisers"—this may have been beside the point under the circumstances.[39] For all their talk of "self-determination," Lindsay, Allen, and Doar never really tried community control in Ocean Hill–Brownsville. If Powis and Oliver felt as "sold out" by their ostensible friends as by enemies like Shanker, they had much justification.

Much of the UFT membership also felt sold out, albeit for different reasons. When Shanker took the proposed settlement to the union's Delegate Assembly for ratification on the evening of Sunday, November 17, he was shouted off the stage by furious rejectionists. Shanker had overplayed his hand with his membership by demanding the permanent removal of McCoy and the local board, and the dismantling of the Ocean Hill–Brownsville experimental district. When he did not deliver, the delegates shouted him down with cries of "sellout." Shanker, usually

15. Fred Nauman enters Junior High School 271 under police escort, November 22, 1968. James Garrett, *New York Daily News.*

the master of his membership, could not even bring the proposed settlement to a vote, and stalked off the stage, muttering that his own delegates resembled the "mobs" and "extremists" he had so recently encountered in the city's black community.[40]

Shanker was able to have the settlement ratified only because the UFT constitution permitted the full membership to override an action, or in this case, a nonaction, of the Delegate Assembly. Given an extra day to allow cooler heads to prevail, the rank-and-file members, the vast majority of whom had supported the strikes, and who were facing the prospect of more payless paydays, ratified the agreement by 17,658 to 2,738. At a mass UFT "victory rally" in Madison Square Garden, dissidents were in short supply. Shanker and the other top union officials received loud ovations from the assembled teachers, who booed ritualistically each time the names "Lindsay," "Bundy," "Doar," and "McCoy" were mentioned.

16. African-American Teachers Association President Albert Vann (left) and Ocean Hill–Brownsville local school board chairman C. Herbert Oliver after their arrest for illegally entering Junior High School 271, November 26, 1968. Charles D. Hogan/*The New York Times.*

On Tuesday, November 19, Nauman, his Ocean Hill–Brownsville colleagues, and 57,000 other UFT teachers returned to work.[41]

This time, the settlement held up. There were, to be sure, some rough moments. The suspended Oliver and Vann sought to enter JHS 271 and were arrested, setting off a series of disturbances that prompted the state trustee to close the school temporarily. A pupil at 271 accused Nauman of striking him, forcing the teacher's temporary reassignment to Board of Education headquarters. But on the whole, at least the formalities of the agreement remained in place. McCoy, after some initial difficulties, gradually settled back into his unit administrator's job.

In January 1969, the demonstration principals got their jobs back, when the State Court of Appeals reversed both lower courts and upheld the validity of the position. The court, however, sharply limited the scope of its ruling, allowing the category only as an experiment and refusing to exempt it from the requirement of written examinations in the future.[42] It ruled, in essence, that the demonstration principal idea violated the State Constitution and the merit principle, but that the disputed principals could return in the general interests of racial peace at Ocean Hill–Brownsville. Shanker had lost on the immediate issue, but, once again, received most of what he wanted in the end.

Shanker also moved to settle scores with UFT members who had opposed him during the strike. He took particular aim at those with connections to the Communist-influenced Teachers Union (TU), a longtime rival of the UFT's socialist antecedent, the Teachers Guild. The Teachers Union, which had disbanded in 1964, had long championed the study of black history, producing a series of annual "Negro History Week" supplements in its newspaper.[43] TU alumni were active on the UFT's Committee on African-American History, and had chafed at Shanker's attempts to control its work.

In 1969, the committee produced a volume entitled "Lesson Plans on African-American History," containing material almost guaranteed to raise Shanker's hackles. TU veterans on the committee, who had opposed the Ocean Hill–Brownsville strikes, inserted in "Lesson Plans" a passage endorsing a report issued by the New York Civil Liberties Union which was highly critical of the UFT. Shanker had the passage removed, and deleted the names of the authors of "Lesson Plans" from the final version of the volume, to punish the TU-affiliated members of the committee for their apostasy on Ocean Hill–Brownsville. He also removed material that he considered too incendiary, including two chapters on Malcolm X; the Kerner Commission's conclusion that "our nation is moving toward two societies, one black, one white — separate and unequal"; and Frederick Douglass's assertion that "power concedes nothing without demand."[44]

The Ocean Hill–Brownsville controversy had been the UFT's version of civil war, and by 1969, it was clear that Shanker had emerged victorious in his struggle, having branded opponents of the strikes, like the former TU members, as disloyal. His leadership position within the union was virtually impregnable. Thanks in large part to Ocean Hill–Brownsville, Shanker and his allies would dominate the UFT for the next three decades.

In March 1969, the state trustee recommended that Allen reinstate the local board, which he did, on Oliver's promise to obey the orders of the central Board of Education. By this time, most of the white UFT teachers in Ocean Hill–Brownsville, having made their point, had left the district. Nauman himself would depart at the end of the school year. Even the replacement teachers who had come to the district to work for community control were leaving, many disillusioned by the hostility of the ATA-ers. Vann and Campbell, stung by the local board's defeat, had retreated behind a wall of racial separatism. It was as if they could not abide the sight of any white teachers, even sympathetic ones. Less than half of the original cohort of replacement teachers remained in Ocean Hill–Brownsville after the 1968–69 school year.[45]

By early 1969, Ocean Hill–Brownsville began to lose its daily spot on the front pages of the city's newspapers, as the district quieted down. But it had left a sour, angry taste in the mouth of the city as a whole, one that did not easily fade. It was as if, in the words of one observer, blacks and whites in the city were "talking a different language."[46] Polls taken after the strikes showed blacks and whites inhabiting different interpretive universes on the issue of whether racism even existed in New York, with a large percentage of whites denying its presence altogether.[47]

The strikes, moreover, had clearly affected Jews more than any other white group. Jews now were the most likely to report that they feared black-inspired racial violence in the city, as well as black crime. Blacks and white Protestants had replaced white Catholics as the groups Jews feared most.[48] Campbell certainly did not help matters when he read a poem on alternative radio station WBAI in December 1968 dedicated to Albert Shanker, the first two lines of which were "Hey, Jew boy, with that yarmulke on your head / You pale faced Jew boy—I wish you were dead."[49]And Thomas Hoving, the blueblood director of the Metropolitan Museum of Art, also raised Jewish hackles with his handling of the furor over the gallery's January 1969 "Harlem On My Mind" exhibit, a multimedia display of work by Harlem residents. The exhibit catalogue contained statements such as "Our contempt for the Jew makes us feel more completely American in sharing a national prejudice . . . ," and "behind every hurdle that the Afro-American has yet to jump stands the Jew who has already cleared it." In the face of Jewish protests, Hoving at first defended this language as "anything but racist." The author's statements, he averred, "are true. So be it," before Jewish community pressure forced him to withdraw the catalogue from circulation. The exhibit, ironically, had also been criticized and picketed by black leaders, who contended it portrayed a "white man's view of Harlem."[50]

Two reports on bias during the Ocean Hill–Brownsville controversy, one commissioned by Lindsay, the other by the Anti-Defamation League, illustrated the perceptual differences between white Protestants and Jews in the aftermath of the crisis. Lindsay's report cited an "appalling amount of racial prejudice" on both sides during the strikes without emphasizing specific instances of anti-Jewish words or behavior by members of the black community. The Anti-Defamation League, in contrast, found a "crisis level" of anti-Semitism in the city, originating in the black community, but abetted by Lindsay, Doar, Bundy, and other members of the "Establishment," who looked the other way in the interests of preserving community control.[51]

New York's Jewish community exacted retribution against blacks and city elites for their behavior during the Ocean Hill–Brownsville crisis, shifting the city's political landscape rightward. In the wake of Ocean Hill–Brownsville, Jewish support for social welfare programs in New York dropped sharply, to a level close to that of traditionally fiscally conservative white Catholics. A post–Ocean Hill poll showed Jews supporting welfare cuts, in fact, even more enthusiastically than white Catholics, by a margin of 45 to 35 percent.[52] And in the 1969 mayoral race, Jews, who had helped elect John Lindsay four years earlier despite the fact that he was opposed by a Jew, turned to two conservative Italian-American candidates; they received 55 percent of the total Jewish vote. A chastened Lindsay won only because of the divisions among his opponents. His second term featured fewer of the bold pronouncements and initiatives on racial matters that had characterized his first. In the post–Ocean Hill–Brownsville city, the road to electoral success ran through the Jewish and Catholic neighborhoods of Brooklyn, Queens, the Bronx, and Staten Island.

Ocean Hill–Brownsville had helped reconfigure the political landscape of the city. While historian Godfrey Hodgson's pronouncement that outer-borough Jewish defections to white Catholics "tipped the balance from liberal to conservative predominance" in New York may have overstated the case, there was little doubt that the city was a more conservative place after Ocean Hill–Brownsville than before.[53] A diminished liberal coalition of blacks, white Protestants, and Manhattan Jews simply did not possess the electoral muscle to enact Lindsay's ambitious racial agenda: a civilian review board for police, increased levels of spending for social services, and community control of education in black neighborhoods. In this sense, Ocean Hill–Brownsville helped make what was possible in 1965, impossible by 1969.

But Ocean Hill–Brownsville, and the realignment of outer-borough Jews it produced, changed the city in a more elemental way. Jews had traditionally served as mediators between black and white New Yorks, a cosmopolitan influence that helped blunt the force of more primal racial passions. Ocean Hill–Brownsville, in the words of sociologist Jonathan Rieder, turned outer-borough Jews from "optimistic universalism" toward "nervous provincialism," aligning them with most of the rest of the city's white population.[54] By marking the Jewish passage from racial ambivalence to unmistakable white identity, Ocean Hill–Brownsville helped reify the "white" and "black" New Yorks that had gestated over the past three decades.

If it had changed Jewish attitudes, Ocean Hill–Brownsville merely confirmed and made public those held by other groups, both black and white, in the city. In this sense, John Lindsay and Albert Shanker—and Rhody McCoy and Fred Nauman, as well—had severely damaged New York's pluralist experiment, bequeathing a city so simmering with racial resentments that religion and ethnicity, which once seemed to matter so much, paled before the starker realities of black and white. Of course, race had always "mattered" in New York, and the city's veneer of cosmopolitanism and pluralism had often had a self-delusional quality to it. But myths have their uses, and New Yorkers enjoyed at least the outward accoutrements of municipal civility between the end of World War II and the mid-1960s. Ocean Hill–Brownsville's legacy was a New York more realistic about itself, to be sure, but also more openly unapologetic about its prejudices. The crisis may have taught black and white New Yorkers more about each other than they needed to know. Ocean Hill–Brownsville, destroyer of illusions, stripped away a facade of civility to reveal a city of strangers.

Albert Shanker had received most of what he wanted from the strike settlement, but not everything. Above all, he had not been able to destroy the Ocean Hill–Brownsville community control experiment in its entirety. In the spring of 1969, he moved to complete this unfinished business. The Marchi Law, which had delayed a final resolution of the school decentralization issue in the State Legislature for one year, expired in May. The permanent law to be passed by the legislature would determine the fate of the Ocean Hill–Brownsville district. As he had the previous year, Shanker began calling in political chips. Thanks to the fallout from the strikes, he found allies among traumatized outer-borough Democratic legislators, as well as upstate Republicans. Shanker knew that some type of decentralization bill was certain to pass, but if he could limit its scope, the UFT might still retain its co-managerial prerogatives in the New York public school system.

In many respects, the battle over the permanent decentralization law in the State Legislature reprised that of Ocean Hill–Brownsville, with a similar cast of characters. Lindsay, Doar, Allen, Galamison, and Clark, along with the Ford Foundation, the New York Urban Coalition, and the major civil rights organizations, lined up behind a proposed bill that permitted local boards to hire and promote teachers, set New York State certification as the basic qualification for educational personnel, and ended the examination system in its entirety. In these and most other respects, the so-called "Regents" bill echoed the long-standing demands of the Ocean Hill–Brownsville local board.

This battle, however, would not be anywhere near as long or as bruising as the one at Ocean Hill–Brownsville the previous fall. Except for the relatively small number of black and Puerto Rican legislators, who were joined by an equally small group of "New Politics"–oriented white Democrats from Manhattan, the Regents bill simply did not have the votes. The upstate Republicans who had supported community control for New York City a year earlier had not done so out of any great concern for civil rights; they merely wished to permit schools in the city the same local prerogatives that their own schools enjoyed. But the dislocations of Ocean Hill–Brownsville had aroused their conservative instincts, and the Republicans were now in a mood to punish community control supporters for their "misbehavior." The Ocean Hill–Brownsville controversy had also cemented Shanker's relationship with outer-borough Democratic legislators whose constituents were also in a vengeful mood. As one such legislator put it, "my people were so frightened by the character of the Ocean Hill–Brownsville controversy, I'd be a fool to vote for a liberal bill." Governor Nelson Rockefeller, a Republican keenly interested in expanding his party's base among the state's unions, also came in on the side of the UFT, and applied the coup de grace to the Regents bill.

On April 30, the State legislature passed a final decentralization law that would govern the New York City public school system until 1996. The new law had Shanker's fingerprints all over it. It was, emphatically, a decentralization and not a community control law. Shanker had argued strenuously during the lobbying process that "objective standards must not be lowered," and he got his wish. The Board of Examiners, long-standing target for community control supporters, remained in place, along with its array of competitive examinations governing hiring and advancement. The "rule of three" would continue to govern teacher selection, although Shanker did agree to a compromise under which school districts ranking in the city's bottom 45 percent in reading could choose any applicant who passed the National Teacher Examination. Principals would also continue to be chosen by examination, although no longer in strict rank order, and existing principal eligibility lists—which were composed almost entirely of whites—would be used until exhausted. A new seven-member Board of Education, with one member to be chosen by each of the five borough presidents, and the other two by the mayor, would replace Doar, Galamison, and the rest of the Lindsay-appointed Board. Local school boards would have the power to select district superintendents and principals, choose textbooks from a Board of Education–approved list, and allocate monies independently up to a maximum amount of $250,000. In a crucial victory for Shanker and the UFT, all involuntary interdistrict transfers by local boards would be prohibited. And finally, the city would be divided into approximately thirty school districts, each with a minimum student enrollment of twenty thousand. This meant that the Ocean Hill–Brownsville district, with far fewer students, would be folded into a new and larger District 23.[55]

In this backhanded way, the Decentralization Law of 1969 announced the demise of the Ocean Hill–Brownsville community control experiment. The law set elections for local board positions in each of the new districts, including District 23, for March 1970. A little over three months later, on July 1, 1970, when the elected local boards officially took office, the Ocean Hill–Brownsville school district would pass out of existence. It had taken Albert Shanker two years, but he had, yet again, gotten what he wanted.

But McCoy, Oliver, Powis and the Ocean Hill–Brownsville local board did not plan to go quietly. The new law gave them almost a year until the new local board elections, ample time to organize a counterattack. They made a crucial tactical mistake, however, that destroyed any chance they had to retain influence in the new district. McCoy and Oliver called for a boycott of the local board elections, arguing that the "community" had already chosen a local board—theirs. In addition to the questionable logic of their claim—since their local board had been chosen in August 1967, and had never stood for reelection—they overlooked Samuel Wright's preparations to wrest power from them.

Wright, the local assemblyman, was already a member of the Oliver/Powis local board. He had, in fact, been a member when it drafted the termination letters to Fred Nauman and his colleagues. Wright had dissented from that decision, as he had from many others taken by that body. But he did not proceed out of any great affection for the UFT, due process protections, or, indeed, any ideological predilections whatsoever. Wright was an old-fashioned political spoilsman, who rewarded his friends and punished his enemies according to what they could do for, or to, him. He had long coveted the jobs and influence that the Ocean Hill–Brownsville school district offered, and now that the new decentralization law had created a perpetual source of patronage, he was ready to make his move. He put together a slate of candidates for election to the new District 23 local board, and began campaigning.

Oliver and McCoy, however, continued to follow the imperatives of ideology. To them, the upcoming local board elections were just another battle in the long war for community control of education. Once again, as they saw it, the white power structure, this time through the new decentralization law, sought to deprive blacks of control over their schools. And they regarded Wright, who had maintained civil relations with Shanker even during the darkest days of the Ocean Hill–Brownsville strikes, as just another white man's lackey. A boycott of the local board election, then, appeared to be in keeping with everything Oliver and McCoy had fought for at Ocean Hill–Brownsville.

But they miscalculated badly. The historical momentum that had driven the Ocean Hill–Brownsville experiment had dissipated. The strikes were over, Nauman and most of the striking UFT teachers were gone, and the district was struggling with the more mundane, day-to-day demands of running its schools. The election results would be binding no matter how few people voted; the Board of

Education would not allow the old local board to remain in power simply because of a low turnout in District 23. McCoy and Oliver's boycott plan, then, was a last-ditch, romantic gesture, a defiant tilt at an institutional windmill. But their moment had passed. McCoy and Oliver may have preserved their ideological purity, but at a high price. As far as the electoral process was concerned, they were now outsiders looking in.

Two weeks before the scheduled local board election, McCoy sent a letter to Ocean Hill–Brownsville parents touting the gains the district's children had made in reading under his regime, a sign of how desperate he had become. McCoy had refused to administer standardized reading tests during his tenure, viewing them as culturally biased, but he now informed parents that "64 percent" of Ocean Hill–Brownsville third-, fourth-, and fifth-grade students had made "substantial progress," a term he did not define.[56] "If you vote in the school board elections," he told the parents, "you will [l]egalize your child's failure . . . [and] be forced to follow all of the rules and regulations that have caused such massive and severe failure for our children." "When the city-state know you are dissatisfied," he predicted, "they will have to come to you."[57] In another appeal to parents, Oliver raised the specter of Albert Shanker, who he referred to as "Mr. Charlie," returning to run the Ocean Hill–Brownsville schools. "Don't be fooled or used by the UFT," he warned.[58]

But on election day, March 19, 1970, Wright's slate, running virtually unopposed, won every seat on the new District 23 local board. McCoy's boycott had kept turnout down to a city-low 5 percent, as compared to 13 to 22 percent elsewhere, but as he should have anticipated, the results stood nonetheless. On July 1, 1970, police removed Oliver, Powis, and their supporters, who had refused to leave the district offices, and Wright's new board moved in. A few weeks later, a state court judge dismissed Oliver's legal challenge to the election results—he had claimed "we are operating to do what the community wants"—in a scathing decision. The judge noted pointedly that the low turnout Oliver complained of approximated the number of voters who had elected him in 1967. McCoy and Oliver, the court observed, acted as if "the perpetuation of their own rule is the only answer to the needs of the community."[59] Dismissing their challenge, he declared the Wright slate the legally constituted local board of the new District 23. His pen stroke on the decision officially ended the Ocean Hill–Brownsville community control experiment.

Across the rest of the city, Shanker had moved to co-opt the new school decentralization process. He put together slates of UFT-affiliated candidates to run in each of the districts, and elected enough of them to protect the union's co-managerial status in the public schools, a status it retains today. Shanker also thrived professionally under the new decentralization structure. Already wildly popular in his own local union in the aftermath of the Ocean Hill–Brownsville strikes, he ran successfully for the presidency of the UFT's national parent union, the American Federation of Teachers, in 1974. He held both AFT and UFT presidencies simultaneously until 1982, when he bequeathed the latter office to his protégé, Sandra Feldman. At his death in early 1997, Shanker was the most powerful and influential education union official in America. Until the day he died, he never expressed the slightest regret over any of his actions during the Ocean Hill–Brownsville controversy. If he had it to do over again, he always maintained, he would not have changed a thing.

The years after Ocean Hill–Brownsville were less kind to many of the dispute's other major principals. Bernard Donovan, his reputation badly damaged, retired at the first available opportunity, in September 1969. In what may have been an unconscious comment on his thirty-year career in public education, he became an adviser to the New York City parochial school system. John Doar and Milton Galamison lost their positions as president and vice president, respectively, of the Board of Education, when that body was dissolved by the 1969 Decentralization Law. James Allen, realizing his ambition, became U.S. commissioner of education under Richard Nixon. After a brief and relatively unsuccessful tenure, he died in a 1971 plane crash. McGeorge Bundy fought unsuccessfully against UFT-inspired federal legislation that restricted the scope of permissible foundation-sponsored political activities and narrowed foundation tax exemptions. He cut off Ford Foundation funding to the Ocean Hill–Brownsville experimental district after the strikes ended, and instructed his aide Mario Fantini to steer clear of such controversial projects—or at least those that would bring him into conflict with Albert Shanker—in the future. After leaving the foundation, he taught in the History Department of New York University.

And John Lindsay, reelected mayor in 1969 only because he had the good fortune to run against two conservative Italian-American candidates who split the vote against him, found himself at a political dead end. Permanently tainted by Ocean Hill–Brownsville among the city's white middle-class population, blocked from higher statewide office by his rival fellow Republican Nelson Rockefeller, and out of step philosophically with the national Republican leadership, he became a Democrat in 1971, and sought his new party's presidential nomination the following year. His campaign was a disaster, highlighted by his almost comically wrongheaded decision to concentrate his energies on the Florida primary. Walking the sands of Miami Beach in search of votes from former New Yorkers, he instead encountered angry expatriates who eagerly told trailing reporters that they had left the city because of Lindsay. The press was treated to the sight of the candidate re-treating from his own "constituency," some shouting "Lindsay go home!" It was, one reporter mused, just like New York.[60]

By 1971, both Fred Nauman and Rhody McCoy had left Ocean Hill–Browns-ville. Both had been taken care of, so to speak, by their own. Shanker rewarded Nauman for his perseverance during the strikes with the ultimate "perk" for any New York City public school teacher: a ticket out of the classroom. He gave Nau-man a succession of UFT administrative positions, including one with the union's Albany office. McCoy also left the New York public school system. After Samuel Wright's takeover of the new District 23, Fantini helped McCoy matriculate at the University of Massachusetts, where he earned a doctorate in education. He wrote his dissertation, not surprisingly, on the Ocean Hill–Brownsville contro-versy. Later, after a fellowship at Harvard, he worked for the U.S. Department of Education. McCoy, like Shanker, never expressed regret about any of his decisions during the Ocean Hill–Brownsville dispute.

After assuming control of the new District 23 in July 1970, Samuel Wright quickly removed the last vestiges of the Ocean Hill–Brownsville experimental dis-trict. One by one, he rid himself of the principals appointed during the McCoy-Oliver regime, replacing them with political allies. Wright, in fact, viewed the en-tire school district as little more than an employment agency for his friends. He made sure that seats on the local board, principalships, administrative jobs, and contracting opportunities went to those who helped him. Eventually, Wright over-stepped himself, was convicted on bribery charges, and sentenced to prison.

Wright's reign was an example, albeit a rather extreme one, of the corrup-tion and influence-peddling that characterized most of the city's school districts under the 1969 Decentralization Law. During the twenty-seven years the law was in effect, the city's schools were wracked by scandals involving contract kickbacks, personal use of school funds by local board personnel, and the buying and selling of principalships. Turnouts for school board elections were low, usually below 10 percent of eligible voters, permitting organized cliques to monopolize power. The rules governing entry into the public education system, however, had changed by the mid-1970s to favor black applicants for teaching and principalship posi-tions. Inspired by the challenges to the examination system that developed out of the events at Ocean Hill–Brownsville, a group of minority educators, backed by the NAACP Legal Defense Fund, filed suit in federal court in 1970 to have the New York City principals examination and eligibility list invalidated as racially dis-criminatory under the Civil Rights Act of 1964 and the Fourteenth Amendment. The next year, in *Chance v. Board of Examiners,* a United States District Court judge enjoined the use of the examination and list, and ordered that new procedures be instituted that would result in more equitable hiring practices. The requirements for principal selection were revised to permit greater community involvement and the use of on-the-job performance tests; by the mid-1970s, 15 percent of the supervisors in the city's schools were members of minority groups, five times as many as had been in the system ten years earlier.[61] And in 1976, a black teacher filed an administrative class action complaint with the Office of Civil Rights of the Department of Health, Education, and Welfare against the Board of Education, seeking to invalidate their teacher selection policies. The complaint resulted in an investigation of the Board that eventually expanded to include its student tracking procedures. Faced with an Office of Civil Rights finding that its teacher testing system was racially discriminatory, the Board agreed to a memorandum of understanding in 1977 that required it to take steps to significantly increase the percentage of minority teachers in the New York public schools. A subsequent agreement substantially reduced the use of student tracking procedures in the school system. By 1980, the percentage of minority teachers in the city's elementary and junior high schools was over 20 percent, more than double what it had been at the time of the Ocean Hill–Brownsville strikes.[62]

In addition, the New York public education system began to change its overall philosophy. By the 1990s, much of the educational program instituted in Ocean Hill–Brownsville during the UFT strikes had become the official policy of the Board of Education. Multicultural curricula, affective learning techniques, noncompetitive instructional environments, community-based educational systems — all trace their roots to the Ocean Hill–Brownsville experiment. The New York City public education market changed to accommodate and reward attributes and behaviors offered by the black community as currency for upward advancement. Yet both the increased percentage of minorities in teaching and administrative positions and the changed pedagogical atmosphere in the city school system turned out to be pyrrhic victories of sorts for both black educators and black schoolchildren in New York. Despite the absorption by the system as a whole of much of the philosophical underpinnings of the Ocean Hill–Brownsville experiment, achievement levels for black public school students, as measured both by standardized test scores and by classroom performance, declined throughout the 1970s, 1980s, and 1990s. The "new" rules of public education in New York may have produced more jobs for black educators, but none but the most naively optimistic of them would argue that the city schools are educating black children better today than they did before Ocean Hill–Brownsville.

In 1996, fed up with the corruption, lack of accountability, and academic failure associated with local control, New York City Mayor Rudolph Giuliani and

Governor George Pataki engineered legislation to replace the 1969 decentralization law. Ignoring the protests of both community leaders, as well as John Powis, who was still living and organizing in Brooklyn, the two Republicans engineered the passage of a new law that effectively recentralized the New York City public school system. It gave the Schools Chancellor the power to remove local board members, veto principal and district superintendent selections, and reject local budgets. In extreme cases, it permitted him to take over a school district and run it himself. Today, over thirty years after Ocean Hill–Brownsville, the administrative structure of the New York public school system resembles something Bernard Donovan might have recognized in 1966.

Rhody McCoy did not produce anything resembling a legacy of academic achievement in the Ocean Hill–Brownsville schools. He had refused to administer standardized reading tests, but when they were given by Wright's newly installed board in the spring of 1971, the results showed the community's students moving backwards. Reading scores for seventh- and eighth-graders at JHS 271 had decreased during McCoy's three-year tenure. The typical JHS 271 student now read three years behind the national average, and only 5.5 percent were at grade level. 271 was the second lowest–ranked junior high school in Brooklyn. All Ocean Hill–Brownsville schools, in fact, had higher average reading levels in 1967, before the community control experiment began, than in 1971.[63]

The community of Ocean Hill–Brownsville was dying as well. Every measure of social and economic distress had worsened by the early 1970s, including unemployment, crime, welfare assistance, out-of-wedlock births, and drug addiction. None of the antagonists at Ocean Hill–Brownsville—John Lindsay, Albert Shanker, McGeorge Bundy, or, for that matter, Rhody McCoy or Fred Nauman—had left the neighborhood in better condition than he found it. By the mid-1970s, black residents of Ocean Hill–Brownsville and white New Yorkers lived in different social, economic, and political universes. It was, however, culture, and specifically, the cultures of black and white New Yorks, that lay at the heart of these profound differences. During the Ocean Hill–Brownsville dispute, the African-American Teachers Association was the main vehicle through which the black community's critique of the values of white New York was articulated. The ATA's bitter cultural war with the UFT would eventually spill out into the everyday dialogue of the city as a whole. It ensured that beneath the surface of every municipal policy issue—from mayoral elections, to labor negotiations, to budget decisions—would lie racialized, value-laden arguments between black and white New Yorkers. The ATA and UFT, then, fought for more than control of the public school system before, during, and after the Ocean Hill–Brownsville crisis: they fought for control of the city's culture.

7

CULTURE WAR

By the time of the Ocean Hill–Brownsville crisis, the African-American Teachers Association, fueled by the ideas of black critics of New York's dominant civic and educational culture, had emerged as a serious philosophical rival to the UFT. Modeled on the already existing Jewish, Catholic, and Italian-American Teachers Associations, it was founded in March 1964 as the Negro Teachers Association, by UFT teachers intending to maintain dual affiliations. The ATA drew its initial impetus from black teacher dissatisfaction with the tepid reaction of the UFT leadership to the February 3, 1964, public school integration boycott led by Milton Galamison and Bayard Rustin.[1] To black educators, Albert Shanker's unwillingness to officially endorse the boycott, and his suggestion that sympathetic teachers take February 3 as a sick or personal day, epitomized the union hierarchy's equivocal response to the public school integration issue as a whole.[2] While the core of the resistance to the integration of the New York City public schools came from white parents, black teachers believed that neither the central Board of Education nor the UFT were the innocent bystanders they claimed to be. The Board had underpublicized open enrollment and free choice transfer plans designed to move black pupils into schools in white communities, and balked at expanding a pairing program, in which children in adjoining black and white neighborhoods attended the same school, beyond a few experimental areas. The UFT, for its part, strongly supported the idea of public school integration in word, but not always in deed, as its cautious response to the Galamison/Rustin boycott illustrated. Many black teachers believed the UFT leadership used the bureaucratic unwieldiness of the Board of Education as a convenient excuse for its own inaction while preserving its rhetorical pro-integration credentials.[3]

The members of the ATA were also motivated by a belief that the public education system was working for whites but failing blacks in New York City. By 1964, black educators could see the impact of the city's postindustrial economy on a black community already plagued by unemployment, crime, drug addiction, and a rising tide of out-of-wedlock births. The situation was especially bleak in the area of education. The number of pupils in the New York public schools had doubled since 1950, largely as a result of in-migration from the South.[4] Overcrowded, poorly maintained, and often staffed by teachers who had "washed out" elsewhere in the system, ghetto schools stood in marked contrast to those in white areas. Blacks constituted approximately 30 percent of the city's public school students by the mid-1960s, but earned only 2.3 percent of the academic diplomas. In Harlem, 85 percent of sixth-graders were two or more years behind grade level in reading. At Ocean Hill–Brownsville's JHS 271, 75 percent of the students were classified as not possessing the "minimum competence" to learn effectively, twice the city average.[5] Almost perversely, the more time black pupils spent in the city's public education system, the more they appeared to regress. The IQs of Harlem elementary school pupils, according to the HARYOU-sponsored study, *Youth in the Ghetto,* actually declined between the third and sixth grades.[6]

ATA members were also angered by what they perceived as the matter-of-fact acceptance by white teachers of black underachievement in the public school system. White teachers, they believed, were convinced that the culture of poverty doomed black students, and responded to this self-fulfilling prophecy with indifference and benign neglect.[7] Such teachers demanded too little of their students, on the misguided assumption they were performing acts of kindness. The ATA wanted no part of such beneficence. Its members were enraged by reports from black parents of white teachers' condescension toward their children.[8]

Black teachers joined the ATA, in large measure, because a generation of black schoolchildren seemed to be disappearing before their eyes, condemned under the tracking system to the netherworld of the "slow" classes, and, in the words of the education reformer Jonathan Kozol, "death at an early age." To ATA teachers, the mind-set of the white teacher held the key to the fate of this generation: whites had to look beyond the facts of poverty and racial difference, and believe in their students. "One can be black, reside and attend school in an enforced ghetto and still be successfully educated to the limits of his potentialities," argued one member in 1966. And even school integration, such as it existed in New York City in the mid-1960s, was not by itself enough, since the tracking system effected, in the view of another ATA member, a new form of "segregation" in integrated schools.[9] The ATA thus represented an attempt by black teachers to head off a developing educational catastrophe among black pupils in the New York City public schools.

Black teachers also had a pragmatic reason for joining the ATA. At mid-decade, despite the fact that the city's public school system was approximately 30 percent black and less than 50 percent white, blacks constituted only 8 percent of the teaching staff and 2.8 percent of the supervisors.[10] The contrast with most other major American cities, in which the proportion of black teachers averaged approximately 30 percent, was not lost on ATA members.[11] The ATA viewed these statistics as prima facie proof that the Board of Examiners recruitment system, and the city's public education market generally, discriminated against nonwhites.

There were, to be sure, extenuating circumstances. New York's public schools had undergone an extremely rapid shift in racial balance over the previous decade; as recently as 1957, whites had represented 68 percent of the student population, and blacks only 18 percent.[12] Some degree of lag in the pace of adjustment to this abrupt change was to be expected. And, of course, the promotional examinations administered by the Board of Examiners were race-neutral on their face. Nonetheless, ATA members viewed the system as exclusionary in effect. Particularly galling was the fact that much larger percentages of "acting" than "permanently licensed" supervisors in the public schools were black.[13] The first category was composed of those who had not passed the requisite promotional examination for a particular post, but who were temporarily serving until a representative from the latter category was available. Thus, blacks who were actually performing in supervisory positions throughout the city were routinely pushed aside by examination-qualified, and invariably white, applicants. Black teachers believed that New York's public education market was not the level playing field it purported to be. It was not, of course, discriminatory on an individual basis: no black applicant was ever rejected simply because he was black. But the preponderance of whites—and, specifically, Jews—in the public schools represented, for many ATA members, a more subtle, institutionally based form of racism.

There were, again, reasons for the large number of Jews in the city educational system. Excluded from many areas of the private sector, and attracted by the objective nature of the examinations and the job security offered by civil service employment, Jews had gravitated toward the New York City public schools since the 1930s. As was customary under such circumstances, and like other ethnic groups in other city agencies (notably the Irish in the Police Department and Italians in sanitation), Jews had established an informal network that operated to draw co-religionists into the system, providing information on vacancies, job contacts, and test preparation assistance, among other advantages.[14] By the 1960s, in New York, it was almost an instinctive reaction for a Jewish college graduate, especially a graduate of the city colleges, to consider teaching in the city's schools as a career option. Black teachers were reminded almost on a daily basis that this network did not exist in their communities. The ATA, in part, represented an attempt to replicate the institutional arrangements that had served Jews so well in the public education market over the past thirty years. The organization was at once an indictment of the racism of institutions—in its focus on numbers and outcomes— and an effort to achieve group power by constructing similar institutions. As such, the ATA both challenged and sought to imitate the Jewish community in New York City.

The ATA at mid-decade, then, was a combination of trade association and advocacy group. It was critical of white teachers and the Board of Examiners promotional system, to be sure, but its demands were still couched in the traditional language of interest group politics. It sought, essentially, more jobs for black teachers and administrators, and more sympathetic treatment of black schoolchildren. It still supported school integration. Its members still belonged to the UFT. It offered no critique of or challenge to the prevailing culture of the educational market or the city at large. It was, indeed, still the "Negro Teachers Association."[15] All this would change in 1966 and 1967, as two new leaders, Leslie Campbell and Albert Vann, introduced an ideological focus, and transformed the ATA into an organization that would challenge the UFT, the city's public education market, and white New York generally, on first principles.

Together, these two leaders epitomized both the demographics and the politics of Brooklyn's black community. Campbell, of West Indian descent, and the son of a local Communist party official, had grown up in New York as a "red diaper baby" during the 1950s. After graduating from Long Island University in 1964, he began his teaching career in the Social Studies Department at Junior High School 35 in the Bedford-Stuyvesant section of Brooklyn. As a young teacher in the Brooklyn public schools, Campbell sought to combine Marxism-Leninism with black nationalism.[16] He infused his lessons with material on black history and the class struggle, becoming a political mentor to—or, in the opinion of his superiors, an indoctrinator of—his students.[17] In February 1968, after he defied the orders of Schools Superintendent Bernard Donovan and took one of his classes to a memorial service for Malcolm X in Harlem, he was transferred to Ocean Hill–

Brownsville's JHS 271—a move Donovan inexplicably viewed as punishment and Campbell saw as providential.

In keeping with his Marxist-Leninist orientation, Campbell portrayed himself as a vanguard leader of the black masses. He also viewed the city's lower-class black community as the embodiment of authentic racial identity. His contempt for the black middle class—including his fellow teachers, whom he viewed as estranged from their roots—was palpable and constant. Black teachers, he wrote in 1966, were "too secure and comfortable" and "obsessed with the amassing of wealth and aesthetic comfort." They held back "the struggle of the black masses. What the black masses demand cannot be granted because the Negro professional refuses to associate himself with the man on the street."[18] "The black teacher," he argued the next year, "must begin to identify with and speak the language of the black community. He cannot come to the community like a 'stranger bearing gifts.'"[19] Campbell would spend the rest of the decade transforming the ATA, a group composed of middle-income black professionals, into an aggressive defender of the city's lower-class black population and its culture.

Vann, the ATA's president, had come to Brooklyn from South Carolina as a youngster in the 1950s, during the great postwar migration. Vann was not a Marxist like Campbell, and his cultural nationalism proceeded along more traditional lines. He was a "race man," influenced by the philosophy of Marcus Garvey. Vann helped organize campaigns for increased black hiring levels at Brooklyn's Sealtest Dairies and Downstate Medical Center during the early and mid-1960s, as he sought to rise through the ranks in the local public schools. By 1967, he was also in the Ocean Hill–Brownsville district, where he was a frustrated acting assistant principal at JHS 271.[20] Vann applied the lessons of his earlier struggles against employment discrimination to his own career, concluding that the city's school system, notwithstanding its pretensions to standards of individual merit, was a racist institution. Under his presidency, the ATA spoke out forcefully against the impact of the "merit system" on black teachers as a group. Results, not intentions, were what mattered to Vann. Numbers, he believed, did not lie, and the low number of black teachers and administrators in the New York public school system proved it discriminatory.

Campbell and Vann, then, had by 1966 played a major role in crystallizing the most important elements of what would become the ATA's public posture: a defense of the black lower class; a rejection of the culture of the middle class, both black and white; an adherence to group identity; and an embrace of the idea of institutional racism. Over the next two years, the ATA would engage in two emotional battles with the UFT—one involving the hiring of a black principal at

7. African-American Teachers Association President Albert Vann. Ed Giorandino, *New York Daily News.*

Harlem's Intermediate School 201, the other over the behavior of black school-children—and begin to articulate an alternative vision of the culture of New York's public education market. It would seek to define a set of "black" values that could be used as a form of alternative currency in that market and in the city at large, and initiate a struggle with the UFT over these values that would continue through the events of the Ocean Hill–Brownsville crisis and the succeeding decades.

The first of these battles took place in September 1966 over whether the newly-opened IS 201 in Harlem would have a black or white principal. Donovan's choice of Stanley Lisser, a white, as the school's first principal outraged the ATA.[21] Its members were prominent among the demonstrators protesting the Lisser appointment at the beginning of the 1966–67 academic year.[22] Lisser soon bowed to this pressure and tearfully asked the Board of Education to transfer him to another school.

Superintendent Donovan, a careful man with the lifelong bureaucrat's instinct for self-preservation and deal-cutting, sought to finesse the question of the racial identity of the next principal. He promised the anti-Lisser protesters that, while he could not guarantee explicitly that the principal of IS 201 would be black, he would grant community representatives veto power over the selection as long as the objections were "sound and serious."[23] Now it was the equally outraged UFT's turn to protest. It denounced the "sound and serious" veto as an affront to its most cherished principle: color-blind, individual merit. "'Sound and serious' objections," Albert Shanker argued, "could never be made on the basis of race, color, sex, creed, national origin, or mere unpopularity."[24]

The union leadership's demand for the reinstatement of Lisser was joined by the teachers at IS 201. Virtually the entire staff, blacks as well as whites, boycotted the school and picketed the headquarters of the Board of Education on Lisser's behalf, carrying signs that read "All Of Us Or None Of Us," and "Should Principals Be Ousted Because They Are Not Black?" "The only reason I volunteered for this school was because I wanted to serve with Dr. Lisser," one black teacher told a reporter. Back inside IS 201, a black acting assistant principal refused Donovan's offer to succeed Lisser, explaining that she objected to being selected on the basis of "color, not competence."[25]

This protest carried the day, and Lisser was returned as principal of IS 201.[26] The UFT leadership celebrated the triumph of what it considered bedrock principles. "The very integrity of the school system was at stake," wrote Shanker, "for if we had not prevailed, we would enter an era where only a Jewish principal could be appointed in schools located in a predominantly Jewish neighborhood, Italians in Italian neighborhoods, Irish in Irish. It was because the integrity of our schools was at stake that I demanded Dr. Donovan refuse to accept Dr. Lisser's request for transfer." The union singled out the black teachers at 201, who had supported Lisser, and the black assistant principal who had turned down a chance to succeed him, for special praise.[27]

The ATA, however, saw things differently. Campbell ridiculed the "color-blind" black teachers and administrators who had supported Lisser, and viewed the controversy as another example of the black middle class betraying the black poor. During the dispute, he wrote, "the establishment turned to its secret weapon, the Negro professional. The Negro teachers at 201 helped transform the victory into defeat. How can we dismiss the white principal when the Negro teachers refuse to allow his dismissal? How can we replace the white supervisor when Negro candidates readily admit they are not qualified? These are the echoed words of the white press and the Board of Education." The IS 201 incident, he argued, was one of many "in which the Establishment used the schism between the black masses and the Negro professional to wipe out significant gains. The new weapon will be used frequently." "How is it possible," he asked in frustration, "to wed black masses and black professionals into a oneness?"[28]

Vann also blamed the UFT and the white educational establishment for denying blacks at IS 201 and elsewhere "the supervisory positions they so justly deserve." At the same time, he complained that black teachers, and black professionals in general, "have had to fit a certain pattern," and that, due to the constraints of white society, "many of us find it difficult to be ourselves."[29] This ambivalence—anger at restricted opportunities within a white-dominated educational market, coupled with criticism of the legitimacy of the values undergirding that market—would characterize the ATA's relationship with the UFT in the years to come.

The second, and even more serious, battle between the ATA and UFT centered on the latter's attempt to address the issue of black pupil misbehavior in the public schools, and the related question of the validity of black lower-class culture in general. By 1967, school violence had become a hot-button issue among the UFT rank and file. In 1963, sixty teachers had been assaulted by students in the city's public schools. By 1966, this number had grown to 213, and would rise even higher in 1967.[30] Reports of acts of student vandalism, including window breakage, fires, and unlawful entry, also shot upward in 1966.[31] Early in 1967, at JHS 98 in the Bronx, seventy-nine white teachers staged a wildcat strike—which the black teachers at the school refused to join—over the issue of student behavior, returning only when school administrators promised them the right to unilaterally remove misbehaving pupils from their classrooms after a certain number of serious incidents.[32] A group of white teachers also walked out at PS 284 in Brooklyn over the same issue.[33]

In February 1967, under strong pressure from the union rank and file, the UFT

Executive Board passed a resolution demanding that a "disruptive child" clause, under which a teacher could expel a "seriously misbehaving" student from his class and send him to a "special service" school, be included in the collective bargaining agreement which was to be negotiated with the Board of Education for the following September. This demand to "place in the hands of the classroom teacher a major share of power of decision regarding action to be taken in the case of a disruptive child," was interpreted by Board of Education negotiators as a union attempt to assert managerial control over the operation of the school system, and thus outside the scope of collective bargaining.[34]

The reaction of black teachers, and of the ATA in particular, to the proposed disruptive child clause was sharp and emotional. To them, the clause represented more than an attempt to ensure order in the classroom: it was a white assault on the culture of poor black children and the black lower-class community. In an acid exchange with Shanker, Vann charged that the clause would "only provide teachers with police powers rather than solve any of the problems." The "so-called 'disruptive child,'" he wrote, was a function of "miseducation and ineffectiveness of education for black youth, coupled with the frustrations of being black in white America." "Improvements of education within the black community," he told Shanker, ". . . would eliminate the so-called 'disruptive child.'"[35] When Shanker sought to convince Vann that the disruptive child clause would allow "improved education for the overwhelming majority of our students whose classrooms are disturbed by students who need special treatment," Vann accused Shanker of being "obviously concerned with material matters and . . . unconcerned with matters of moral and social justice."[36]

During the spring of 1967, the ATA offered its own proposal for addressing the issue of the "disruptive child"—a term the organization invariably placed in quotation marks. It advised teachers to practice "complete openness," employ "judicious praise," "accept the student's challenge to authority," and take "an objective view of a child's obscenities." Administratively, its plan required a misbehaving child to be evaluated by a school supervisor who was "indigenous" to the community and approved by the child's parent. The supervisor would use a "guideline-oriented approach" with the student, with numerous hearings, and a special guidance class within the school itself as a last resort. There were to be no expulsions, and no "dumping" into special service schools. "The ATA submits," the proposal concluded, "that 90 percent of students will respond to effective classroom management administered by dedicated teachers able to place in perspective . . . social, emotional and pedagogical problems."[37]

The UFT rejected the ATA plan out of hand. White UFT rank-and-filers ridiculed its premises. "Young jackanapes and emotionally unstrung hoodlums," wrote one, "will tax the patience of the most saintly and ingenious teacher. An energetic youngster [from] a family where authority is respected has no problem conforming with acceptable behavior patterns. If the Afro-American teachers find it discriminatory to remove problem children from the room, their objectivity is greatly suspect." The ATA, she argued, "oversimplified" when it assumed "that all a good teacher has to do is put a gentle hand on the shoulder of the obstreperous child and lead him to his seat. Anyone who has tried this procedure on such a child has rued the day."[38]

Neither the UFT, the ATA, nor the Board of Education retreated from their respective positions during the summer of 1967. In September, the union struck the city's schools over the disruptive child clause, as well as over funding for its More Effective Schools program and salary issues.[39] ATA members refused to join the strike, and worked to keep their schools open; all schools in the Ocean Hill–Brownsville district, thanks in large part to the efforts of Vann, operated throughout the strike. The UFT, aware of the racial volatility of the disruptive child issue, sought to portray the strike in race-neutral terms. A union flyer, for example, did not mention the disruptive child clause specifically, but instead referred euphemistically to "special facilities" for such children.[40]

Longtime UFT ally Martin Luther King Jr. sent Shanker a telegram voicing his concern over the handling of the disruptive child issue. "To avoid misunderstanding and confusion," he wrote, "I urge you to pay special attention to clarifying the issue of the disruptive child. The utmost care is necessary to avoid oversimplified illusory solutions."[41] Shanker's deliberately evasive reply to King was an indication of the union president's determination to downplay the racial implications of the disruptive child contract demand: "We share your concern that proper facilities be provided for those children who cannot now be educated in regular classes and whose disruptive behavior makes it impossible for others as well."[42] Despite Shanker's indirections, however, there was no way to finesse the racial issue. To the black community in New York, the disruptive child clause was about their children, and their culture. A Harlem parent at IS 201, which also remained open during the strike, captured the prevailing sentiment: "We don't have disruptive children. We do have a lot of disruptive teachers, however."[43]

After a two-week strike, a combination of resistance in the black community and Board of Education insistence on its "right to manage" the school system — not to mention a generous wage offer — had worn the UFT down on the disruptive child issue. The union agreed to a compromise whereby a teacher, after lodging formal complaints with his principal and district superintendent, could request an outside committee, on which UFT representatives would be in a minority, to discipline a misbehaving pupil. Since in practice matters rarely would proceed beyond the level of the principal, the UFT had lost this round. But this was little consolation to the embittered ATA members, most of whom left the UFT over the issue.[44] It would continue to divide the two organizations—now independent of each other—in the future, as increasingly angry rhetoric served to illustrate the magnitude of the perceptual gap between them.

By early 1968, Vann would go so far as to argue that an assault by black intruders on two white principals and a teacher at JHS 117 in Brooklyn was merely a reaction to "a kick in the community's rear [by] the UFT," and the realization "that [blacks] have no control over forces that directly and adversely affect their lives and the lives of their children." "The initial precipitating act," he wrote, "is quite inconsequential as we view the total atmosphere in our schools. It is a wonder that black and Puerto Rican people have kept their emotions restrained for so long. . . . One day a principal and two teachers [sic] get punched around a bit. Daily, hundreds of children are psychologically and academically whipped. Daily, our community dies a little."[45]

Support for Vann's position came from the ATA's allies among grassroots black community organizations and New Left–influenced intellectuals and educators. Brooklyn CORE defended the so-called "disruptive child" as a "high-spirited non-conformist" with a "highly creative imagination," who was "not willing to accept mediocre education." Cursing and even physical confrontations, CORE argued, "are commonplace occurrences in ghetto communities. . . expected and understood," albeit "shocking to most teachers whose frame of reference is totally alien to those in neighborhoods in which they work."[46] Joseph Laspro of the New Coalition, a pro–community control dissident group within the UFT, echoed Vann's sentiments, arguing that "teachers overlook the open and subtle forms of violence perpetrated on minority groups in education. The violence done to [minorities] by failing to provide them with the fundamental skills . . . far outweighs the individual acts of students whose occasional outbursts reflect the horrible frustrations they have been made to suffer every day of their lives." In the future, he predicted, "the great majority of our student population will become so-called 'disruptive children.' Perhaps then, a more appropriate epithet for these youth will be 'revolutionaries.'"[47]

In contrast, an angry UFT leadership complained, in an advertisement placed in the New York Amsterdam News, that "teachers are beaten in classrooms by self-styled prophets of educational reform." It vowed that it "would not permit our teachers to be used as scapegoats for the failures of a system for which we are not responsible."[48] White rank-and-file teachers also expressed their frustration. The minutes of a March 1968 meeting between Ralph Rogers, the black principal of PS 144 in the Ocean Hill–Brownsville district, and three white UFT teachers, provide an illustration of the philosophical and perceptual gap between black and white educators on the subject of the disruptive child:

> MISS FLISS [TEACHER]: The whole atmosphere is very unschool-like. My children are afraid to go out of their rooms because they will be beaten up.
>
> MISS GOLDSTEIN [TEACHER]: There is a tendency for the older disruptive children to be the troublemakers.
>
> MR. ROGERS [PRINCIPAL]: This is a community-controlled school. The policy is no suspension. We do not want children out in the streets.
>
> GOLDSTEIN: Teachers are exhausted with discipline problems. Children see others striking teachers . . . and nothing is done. . . .
>
> FLISS: A child came into my room, shouted and hit children. When I tried to take him by his arm he practically tore my arm off. The child is still in the school. He later slammed another child with a window pole. This is not an isolated case. It happens every day. . . .
>
> MR. RUBINSTEIN [TEACHER]: . . . . You cannot teach when a child comes over to a teacher and uses foul language continually. Something has to be done. . . .
>
> ROGERS: You have to devise your own method of dealing with discipline. Most of the time it is the teacher and not the child. . . ."[49]

The issue of the disruptive child, then, had created serious fault lines between the UFT and ATA, and between black and white educators in New York City, by early 1968. Most white teachers viewed the disruptive child phenomenon as a result of the culture of poverty's impact on young black lives. To the ATA, however, it was merely an excuse for an attack on the culture and values of poor blacks in the city. The disruptive child issue catalyzed a debate between the UFT and ATA over related questions which were already points of contention between black and white intellectuals and activists in New York, and which, by the late 1960s, had filtered into the dialogue of the city as a whole. These broader questions—relating to the legitimacy of lower-class black culture, and the applicability of "middle-class" values to the city's black population—pitted the ATA against the UFT in a cultural war characterized by clashing assumptions, perceptions, and proposed solutions. It would spill out beyond the specific events of the Ocean Hill–Brownsville crisis and outlive them, dividing black and white teachers, and to a large extent, black and white New Yorkers, for years to come.

Even as its argument with the UFT over the disruptive child was developing, the ATA was moving to place the values of both the black lower class and the white middle class in New York at the center of its critique of the culture of the school system and the city. Vann attempted to align his organization with the black poor, seeking to overcome what he considered the stigma of the group's middle-class economic status. "In spite of our material gains and educational achievements and adopted attitudes," he wrote in November 1966, "[poor black children] really are our brothers and sisters." The following month he asked his colleagues: "Are we suffering from a middle-class syndrome, fear, self-hate or plain apathy? We can reach no higher esteem, nor be any better, than our downtrodden brother unless we help him, and by doing so, help ourselves."[50]

ATA members rarely missed an opportunity to articulate their vision of what an "authentic" black culture was—and was not. They appropriated what they perceived to be the values and attributes of the lower-class black community—mutualism, cooperation, and egalitarianism—and sought to use them as a new form of currency in the city's public education market. ATA members counterposed these "authentic" black values to those they associated with whites. To them, "white" values—individualism, competition, materialism, elitism—constituted those of the "anti-community," a dog-eat-dog world with overtones of Social Darwinism and Calvinism. ATA members believed that the UFT epitomized this cold, acquisitive white culture. During the Ocean Hill–Brownsville dispute and beyond, the ATA would move from a defense of the culture of the black community, as in the disruptive child controversy, to an attack on the values of the middle class in the educational system and city, values which the organization sought to link exclusively to whites. In this endeavor, it received assistance from an ironic source — white teachers themselves, who, with rare exceptions, seemed as willing as ATA members to define middle-class values as "white."

In December 1967, ATA member John Hatchett, a probationary teacher at a Harlem elementary school, published an article in the organization's newsletter, the *African-American Teachers Forum*, entitled "The Phenomenon of the Anti-Black Jews and the Black Anglo-Saxon: A Study in Educational Perfidy." In it, Hatchett argued that Jewish schoolteachers had "educationally castrated" black pupils and had engaged in "horrendous abuse of the [black] family, associates and culture." Overshadowed in the furor over the issue of black anti-Semitism that resulted from the article, however, was Hatchett's attack on blacks in the educational system who, in his view, had adopted "white" attributes. He saw these "power-starved imitators" of Jews as "black Anglo-Saxons," who wished to be white.[51]

Hatchett believed that "black Anglo-Saxons" became "white" by becoming middle-class. The black teachers he criticized in the article were those who accepted the premises of the Board of Examiners system, who studied for tests and advanced degrees, who were upwardly mobile, and whose behavior appeared indistinguishable from that of the white middle-class UFT teachers he scorned. When Hatchett criticized the "cowardly black Anglo-Saxon, who has become so

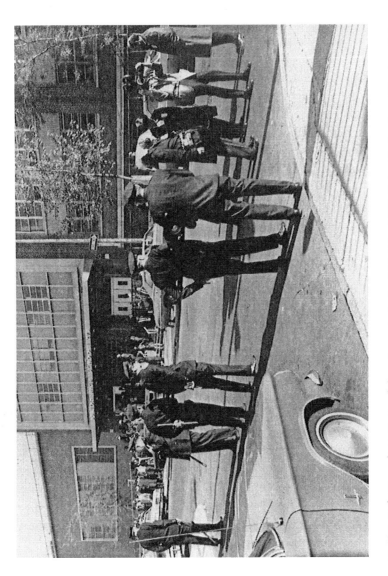

18. New York City policemen guard the entrance to Junior High School 271. United Federation of Teachers Collection, UFT Photo Collection, Robert F. Wagner Labor Archives, New York University.

assimilated that he believes only middle-class people pay taxes," he was arguing, in effect, that they were "assimilated," or "white," because they were behaving like, or "imitating," middle-class whites.[52] To Hatchett, middle-class values could never inform any conception of "authentic" black culture because of their association with whites, and because they were antithetical to those of the black lower class as he envisioned them. This direct linkage of "middle-class" behavior to "whiteness" would become a central theme in the ATA's philosophical challenge to the UFT in the ensuing years.

By late 1967, the ATA, having changed its name from the Negro Teachers Association earlier in the year at Vann's behest, claimed approximately two thousand members, representing almost half the total number of black teachers in the city's public school system. It was especially strong in the Ocean Hill–Brownsville district.[53] In February 1968, Campbell joined Vann at the district's flagship school, JHS 271. There, the two brushed aside the nominal but ineffectual principal to become its most influential figures—Vann as an administrator from the assistant principal's office, and Campbell as a pedagogical leader and cultural gatekeeper from his position in the Social Studies department.

The Ocean Hill–Brownsville local board's termination letters to Fred Nauman and his colleagues in May 1968 served a dual purpose for Vann and Campbell. The dismissals would, they hoped, establish the local board's right to govern the Ocean Hill–Brownsville district independent of the UFT and the central Board of Education. The ATA leaders also expected them to consolidate the organization's influence in the Ocean Hill–Brownsville schools, since the rest of the union teachers in the district were likely to walk out in protest of the local board's action; this was, in fact, what occurred two weeks later. Except for brief intervals, UFT teachers would not return to Ocean Hill–Brownsville until November, some six months later, at the conclusion of the last of the citywide teachers' strikes.[54]

The walkout gave District Administrator McCoy, the local school board, and the ATA the opportunity to choose a group of replacement teachers from outside the Board of Examiners system, to staff the Ocean Hill–Brownsville schools. They recruited an inexperienced, politically radical, and racially mixed group from Ivy League college campuses, Ph.D. programs, and law schools. Eager to participate in what appeared to be an innovative experiment in community-controlled educational democracy, the replacement teachers were willing to defer to Vann, Campbell, and other ATA members in the Ocean Hill–Brownsville schools—on philosophical grounds as well as practical ones, since the latter were among the small number of experienced teachers remaining after the UFT walkout. With a sympathetic teaching staff, support from the local administration, and no interference from a striking UFT membership, the ATA was positioned to impose its will on the Ocean Hill–Brownsville schools.

The Ocean Hill–Brownsville schools during this period of ATA dominance featured a new educational approach that focused on the student as an individual. The ATA's stress on what educational theorists termed the "affective" component of learning—developing feelings of self-worth, of control over one's surroundings, and of personal identity and growth—was a departure from the prevailing focus in the city's public schools on "cognitive" pedagogy, which stressed rational thought, substantive knowledge, and adjustment to one's surroundings.

This concern with the pupil as an "affective" being derived from two other aspects of the philosophy of the ATA and its allies. The first was opportunity theory, the germinal idea behind the War on Poverty's community action program, and the Ocean Hill–Brownsville experiment itself. Opportunity theory provided an alternative for critics of the UFT-endorsed culture of poverty and cultural deprivation ideas. Instead of viewing poor students as needing to overcome their lower-class environments, opportunity theory argued that their culture was essentially sound as it was: the poor simply required a sense of control and empowerment. As an educational theorist sympathetic to the ATA argued, "the values of the community must become those of the school . . . [and] values in education incompatible with the child's life conditions [must be] changed to become natural extensions of those values and beliefs which already exist in the community. Those goals which are deemed worth striving for—equality, freedom, etc.,—can be reflected in the operations of the school."[55]

The ATA and its supporters combined this idea with one of the central tenets of the Progressive education movement as popularized by John Dewey—that children learned from their own surroundings. They argued that if teachers showed respect for the culture of lower-class black students, made instruction relevant to their lives outside the classroom, and accepted them as they were, they would respond as they had not for the UFT teachers. In the context of the Ocean Hill–Brownsville district in the spring and fall of 1968, "affective" education meant giving students a clear sense of racial identity. Vann's goal, as he once put it to an interviewer, was to create "big black men, not little white men."[56] The ATA, accordingly, launched a campaign against attributes and values it associated with white teachers and the UFT. These included examination-based competition and materialism, as well as the cultural idea of the middle class in general, which ATA members viewed as embodying a rigid, stifling belief system that, like the examination structure itself, rewarded blind obedience and conformity.

Two of the major educational programs instituted in the Ocean Hill–Brownsville schools, Project Learn and the Bereiter-Engelmann reading program, were notable for their emphasis on individual self-actualization and on cooperative instruction. Project Learn featured programmed learning materials in a variety of academic subjects, through which pupils proceeded at their own pace. Academic tracking, grade levels past the first grade, and even marks themselves were eliminated, and, in a precursor of "elective" systems, students were encouraged to "set their own goals" and to study subjects that interested them.[57] The Bereiter-Engelmann program provided individualized reading instruction in a self-consciously egalitarian setting, one in which, in the words of one of its administrators, "the onus of school failure is taken from the child and placed on the school." It operated on the assumption "that every child can achieve, if he receives adequate instruction," and that "a child who fails is a child who has received inadequate instruction." Children who showed progress in this ungraded program were rewarded with ritualized and repeated chants of "Are you smart!"[58]

The ATA and replacement teachers sought to create a flexible, encouraging, and non-hierarchical atmosphere in the Ocean Hill–Brownsville schools. "If they think you like them, they respond a lot better," said one replacement teacher, describing his philosophy of instruction.[59] Students were encouraged to help teachers build lessons around their everyday life experiences, so that, in the words of an Ocean Hill–Brownsville student, "the system will fit our community, not some community in Queens."[60] "We approach the children with an expectation of success which we communicate to them and to which they are responding," wrote a group of replacement teachers in a published newspaper advertisement, referring with pride to their "relationships of mutual trust and respect" with the students. Another attributed his class's progress almost entirely to such positive expectations: "I decided mine was going to be the brightest class and that's just what happened."[61]

Sympathetic visitors to the district from New York's intellectual and literary communities, including I. F. Stone, Alfred Kazin, and Dwight Macdonald, praised the cooperative, positive relations with students that the replacement teachers had produced, as contrasted with the more heavy-handed tactics of the UFT teachers. "The flame [of learning] burns hotter than ever" in Ocean Hill, wrote Kazin, comparing the schools favorably with those he had attended as a child growing up in the same neighborhood decades before:[62] Macdonald praised the "hum of cooperative effort" in the Ocean Hill classrooms. They and other observers reported reduced incidents of vandalism and student misbehavior.[63] Rhody McCoy summarized the operative philosophy of the Ocean Hill–Brownsville schools during this time: "What is [teacher] 'competence'? It isn't the grasp of your subject or your ability to make an effective lesson plan. The absolutely rock-bottom minimal aspect of competence today for teaching in the ghetto schools is respect for the kid. . . . If you go into your classroom with a string of Ph.D.'s and all sorts of other 'qualifications' and still you're convinced that this kid is doomed by nature or by something else to lead a shrunken and curtailed life, then you're basically incompetent to teach that child."[64]

The ATA and replacement teachers believed that the most important element of "affective" pedagogy in the Ocean Hill–Brownsville schools during the months of the UFT walkout involved defining a clear sense of black identity for their students. Given the cultural climate in the city's schools at the time, it was hardly surprising that this effort would be driven by what was "not white," and, specifically, by attempts to avoid or denigrate values and practices which the ATA and its supporters defined as "white."

They were, for example, determined that "white standards" not be used to judge the achievements of black students. When a white replacement teacher at JHS 271 sought to motivate his English class by telling them to think of themselves as being in competition with middle-class white schools, Vann called him into his office and dressed him down. He told the teacher that his use of whites as a point of comparison was a manifestation of racial prejudice. The teacher was reprimanded on another occasion for including the works of William Shakespeare in his curriculum.[65]

The Ocean Hill–Brownsville district's refusal to administer standardized reading and mathematics tests between 1967 and 1970 was also a challenge to what ATA and replacement teachers viewed as a mindlessly overcompetitive, white-dominated educational system designed to measure only the "cognitive" abilities it associated with whites. Standardized achievement tests might well be appropriate for "middle-class children," a replacement teacher charged, but were useless in evaluating black lower-class students. Such tests, he wrote, "fail to measure the extent to which a child has been educated; they simply test rote memorization [and] stifling of initiative. . . . Unleashed creativity or a critical outlook would probably lower a child's scores on these examinations rather than raise them."[66] McCoy, describing his philosophy of education in Ocean Hill–Brownsville, said: "The schools were not there to teach the skills, i.e., reading, writing, and arithmetic, but to present or prepare a learning environment where youngsters would be educated. Too often, we got caught up in saying, 'Our kids can't read and write, and they don't do well on standardized tests,' and we lost sight of the fact that we've got millions of our kids who *can* read and write, and who can pass standardized tests, who are basically not educated in terms of what's going on in the real world."[67]

The ATA also took aim at the competitive ethos of the Board of Examiners system, which it also linked directly to whites. One member, explaining the paucity of black personnel in the city's educational system, argued that "if a [black] wants to succeed, he has to 'become white,' and the degree to which he becomes successful is directly related to the degree to which he becomes white—mentally."[68] Another argued that white society had attempted to force its competitive ethos down the throats of the black community. "The point of pivot," he wrote, "is competition. Competition for what America is calling the basic economic and cultural goods. The question to be asked is can anyone be expected to love, to have compassion, or even to have a mind of one's own? America has propagated not the myth of success, but the obsession with failure." An ATA supporter distinguished between a "destructive," "white" style of capitalism, characterized by "cutthroat competition and heartless dealings," and a "black" style, in which "black businessmen help each other."[69]

The ATA also attacked what it viewed as the rampant materialism of the white UFT teachers. The white teachers' "greatest joy," charged a black teacher at JHS 271, "is the security of the job."[70] Another described them as "petty civil servants" who "like their jobs because of the nice salaries, health plans, and medical coverage."[71] John Hatchett said the UFT was the epitome of "white decadence."[72] An ATA supporter accused whites of seeking to subvert blacks "by the traps of individualism, materialism and integration."[73] Implicit in this rhetoric was the idea that black educational and social structures would not repeat the mistakes of the "joyless, grasping white man."[74] Thus, when an ATA teacher complained that "I was educated to be what I could not possibly be—a white person," he was indicting an educational system that, in his organization's view, condoned the worst excesses of the white middle class.[75] Striking white UFT teachers, however, answered back, angrily defending as virtues what the ATA and its allies condemned as vices.

White UFT teachers went to great lengths during the Ocean Hill–Brownsville controversy to justify the same competitive and individualist values that black teachers attacked. They sought to link them to a well-established American culture of opportunity and advancement. A white teacher accused critics of the Board of Examiners of fomenting "an irresponsible revolution to uproot the whole structure of a competitive merit system, which is embedded in our democratic tradition and state constitution."[76] Another wrote that black underrepresentation in teaching and administrative positions was not the fault of whites, but a result of "the failure of black people to compete successfully in the open marketplace of the merit test system." "The end of the merit system," he continued, "will enable those who can't make it on ability to reach the top on the basis of their skin color."[77] Still another noted that the costs for the Ocean Hill–Brownsville community control experiment "will be borne principally by the tax dollars collected from those who live and work elsewhere," referring to middle-class whites, and charged that the leaders of the Ocean Hill–Brownsville district did not understand that the purpose of the school system was to instill in the student "a desire to learn, and a desire to behave, and a desire to advance by merit."[78] "50,000 of us," wrote a Brooklyn teacher, "are striking to preserve the sanctity of the Civil Service System, and particularly, the merit system . . ."[79] "The curriculum at Ocean Hill," charged a striker in the *United Teacher*, "is not designed to produce young American citizens well prepared to enter the job market—just well prepared to hate whitey."[80]

White teachers also openly flaunted their materialistic lifestyles. No reader of the *United Teacher* during this period could fail to notice the advertisements for vacation trips, summer camps, furniture, appliances, and other creature comforts—conspicuous testaments to the material success of UFT members.[81] Most white UFTers, moreover, shrugged off criticism that their "attitudes [were] as middle class as [their] possessions."[82] Writing in the *Village Voice* during the strike, a white teacher articulated the rationale behind this impulse, justifying it as, like the related ethos of competition, a typically "American" characteristic:

> We hear the charge that teachers today are acting like "plumbers," that they are not "dedicated." What is interesting to me about these charges is not that they are false (there is much truth in them), but that if teachers act like this it should really be surprising to anybody. The public school teachers in this city are in the main a "lower-middle-class" group of people; that is, they reflect the values, thinking, goals and life-style of a group of people whose parents were working-class. They are people who did not have "things" and now want "things," the same things that everybody in our consumer culture wants—and if they have to act like members of an electricians union to get them, they will.

The age of the self-abnegating teacher, who was rewarded "not in the money he was paid but in the shining eyes of a child mastering his numbers" was over, he argued, and critics of the UFT in the black community would simply have to get used to it.[83]

The union leadership, which had won unprecedented wage increases for its members during the 1960s, agreed. Shanker scoffed at those who criticized teachers for acting in their own interests. "The Board of Education does, the teachers do, and so does Lindsay," he retorted.[84] Shanker argued that the role of education was not primarily to cultivate the student as an "affective" being, but to teach him how "to *make it* within our society."[85] And David Selden, the president of the UFT's parent, the American Federation of Teachers, and a supporter of the strike, responded to critics in the black community who complained that "schools teach white, middle-class values and skills," by defending "those middle-class skills and values—reading, mathematics, respect for work and initiative—which serve as the basis for upward social mobility." "Slum life," he maintained, "no matter how romanticized in current literature, has a deadly intellectual undertow which only the exceptionally able or lucky can survive."[86]

It was, indeed, the linked ideas of the culture of poverty and the ethos of the middle class that informed the white teachers' critique of the Ocean Hill–Brownsville educational experiment, and of the culture of the lower-class black community in New York. By the time of the Ocean Hill crisis, many white teachers were using the culture of poverty to "explain" black behavior, and appeared to be as convinced as the ATA that a "middle-class" culture was by definition a "white" one. The problem with education at Ocean Hill–Brownsville, and in the black community generally, a UFT member wrote, was "a situation where a shift of population results in a broken-down student potential," that was "beyond the control of the Board of Education" and the classroom teacher. "The deterioration of the neighborhood," he argued, "was accompanied by the deterioration of the schools not only scholastically but physically."[87]

Others cited the black family, and not the school, as the key determinant of a black student's achievement level: "If pupils have 'environmental handicaps,' no school can do much to make them learn at a faster rate than they are learning anywhere else."[88] The primary goal of the schools in Ocean Hill–Brownsville and other black neighborhoods, wrote a white teacher pointedly, should be to promote "education for family living."[89] Other teachers were even more blunt. "If only these people took an interest in their children," lamented one. "If only they had a male symbol."[90] And a white teacher at JHS 271, commenting on community control at Ocean Hill–Brownsville, said: "We believe that the people of this community are not educated enough to run the schools. They must become middle-class before they can participate."[91]

It would fall to Shanker to make the most explicit connection between middle-class values and those of the Ocean Hill–Brownsville educational experiment. In an interview immediately after the conclusion of the strike, he described education in the Ocean Hill schools as a "cruel hoax . . . where they take over a school in the name of rectifying this horrible tragedy and say: 'We're going to run a good school and teach your children a lot of good things. But forget about the middle-class values of reading, writing and arithmetic. Don't evaluate us by that standard.' The hoax is perpetrated by these community control people when they experience failure in getting kids to achieve. Then they say forget middle-class virtues and they try to convince parents that reading and writing don't count."[92]

By the time the Ocean Hill–Brownsville crisis ended, then, blacks and whites had developed clashing approaches to the values that would govern both the public education system and the city as a whole. Vann, Campbell, the ATA, and the replacement teachers had sought to create an alternative culture in the Ocean Hill–Brownsville schools, one that would reward those who held values they associated with blacks and "blackness" by facilitating success in the public education system. The curricula and activities in the Ocean Hill–Brownsville schools during the UFT strikes were an attempt to use attributes that these educators considered unique to black New Yorkers as a new form of currency, a means to empowerment, identity, and respect. White educators, however, would not allow the rules of this system to change without a struggle. These differences—in perception, prescription, and understanding—would only widen in the years that followed.

The battle between the UFT and the ATA continued after the Ocean Hill–Brownsville strikes ended in November 1968. If anything, the rhetoric on both sides became more inflamed, and divisions more pronounced. The ATA and its allies, stung by the resolution of the immediate issues of the Ocean Hill controversy substantially on the UFT's terms, lashed out at the culture of poverty idea in the years following the crisis. "The concepts of poverty, broken homes and emotional traumas permit an easy exit for [white teachers]," wrote one ATA member. "You may always blame the runaway father for the school's failures." Another ATA teacher took this a step further, seeking to distinguish the extended African-American family structure from that of whites on the basis of its African roots. "In Africa," she argued, "'family' defines individuals beyond the immediate members. The structure of black family life differs from the family organization of the white majority in America. Adoption does not undergo the many 'legal' processes necessary for upper and middle-class Americans. Instead, maternal love [an inheritance from Africa] governs." Behavior whites labeled as "illegitimacy," she argued, was "generally accepted" in black families, "because we as black people consider life as sacred." "The black family," she concluded, "is being judged by the standards of white society and not by Africa from which it stemmed."[93]

The ATA's white allies during the Ocean Hill–Brownsville controversy—New Left–influenced intellectuals, educational activists, and community action organization leaders—took similar positions. The Institute for Community Studies, through which Ford Foundation had funneled funds for the Ocean Hill experimental district, argued in its newsletter that community control was "a challenge to the prevalent middle-class vision of what education entails, to the attitude that the black poor are unteachable in the absence of a drastic reform of their social, cultural and familial conditions in directions accepted as normal by middle-class whites." "The crisis in education," it argued, "is a crisis in values," and "what is holding up the education of poor blacks is a set of values masquerading as facts, which are held by middle-class whites."[94]

Ellen Lurie of EQUAL and United Bronx Parents viewed the culture of poverty idea as a means for white teachers to assert an unwarranted cultural superiority over their black students. In her 1970 book, *How to Change the Schools,* she asked rhetorically, "if a student talks about Garvey and a teacher quotes Roosevelt . . . if a teacher loves Berlin, and a child sings plenas and bombas . . . if a teacher enjoys reading erotic novels with off-color language and a student enjoys using those words and talking about sex, which one is culturally deprived?" The educational system in New York, she argued, "is based upon the assumption that the child has deficiencies that must be overcome: his family background is deficient, his language is deficient, his cultural heritage is deficient, his life experiences are deficient. . . . [S]chools teach [students] to be ashamed of their parents and their homes." United Bronx Parents leader Evelina Antonetty dismissed the arguments of white teachers who linked family structure to academic achievement: "What happens to orphans? They learn, don't they?"[95]

The ATA and its supporters also pressed their assault on the values they associated with white teachers and the UFT after the Ocean Hill–Brownsville strike ended. Campbell wrote in 1970 that white-run schools "encourage the individualist instincts . . . [and] perpetuate the idea that any knowledge worthwhile must come from a book, to set the so-called 'educated' apart from the community." He advocated an educational system based on "black values," which he defined as "working and living together for the common good." A year later, Vann blamed a white-dominated competitive ethos for fostering "the concept of individual achievement and success at the expense of fellow human beings." The ATA's 1972 annual convention issued a call for "a black value system, which will make unity a way of life rather than an abstraction," and that would "eliminate the negative concepts of individualism and competition." "Individualism," editorialized Vann in 1971, "is a myth."[96]

The ATA and its allies also continued to attack the "test culture" of the city's educational system, and rejected the use of "cognitive" learning skills they associated with whites as currency for advancement within this culture. "How do we identify giftedness in black children?," it editorialized in 1971. "Shall we use tests? Of course not. The man has been testing for the past two decades. The man has defined the abilities he considers important as being cognitive. Then he defines what he calls cognitive. We maintain that even though we have cognitive abilities, there are probably more important abilities. For black children in a racist school, giftedness would be identified by pupils' challenge of authority, defending

other students 'in trouble,' independence, and curiosity."[97] Rhody McCoy criticized "the general failure of the philosophy of American education, namely, its excessive preoccupation with grades and test-passing at the expense of 'humanizing'
usages of liberal education."[98] And Ellen Lurie described the city school system
as a place where "[c]hildren learn that competition is important, marks are everything. Knowledge, if it is not going to be on a test, is worthless. A child who helps
another is not cooperating; he is cheating."[99]

As they had during the Ocean Hill–Brownsville crisis itself, ATA members and
supporters strove to distance themselves from attitudes and values they associated
with the white middle class. "During my first year [of teaching]," an ATA member
wrote in 1970, "I felt myself disliking being referred to as a teacher, since, to me,
this term had become synonymous with 'white' and had only negative connota-
tions. . . . I am absolutely speechless when a child in anger refers to me as a 'white
ass' or says 'I'm black and I'm proud and you're white so you know what you can
do!'" "I don't want to be like the white teachers," she continued. "I'm not even
sure whether I want my own children to be or act the way their [white] teachers
want them to act. I know I don't want them to be like their own teachers."[100]

Another black educator defended community control of schools as a challenge
to a system "too based on industrial values—hard work, obedience, conformity—
to even contemplate admitting rebellious, outspoken, noncompliant and 'unedu-
cated' members of the urban population [who seek] equalization of economic and
educational advantage."[101] "Black people are not white people," wrote Vann in
1972. "Their goals and purposes cannot truly be obtained through white schools.
As black educators we must take our proper position in regard to and for the
greatest benefit of the mass of black people."[102] The public schools, complained
another ATA member, "relate only to the dominant non-black middle class."[103]
Rhody McCoy attacked a group of black teacher assistants who had joined the
UFT for "seeking to rise to middle-class professional status at the expense of their
allegiance to their roots."[104] And a black teacher warned his fellow ATA members
to "try not to confuse your 'hustle' with your job! As a black teacher, you are doing
a hustle."[105]

The most comprehensive critique of white middle-class values in the city's educational system by an ATA member, however, came from a principal, Alton Rison.
Rison, who headed JHS 117 in Brooklyn, was one of the few black principals
serving in the New York public schools when he published "How to Teach Black
Children" in the *African-American Teachers Forum* in 1972. He began by distinguishing what he labeled "black" and "white" (or "Middle-European") styles of
learning. Whites, he argued, "are conditioned to a high degree of structured, stiff
learning," and "can tolerate monotonous, boring, mostly lecture or oral teaching.

Their whole tradition programs them to respect their teacher, good or bad. To them, the high mark is more important than short-lived rebellion and failure."

When white students trained in this "Middle-European" style became teachers themselves, Rison argued, they attempted to replicate it in their black students, to whom it was culturally foreign. "There is no way," Rison wrote, "that black children will sit still listening to a verbal lecture assault by teachers of Middle-European, Germanic philosophical structure. In excruciating, tortuous moments, they will misbehave, squirm in their seats and make life miserable for those incompetents who may very well be competent somewhere else, but not among black children."

White teachers, he maintained, misunderstood this reaction, blaming it on the culture of poverty or labeling the students "disruptive," when in reality it was a manifestation of a unique black culture. "Black children," Rison wrote, "are innovators, inventors, creators, actors and performers. They like exciting styles, fashions, colors and constant change." These "healthy, bubbling energies," he argued, were evidence of "rare distributive talents which many whites lack," and thus misinterpret. White teachers, he charged, attempted to impose their cold, abstract, and intellectually elitist educational culture on black children whose frame of reference was concrete and spontaneous.

"White teachers," wrote Rison, "would like blacks to begin with the book. Many black children would rather begin with their talents and create in reality ideas found in books." Unable to understand this, white teachers instead sought to "have black students become identical objects of themselves or their own children and values." Obsessed with competition, they focused solely on "the achievements of their bright black classes. Very seldom do they speak of their larger middle and slower groups." Rison explained this by arguing that high-achieving black pupils "appear to [white teachers] to be more similar to white students than to their fellow blacks. They can act more white. . . . They seem to have similar values as whites. White teachers would like all blacks to follow the white route. This is an error."[106]

Rison thus contrasted the "monolithic talents" of white students with the "many moving talents" he attributed to black children. He explicitly associated competition, individualism, and cognitive learning with whites, and egalitarianism, mutualism, spontaneity, and the affective component with blacks. He and the ATA had, by the early 1970s, drawn a cultural line in the sand in New York City's educational system.[107] They did not act alone, however. White UFT teachers also participated during this period in the process of distinguishing "white middle-class" and "black lower-class" values.

Whites did so by employing the culture of poverty theory to criticize the learning styles and behavior of black youngsters in the school system. The underlying assumption behind white teachers' use of the culture of poverty idea was that blacks, by becoming middle-class, should become like them. The UFT supported a variety of compensatory programs in the 1960s and 1970s with this aim—MES, the Higher Horizons "cultural enrichment" program, school lunch and after-school programs, Head Start, and, more generally, housing, full employment, and guaranteed minimum income programs.[108] White UFT teachers believed that if lower-class blacks could be thus elevated to middle-class economic status, the rest would follow—and the "rest," in this case, would be the jettisoning of a flawed culture for one that more closely resembled their own.

The implications were clear. Becoming middle-class meant approximating whites and whiteness as closely as possible. But by not admitting to the possibility of a distinctively black approach to middle-class culture, and, indeed, by assuming that middle-class culture was the only one appropriate to whites, white teachers made it that much easier for black educators to associate middle-class values exclusively with whiteness. In a similar vein, the strong competitive and individualist ethos of the white teachers—their support for testing, tracking, and the "merit system," their passionate upward mobility and undisguised materialism—allowed frustrated black teachers, who believed that the city's public schools were failing both them and black students, to position themselves in opposition to what appeared to be a white-defined culture.

The UFT and its allies did make some attempts to respond to ATA criticism by defending "middle-class values" as essential for both whites and blacks in New York. The union acknowledged the possible "conflict in the poor urban black community about accepting middle-class values," its "fear of loss of blackness in becoming middle class," and its "criticism of middle-class values and attitudes as essentially 'white.'"[109] Shanker labeled the "romanticization" of black poverty "condescending and insulting," and criticized the projection of poor blacks "into the role of revolutionaries come to save the white middle class from their boredom and their sins."[110] And a UFT supporter wondered whether "a youngster will have a ghost of a chance at securing dignified employment with only the assets of 'walking tall,' [and] being proud of his racial heritage . . ."[111]

But, whatever their motivations, white teachers nonetheless boxed black educators in. Their very act of embracing middle-class values forced many black teachers who were searching for an identity separate from that of whites to a difficult choice: they could either walk in the shadow of whites, or define themselves in terms of what whites were not. Black teachers who, like the members of the ATA, chose the latter course, ceded the realm of middle-class values to whites, in large measure because whites had appropriated them first.

The dangers presented by this choice were not lost on ATA teachers, least of all on their leader, Albert Vann. In an interview with *Ebony* magazine shortly after the end of the Ocean Hill–Brownsville strike, Vann sought to clarify his position regarding "white middle-class" values and behavior. "By no means," he said, "are we saying that it's not important to read, write and manipulate numbers. But we're saying it's also important that you begin to understand yourself, that you've had a glorious past and can have a glorious future, and therefore you can achieve. . . . The Man is not going to give us these values. They have to be earned by a new kind of black man that we don't have yet."[112] Similarly, ATA teachers did not disapprove of discipline in the schools per se, only its administration by whites, as in the case of the "disruptive child" dispute with the UFT. They called for strong black authority figures in the classroom and were particularly outspoken in their attacks on student drug use.[113]

Such attempts by ATA members to construct a black middle-class alternative to white middle-class values were marked by ambivalence, however. On the one hand, they wished to change the rules of the city's public education market to reward attributes they associated with "blackness." On the other, their attacks on the "white" examination system, and on the values they ascribed to it, led many whites to conclude that ATA members rejected that market in its entirety. As a white observer during the Ocean Hill–Brownsville strike noted, Vann "couldn't figure out whether he was an outlaw ranchhand or a fence-building sheepherder," and the often overheated rhetoric of Vann, Campbell, and other ATA supporters distorted their intended message.[114] By insisting on defining themselves primarily as "not white," Vann and his colleagues minimized the more beneficial aspects of the middle-class ethos. While there was, of course, nothing inherently "white" in respect for authority, or a desire to improve one's material condition, the ATA, by taking the position that whites had effectively preempted the field of middle-class values, and that there was only a "white" way to be middle class, lost an opportunity to navigate the waters between the white middle class and black lower class. In attempting to ignore the obvious fact of their own middle-class economic status, and in throwing in their rhetorical lot with the black poor, they preserved their antiwhite credentials, but at a high price.[115]

The ATA had raised important questions about the content of culture in both the public education system and the city as a whole. ATA teachers and supporters had challenged the values of an educational market that equated high examination scores with the acquisition of knowledge, encouraged students and teachers to compete against each other, and disparaged the abilities of children raised in a "culture of poverty" to learn effectively. They offered instead a set of alternative values built around cooperation, mutualism, egalitarianism, and racial identity, one that offered a competing set of values to those of white teachers, and indeed, of New York's white middle class in general. But by failing to distinguish effectively between the middle-class values they wished to discard and those they wished to retain, ATA teachers sent a series of unclear signals to the black poor they hoped to reach. Aiming harsh rhetorical fire at "white" culture, they contributed to what may have been an unnecessarily sharp divide between "white" middle-class and "black" lower-class values. During the Ocean Hill–Brownsville crisis and in its aftermath, ATA members groped for ways to combine racial authenticity and middle-class values in the New York City school system. Trapped both by historical circumstances and by the implications of their own words, they offered a powerful critique, but an ambivalent message.

Thus, both white and black teachers bore some responsibility for the divide between white middle-class and black lower-class culture that existed in New York's public education system by the early 1970s. By failing to acknowledge the possibility of a middle-class culture on anything other than white terms, whites placed blacks in the position of having to reject that culture in order to forge a distinct racial identity. Forced to associate middle-class values with "whiteness," black educators in turn were unable to define a viable middle-class voice of their own, effectively abandoning the field to whites. Driven by what appeared to be ineluctable circumstances, as well as by their own assumptions and biases, blacks and whites in the New York City public education system had formed distinct cultures built largely around negative reactions to attributes each associated with the other. The result was a school system and city in which whites and blacks spoke past each other, inhabiting, both literally and figuratively, two separate New Yorks.

Aided by superior finances, greater manpower, and more favorable public relations, the UFT finally emerged victorious in its battle with the ATA in 1974.[116] The UFT's negotiation of agency shop status in its 1969 collective bargaining agreement with the Board of Education meant that union dues would be deducted from the paychecks of all city teachers, whether or not they were union members. Many black teachers found it too expensive to pay ATA dues as well, and membership in the organization dropped.[117] The UFT and its allies also prevailed upon the New York Urban Coalition and the federal government to cut off over five hundred thousand dollars in ATA funding in the early 1970s, with Shanker enlisting President Richard Nixon himself in this effort.[118] And finally, the UFT exhausted the ATA's treasury in 1973 by winning a judgment against it under the Civil Rights Act of 1964 for excluding a white teacher, who had been sent by Shanker to create a test case, from one of its meetings on public school property.[119]

In the early 1970s, Vann left the public school system, and turned his attention to electoral politics. He did battle with the black representatives of the Brooklyn Democratic political machine, and eventually won a seat in the New York State Assembly. Leslie Campbell also left the public schools to operate a private black nationalist academy. Under his new name, Jitu Weusi, he continued to work as a grassroots activist in Brooklyn, until, in an ironic twist, he regained a position in the public school system. But by the end of the 1990s, there was no ATA for him to lead. It was, in fact, a distant memory. With its finances depleted and its leadership decimated, the group had long since ceased to exist.

While the ATA did not survive its battle with the UFT, its critique of white middle-class values and attitudes, in both the educational system and the city at large, did. Founded as little more than a trade association, it had developed by the time of the Ocean Hill–Brownsville controversy into the cutting edge of a challenge to the culture of white teachers, and New York's white middle-class community. By accepting this challenge, whites joined a debate over the parameters of civic culture in New York, and the relevance of middle-class values to the lives of the black poor. Driven by different impulses and assumptions, whites and blacks came to agree on the essential "whiteness" of attributes that each associated with the middle class in New York, and established a broad cultural demarcation between "white" and "black" values.

Beginning in the late 1960s, an ambivalent, uneasy black middle class in New York would wrestle with the implications of this demarcation. It would be torn between its rising standard of living and discomfort with the ominous levels of social dislocation among poor blacks, on one hand, and anger at persistent white racism and fear of loss of racial authenticity, on the other.

There were, of course, those in New York's black middle-class community during the 1960s and 1970s who sought to defend the authenticity of black middle-class values. One of the most prominent, Roy Wilkins, asked rhetorically, "[does] a man become a 'Tom' simply because he has managed to escape poverty?" He warned that "the supermilitants in their automatic resentment of anyone who has made it may end up making a romantic virtue of deprivation," and attacked their "anti–middle class, anti-professional attitude." Much of this sentiment, however, was indeed "Tommed," chilled and driven undercover by the dominant voices in the black community as a whole. Whatever opinions it may have expressed privately, the New York middle-class black community's public defense of "middle-class values" during this period was muted and defensive.[120]

The fate of John Burrus, a self-described "middle-class Negro" who attempted to drum up support for the UFT in Ocean Hill–Brownsville, is instructive. Burrus was ridiculed as an "Uncle Tom" by virtually every leading personality in the

Ocean Hill experimental district, including McCoy, Vann, Campbell, other ATA leaders, and members of the local school board. Mayor Lindsay viewed him as unrepresentative of the Ocean Hill community and ignored him.[121] It is also significant that after the 1968 incident at Brooklyn's JHS 117 in which two white principals and a white teacher were beaten, the only black parent who wrote the *New York Amsterdam News* in protest, and who described the assailants as "hoodlums," asked that his name be withheld.[122]

Defining a distinct, racially authentic cultural identity would thus prove no easier for black middle-class New Yorkers than for Vann, Campbell, and the other members of the ATA. That process of self-definition continues today, a classic American dilemma made infinitely more difficult by the unique burdens of history, memory, and race.

By thus racializing behaviors that they associated with the other, Ocean Hill–Brownsville sparked a cultural war between blacks and whites that would last for the rest of the twentieth century, and on into the twenty-first. It would affect virtually every public policy choice New Yorkers would make during this time. Whether the specific issue at hand involved a mayoral election, a labor dispute, a budget decision, an anticrime initiative, or a welfare reform plan, culture—and competing black and white cultures—lay at or just beneath the surface. Arguments during the mayoralty of David Dinkins over condom distribution in city schools, "outsider"-run businesses in black neighborhoods, and control of civil disturbances, and during that of Rudolph Giuliani over panhandlers, policing tactics, and workfare, are the lineal descendants of the cultural battle joined at Ocean Hill–Brownsville.

Rhody McCoy once observed that, to white teachers, the behavior of blacks during the Ocean Hill–Brownsville dispute was "a negation of the rules of culture itself."[123] McCoy was correct in more ways than he knew. This phrase encapsulated black views of whites during and after the crisis as well. Neither side had any illusions about the consequences of losing Ocean Hill–Brownsville's cultural war. When a white UFT teacher complained that "our whole way of life is at stake!" a local board supporter's rejoinder was telling: "You got it! That's exactly right."[124] In New York City today, the stakes remain high, and the battle continues.

8

AFTER THE CRISIS

At the height of the third Ocean Hill–Brownsville strike, two major figures of the New York activist Left, Dwight Macdonald and Michael Harrington, debated the merits of community control in the pages of the *New York Times* and the *New York Review of Books*. Along with the personal mudslinging and political posturing customary to such exchanges, they offered a trenchant analysis of the controversy from the rival UFT and local board perspectives. Macdonald, supporting the local board, described the Ocean Hill–Brownsville project as "a deeply imaginative experiment that may have lessons for all ghetto schools." He praised the "friendly, serious, relaxed" atmosphere that prevailed in the Ocean Hill–Brownsville schools when he had visited them, and argued that schools in white neighborhoods, too, could benefit from community control.[1]

But Harrington, supporting the UFT, was much less sanguine. He, unlike Macdonald, had personal experience with groups such as PAT. "It happens," he wrote, "that [the issue of due process for teachers] has arisen first in the ghettos, but it can spread to predominantly white areas [and] local reactionary forces. . . . They are eagerly waiting in the wings for *their* turn."[2]

Harrington was both right and wrong. Whites in New York were indeed using the lessons of Ocean Hill–Brownsville for their own purposes. But they were not all "reactionaries." Indeed, many were members of the UFT, the union whose cause Harrington supported. In the years following the Ocean Hill–Brownsville crisis, white New Yorkers would fuse two powerful impulses—middle-class anger and community control—to establish a political and cultural hegemony in the city that exists to this day. They would turn the words and ideas of local control supporters at Ocean Hill–Brownsville against them, marginalizing both blacks and progressive whites, and choking off the last gasps of the civil rights movement in the city. In the late 1970s, with New York in the throes of its worst fiscal crisis since the Great Depression, they would ally with their erstwhile adversaries at Ocean Hill— white Manhattan elites—through a most unlikely medium, lapsed liberal mayor Edward Koch. The erstwhile rivals would unite behind a financial austerity program aimed at the heart of the city's black community. New York's budget cuts and social service reductions altered a civic culture of municipal government generosity to the city's least-advantaged citizens that had been in place since the mayoralty of Fiorello La Guardia. The cuts were the ironic legacies of community control, an idea that had once seemed so full of promise for black New York.

UFT members moved to capture the momentum of the community control impulse even before the Ocean Hill–Brownsville controversy ended. They directed much of their ire at the Ford Foundation. "Obviously [the foundation] has a high regard for community control," wrote one. "I urge therefore that the community control experiment should be extended to the Ford Foundation itself. Since we pay taxes to subsidize the Ford Foundation, we should demand control of the decisions and funds in the Ford Foundation."[3] The foundation, argued another, "is using tax-exempt money—OUR MONEY without asking us how we feel about it. I urge the UFT to petition the legislature to turn over control of TAX-EXEMPT MONEY to the community—i.e., New York City citizens. WE should control any board that spends TAX-EXEMPT MONEY. Any foundation using tax-exempt money should be controlled by the people of the community."[4] On an even more ominous note, a UFT teacher demanded in a letter to Shanker that "all the white schools should be taken over by the parents of the whites and the blacks . . . let them take care of all their [own] people. . . . [T]he schools should be taken as [blacks] want their schools. We should take over our schools, whites only. . . ."[5]

During the third strike, whites in the Fordham section of the Bronx sought to put their version of community control into practice. After a rumor circulated through this largely middle-class community that "black militants" were planning to "take over" the local school district at a meeting in the Fordham University gymnasium, four thousand whites launched a preemptive strike. They invaded the gymnasium, some arriving more than four hours in advance of the alleged black "takeover," to exercise some "local control" of their own. While the ending was anticlimactic—at the appointed hour, only two dozen Ocean Hill–Brownsville local board supporters appeared, and fled as soon as they saw what awaited them—the whites jamming the gymnasium had made a strong statement about the future uses of the community control impulse in New York City. "We've got to stick together," said one. "It's about time we're demonstrating in reverse." He pointed to the retreating Ocean Hill–Brownsville supporters: "We'll be at every meeting you hold."[6]

As they had before the Ocean Hill–Brownsville controversy began, black and progressive white supporters of community control downplayed or ignored the doctrine's applicability to more conservative white "communities." The *Village Voice*'s Nat Hentoff, for example, argued that the Ocean Hill–Brownsville experiment was an "augury" for white neighborhoods. But he clearly envisioned community control in his familiar Manhattan haunts of Greenwich Village and the Upper West Side, not white outer-borough communities such as Jackson Heights and Canarsie. He predicted expansively that "whites as well as blacks are going to be more concerned with ways of creating communities instead of the cells of isolation that are characteristic of big cities," ignoring the fact that if "communities" were to be found anywhere in the city, they were in white sections of Queens, Brooklyn, and the Bronx. "Whites," Hentoff argued, again apparently referring to Manhattanites, "will see the need for political alliances with blacks and Puerto Ricans so that finally these whites too can have some decision-making power. Once they get a sense of involvement making local schools responsive . . . there is an accompanying rise in their expectations and their own feelings of personal legitimacy."[7]

The New York Civil Liberties Union, or NYCLU, which had strongly supported the Ocean Hill–Brownsville local board during the strikes, and rejected the UFT's due process argument as a "smokescreen" to defeat community control, also was caught off guard by the possibility of white use of local control ideology. In a resolution issued after the strikes, the NYCLU reiterated its stance—one shared by EQUAL, the ATA, the New York Urban Coalition, and most supporters of the Ocean Hill–Brownsville local board—that the community control idea was the exclusive domain of blacks and progressive whites. The NYCLU justified this position by linking community control to its "substantive" definition of equality in city life. To the NYCLU, "equality" meant rough equivalence of group outcomes in economic, social, and political life—"total equality," as it put it—not merely equal treatment under the law. Community control, then, was but a means to an end, and not an end in itself. Accordingly, the NYCLU argued that "in some circumstances, community control is a sound means of achieving equality of educational opportunity. Under other circumstances, it may be used to establish patterns of racial discrimination and educational inequality. When used for the first purpose, the NYCLU will support community control. . . . [I]t is quite possible to support [community control] in one community and oppose it in another."[8]

But this position, well-intentioned as it may have been, led to a philosophical and practical dead end. Bayard Rustin captured its inconsistency when he wrote that in the eyes of organizations like the NYCLU and EQUAL, "community control would be the exclusive province of the poor, while middle-class and affluent neighborhoods would be subject to decisions handed down from some distant agency in a state capital or Washington."[9]

The NYCLU's reasoning was also flawed on a more practical level. Supporters of community control in black neighborhoods such as Ocean Hill–Brownsville made facile comparisons between these areas and more established white communities, assuming that the "positive values to be found in a ghetto atmosphere," as Marilyn Gittell's Institute for Community Studies put it, were the same in both. It was true that poor black communities, as Gittell argued, could "develop their own values and rationale for success," just as white communities had.[10] But given the differences between black and white "communities" in the area of substantive resources, this was almost beside the point. White neighborhoods such as Jackson Heights had permanent residents, long-standing cultural and social institutions, and, perhaps most important, a large degree of economic self-sufficiency. Ocean Hill–Brownsville had none of these. Gittell, the NYCLU, and other community control supporters failed to understand that there were many more white "communities" in New York City during the late 1960s and early 1970s than black ones. And white middle-class New Yorkers, having observed the events at Ocean Hill–Brownsville with great interest, were now, as Harrington had predicted, "waiting in the wings for their turn." That turn would come in the white outer-borough "communities" of Forest Hills and Canarsie.

Forest Hills, a largely Jewish neighborhood of quaint, gingerbread private homes and middle-income apartment buildings, prided itself on its liberal political sensibilities; it had supported Lindsay when he first ran for mayor in 1965. In 1966, Lindsay unveiled a new public housing program for the city. In a major break with Robert Moses, whose philosophy over the preceding twenty years had been to construct large low-income housing projects inside already existing ghettos, the newly elected mayor announced that henceforth, he would build smaller projects on "scattered sites" in white neighborhoods around the city. "This," warned Lindsay, "is a fundamental test as to whether those who argue for integrated communities have the courage of their convictions."[11] Forest Hills, taking up the mayor's challenge, agreed to accept such a small-scale project.

By 1971, however, the scattered-site housing program had fallen far short of Lindsay's goals. Most white middle-class neighborhoods opposed the construction of any low-income housing developments, even small ones, in their midst. Lindsay decided to compensate by increasing the size of the Forest Hills project to three twenty-four-story buildings. They would house some 840, predominantly black, families.

The Forest Hills community responded with a furious grassroots organizing campaign against the project that drew its direct inspiration from what these whites had so recently seen at Ocean Hill–Brownsville. Jerry Birbach, a local businessman, became Forest Hills's Rhody McCoy, C. Herbert Oliver, and John Powis rolled into one. Birbach was a galvanizing speaker, tireless organizer, and resourceful movement theoretician. His three-thousand-member Forest Hills Residents Association made full use of the language and tactics of "community" to advance its cause. Birbach staged loud demonstrations at the site of the proposed project. He invaded public hearings, pillorying Lindsay as "totally unresponsive, pompous and arrogant." He brought thousands to the steps of City Hall. And, like Rhody McCoy, he spoke of the will of the "people," the "community" as an almost monolithic entity. Lindsay's plan, Birbach charged, "rode roughshod over the community." Before the mayor or any city official acted, he "should wait to see what sort of input came from the community."[12]

Birbach's troops fused the idea of community with the same white middle-class anger Shanker's teachers had shown at Ocean Hill–Brownsville. Indeed, these were some of the same people. At a hearing on the project before the City Planning Commission, a Forest Hills Residents Association spokeswoman testified that she had moved to Forest Hills from Ocean Hill–Brownsville ten years earlier because her mother was mugged there. "I will not live with it again," she vowed. The projects, she claimed, would have air-conditioning and wall-to-wall carpeting, subsidized by "taxpayers" like her: "I'm a taxpayer and I don't have it. I will not provide it for anyone else." "This is no longer a case of Sidney Poitier, the star, coming to dinner," charged another speaker, "but Sidney Jones, the porter, planning to move in permanently." Pointing at City Planning Commission chairman Donald Elliott, a white Protestant Lindsay appointee, he sneered, "you don't know what goes on in this city." After Elliott cut off the testimony of a Forest Hills assemblyman allied with Birbach, who had exceeded his time at the speakers' podium, chiding "you often speak of law and order," the legislator shot back, "it's the people who speak, not you."[13]

By the spring of 1972, Lindsay was looking for a way out of what had become, especially in view of his embarrassing presidential campaign, another white middle-class nightmare. He asked Mario Cuomo, a future governor of New York, but at the time a neighborhood Queens lawyer, to devise a plan that would remove Jerry Birbach's teeth from his leg. Cuomo reduced the size of the Forest Hills project to three twelve-story buildings, made most of the apartments cooperatives, and set aside many of the units for the elderly. Birbach and the Forest Hills "community" had won out. Among the parties to this denouement was an ambitious politician from Greenwich Village named Edward Koch, whose liberal politics, like those of the citizens of Forest Hills, were dissolving in New York's racial maelstrom. Forest Hills taught Koch, and a good many of his colleagues as well, a lesson about the power of community—white community—in the city's racial politics.

The events of 1972 and 1973 in another white "community"—the Brooklyn neighborhood of Canarsie—reinforced that lesson. Canarsie, located immediately to the south of Ocean Hill–Brownsville, was an area of Jewish and Italian small homeowners, a prototypical staging ground for the Jewish-Catholic rapprochement that accompanied the Ocean Hill–Brownsville controversy. Canarsie whites had always sought to insulate themselves from their black neighbors, especially in the area of education. Ironically, they were more successful in doing so after the advent of community control of schools than before. Until the passage of the Decentralization Law of 1969, which took effect in 1970, the central Board of Education controlled pupil assignment. Between 1958 and 1970, the central Board ordered black children from the Tilden Houses, a Brownsville public housing project, to be bused into Canarsie schools, and the neighborhood could do nothing about it.

With the advent of local control under the Decentralization Law, however, Canarsie moved to seal off its borders from Ocean Hill–Brownsville. Since the redistricting that accompanied the law placed the two neighborhoods in separate districts, the Canarsie local school board which took office under the new Decentralization Law voted in 1971 to bar the black Tilden Houses children from its schools. Harvey Scribner, Bernard Donovan's successor in the newly renamed position of Schools Chancellor, was an advocate of community control, and had promised not to interfere with local boards except in cases of illegality. The Canarsie board members, accordingly, expected his acquiescence. Scribner shocked them, however, by issuing a direct order: Canarsie's schools were to continue to accept children from the Tilden Houses, and in even greater numbers than before, community control or not.

Scribner's order unleashed a firestorm of protest from Canarsie residents. The addition of the black children they argued, would "tip" the racial balance of Junior High School 211, the school to which Scribner sought to assign the students, causing an exodus of white families from the neighborhood. The Canarsie local board refused to approve the assignment of the Tilden Houses children to JHS 211, claiming the right under community control to determine pupil assignments.[14] White Canarsians staged sit-ins, demonstrations, and two boycotts of the district schools in the fall of 1972 and winter of 1973 which lasted for a total of six weeks. Most of the UFT rank and file supported the protesters.

Sociologist Jonathan Rieder has described the Canarsie antibusing boycotts as "deferred white vengeance for the New York school crisis of 1968."[15] A major element of that vengeance involved appropriating the language of community control that Canarsie whites had heard blacks use at Ocean Hill–Brownsville. "We thought the boycotts during the Ocean Hill–Brownsville crisis were terrible, but we whites learned from the black militance," said one leader. "It all goes back to 1968 and the days of [Brooklyn CORE leader] Sonny Carson." But the white protesters were using community control for more than petty tit-for-tat. Their local control rhetoric expressed their own understanding of racial equality in the city. "Equality," to white Canarsians, meant equivalence of treatment, an equality of procedure, not substance. It was the polar opposite of the definition employed by groups like the NYCLU, EQUAL, and the ATA, and, for that matter, by most of the city's black population. Applied to the Canarsie busing controversy, this "white" understanding of equality led inexorably to one conclusion: if blacks used community control at Ocean Hill–Brownsville, whites were entitled to use it as well.

After Scribner suspended the Canarsie local school board for refusing to approve the transfer of the Tilden Houses children to JHS 211, a white resident expressed his outrage in terms of this view of equality: "Any kind of equity has to be a two-way street or it's a no-way street. If you want equality for you, you damn well better be prepared to give that same kind of equality to me. Don't you dare try to control your district and then try to control mine too." "You and the God-damned liberals," charged another, addressing a busing proponent, "you screamed along with the blacks in 1968 for community control. . . . [N]ow whites want what the blacks have, and you say we can't have it. How come they can do it and we can't?"[16] Canarsie whites coupled this demand for equality of treatment with an individualist orientation reminiscent of PAT ten years earlier. Black children from the Tilden Houses, they argued, would "seriously overcrowd" the "slowest classes."[17]

Altogether, the use of "community" by Canarsie whites was a devastating frontal assault that neither Scribner nor the erstwhile supporters of community control at Ocean Hill–Brownsville quite knew how to handle. The irony of the situation was certainly not lost on Scribner. "The 'quotas' issue which gets so much of this city so uptight so frequently," he observed, "is now raised in reverse. . . . Now I am asked by some of the same people who so adamantly opposed 'quotas' in employment and other areas to assure the boycotting parents that a racial quota—a set limit on the percentage of minority students—will be established for their school . . ."[18] Yet, for all his perspicacity, there was very little Scribner could do. Community control had defined much of his career; he had come from the Vermont Department of Education expressly to institute it in the New York City schools. Now, with a white neighborhood demanding the same community control that he had so ardently championed with blacks in mind, Scribner realized he lacked the stomach for a knock-down, drag-out fight on the issue. He folded his hand, scattering the Tilden Houses children to other districts, and allowing the racial composition of the Canarsie schools to remain the same. By the spring of 1973, he had left the New York public school system.

Unlike Scribner, the supporters of community control at Ocean Hill–Brownsville lacked much of an appreciation for irony. The events at Forest Hills and Canarsie baffled them. One complicating factor, for a group like the ATA, was the integrationist nature of the initiatives in both venues. The group, which had abandoned integration as a goal, was forced into half-hearted denunciations of Canarsians for rejecting black children, combined with simultaneous calls for "independent black educational institutions."[19] Similarly, the Teachers Action Caucus, a pro–community control wing of the UFT that had also dropped integration as a goal during the Ocean Hill–Brownsville controversy, shifted awkwardly as it struggled with the facts of the Canarsie dispute. "We of TAC never rejected the goal of quality integrated schools," it averred, "even though some may have thought so or accused us of it when we supported community control. . . . NO ONE HAS THE RIGHT TO EXCLUDE CHILDREN FROM SCHOOLS ON THE BASIS OF THEIR RACE. NO ONE."[20]

Those who had supported community control at Ocean Hill–Brownsville, moreover, insisted on ignoring the class dimensions of the Forest Hills and Canarsie controversies, viewing them both in strictly racial terms. Certainly the ATA was correct when it charged that Canarsie whites were "united in their disdain at the possibility of black children next to white children."[21] And the Teachers Action Caucus's argument that "'[t]ipping' is also caused by racism—whites leave when minorities arrive" was also accurate, but the group was being disingenuous or naive when it asked Canarsie white parents rhetorically, "what is it about Black and Puerto Rican children that their presence in any school frightens you?"[22] By dismissing "the fears that 'middle-class' whites have that Black and Puerto Rican children, especially the poor, bring with them the problems of vandalism [and] violence and, therefore, cause a declining school," it sidestepped important—and legitimate—questions of class relations that swirled beneath the surface of the Forest Hills and Canarsie disputes.[23]

This, in fact, was nothing new. Whether the adversary was PAT in 1964, the UFT in 1968, or Jerry Birbach in 1972, groups like the ATA and EQUAL, as well as individuals such as John Lindsay, John Doar, and Rhody McCoy, ignored the issues raised by the existence of class gradations among the city's white population. Often they proceeded from the best of motives, so appalled by the racism afoot in the white community they could see little else. But viewing Forest Hills, Canarsie, and Ocean Hill–Brownsville solely through the lens of race imposed a false clarity on a decidedly murky reality. Ultimately, their inability to understand that, while all whites were to some degree privileged, some were much more privileged than others, would cost the supporters of community control at Ocean Hill–Brownsville dearly. It burned whatever bridges existed to the city's white middle class, destroying any chance, however small, to reach an accommodation with them. And, in a practical sense, it ensured that, by dint of sheer numbers, they would lose every battle they fought for their vision of a just, fair, and "equal" New York.

Confused by the use of the community control idea by whites at Forest Hills and Canarsie, members of groups such as EQUAL, ATA, the NYCLU, and the Teachers Action Caucus fell back on claims of prior ownership. Like Canarsie and Forest Hills whites, they linked community control directly to their definition of equality in city life. To them, community control was valid only as a means to achieve the end of substantive equality among racial groups. Just as their view of equality demanded not merely fair rules but fair results, they understood community control not only as a procedural device, but as an instrument of redistributive change. And, in their view, any use of the rhetoric of local control that was not linked to this element of broad redistributive change, as in the cases of Forest Hills and Canarsie, could not be "true" community control. The doctrine, then did not belong to PAT, or to states rights southerners, or to Jerry Birbach, but to them alone.

As the Teachers Action Caucus put it during the Canarsie boycott, "community control is not inviolable or an abstract slogan. It was raised in the context of the need for black and Puerto Rican parents to participate as white parents have always done. We cannot permit a white majority to exclude or oppress a black or Puerto Rican minority under the guise of community control."[24] EQUAL adopted a similar proprietary attitude. "Community control," it observed in mock amazement, "is miraculously reborn as 'power to the neighborhoods'—the white neighborhoods. The black rallying cry of 'community control' has been co-opted. This is not the first time a strategy of black liberation has been turned inside out for the benefit of whites and to the detriment of blacks."[25]

Whether it was "fair" or not, however, these groups should not have been surprised when Forest Hills and Canarsie whites used the language of "community" to justify their actions. There were, of course, the recent precedents of PAT and the states rights South; conservatives had as much historic claim to the idea of community control as did liberals. And Forest Hills and Canarsie, certainly, possessed more of the attributes of "community" than did neighborhoods such as Ocean Hill–Brownsville.

Still, given their vision of an "equal" society, it is also not surprising that members of groups such as EQUAL, the NYCLU, and the ATA acted as they did. They believed that they lived in a city filled with gross disparities and maldistributions, one divided along lines not so much of class, as of racial caste. Decades of strong centralized authority in the city had not seemed to affect the basic parameters of power. Under these circumstances, the argument that community control was a weapon with a potentially vicious boomerang effect carried little weight. Their embrace of the community control impulse was thus a gesture of despair as much as of hope. What choice, in the end, did they have? It is possible, in fact, that the leaders of EQUAL, the ATA, and the others sensed that things would end as they did, with whites taking what was theirs and using it against the black community. Somehow, some way, whites always ended up on top. Wasn't it always this way?

Forest Hills and Canarsie, then, were the vehicles through which middle-class whites applied the "lessons" of Ocean Hill–Brownsville in the early 1970s to capture the community control impulse from blacks and shape it to their own ends. It would take another series of events, however, to complete Ocean Hill–Brownsville's tragic cycle. During New York's fiscal crisis, which began in 1975 and continued for the remainder of the decade, the controversy's scars prevented blacks and white unionists from making common cause to oppose the severe budget and spending cuts that devastated the city's infrastructure of expansive public services. Cut off from the black citizens they served, New York's public employee unions, especially the UFT, were unable to offer an alternative to fiscal austerity. Indeed, the city's financial crisis forced white union leaders like Albert Shanker into a shotgun marriage with New York's financial elite that, by definition, excluded blacks. Thanks in large part to Ocean Hill–Brownsville, he had nowhere else to go.

New York City had spent beyond its means for decades. If Fiorello La Guardia had helped build a city with, in the words of his biographer, Thomas Kessner, a "warmhearted center" for the poor and the dispossessed, he had also created one with extremely high maintenance costs.[26] By the late 1960s, New York had the nation's highest levels of public and social services. It offered the most generous amounts of welfare assistance in the United States. It spent more per public school student than any other city. It maintained a network of public hospitals unmatched in size by any other city. And its free City University was the nation's largest municipal higher education system.[27]

The cost of these services, however, was staggering, and New York had become addicted to high levels of state and federal aid to sustain them. As long as Lyndon Johnson was president, John Lindsay, although nominally a Republican, had a friend in Washington; the mayor was remarkably successful in attracting federal money to New York. But Richard Nixon's inauguration in 1969 marked the beginning of the end of the era of largesse in New York municipal governance. Scrambling to cover the aid shortfall and refusing to cut services, Lindsay began borrowing more heavily from commercial banks, pledging the city's outstanding accounts receivable, in the form of anticipated tax revenues and state or federal aid, as collateral. As the city become more desperate for funds, it exaggerated the amounts of, and the probability of ever receiving, these anticipated funds, until it was asking the banks to lend based on little more than hopeful intentions. The nationwide recession of the early 1970s made matters even worse. As city businesses earned less, they paid less in taxes, and city coffers diminished accordingly. The city also hemorrhaged jobs in the early 1970s, losing a total of 260,000 in the manufacturing sector alone, and 500,000 in all, between 1969 and 1975; its unemployment rate more than doubled during this period to 10.6 percent.[28] By 1974, when a dispirited Lindsay relinquished the mayoralty to machine Democrat Abraham Beame, the city was using bank loans to cover its day-to-day operating expenses. The municipal deficit stood at $12 billion. The interest alone on this sum came to a staggering $1.5 billion a year.[29]

On April 14, 1975, New York's commercial banks, owed more than $6 billion by the city, cut off its money supply. That day, they announced that they would neither purchase municipal commercial paper on their own account, nor sell it to outside buyers, effectively closing off the city's credit sources. New York was broke.

After some initial hesitation, Mayor Beame instituted across-the-board wage freezes for city employees, and began laying off workers. His measures did not go far enough, however, for the commercial banks and for New York's governor, Hugh Carey. They forced Beame to accept the jurisdiction of a newly formed entity, the Emergency Financial Control Board, or EFCB, composed of business leaders and state officials, in September 1975. Mindful of the implications of the EFCB's cost-cutting mission, Carey blocked the appointment of a black representative to the Board. The governor took control of the day-to-day financial affairs of the city away from Beame and lodged it in the EFCB.

The UFT was the first municipal union to negotiate a new contract during the fiscal crisis. The Board of Education, backed by the EFCB, demanded layoffs, a wage freeze, program cuts, and give-backs of previously-won benefits. Shanker's actions set the tone for future collective bargaining under financial austerity. The

UFT's prior contract with the Board of Education expired in September 1975, just after the creation of the EFCB, and at the start of the new school year. That year opened in chaos. Teachers returned to overcrowded classrooms, draconian work rules, and slashed-to-the-bone school programs. Angry teachers pushed a reluctant Shanker into a strike, one that lasted five days. But the union received no organized support from the black community, despite the effect of the Board of Education's service reductions on the community's own students. Ocean Hill–Brownsville's wounds cut too deeply. Even when their interests in restoring what had been lost coincided, white teachers and black parents could not let the past go.

The UFT strike was unsuccessful. The Board of Education held firm, and forced the union to accept the terms of its pre-strike offer. Wages were frozen, work rules were tightened, and although Shanker managed to maintain existing benefit levels, the new contract made layoffs inevitable. In all, fifteen thousand teachers and paraprofessionals lost their jobs in 1975, some 20 percent of the UFT's membership.[30]

Shanker, then, had knuckled under. Defending the new contract as "the best possible outcome in a time of virtual city default," he approved the investment of UFT pension funds in special municipally issued "MAC" bonds, to provide operating capital to the city as it worked its way back to solvency.[31] The union was now, like the commercial banks, New York's creditor. Shanker and Chase Manhattan's David Rockefeller made an unlikely set of partners, but to the extent of being owed money by the city, partners they were. Shanker would have preferred to ally instead with parents and students, including those in black neighborhoods like Ocean Hill–Brownsville, and the irony of his relationship with the banking community could not have been lost on this veteran of the Young People's Socialist League. But the Ocean Hill–Brownsville crisis had so damaged the UFT's standing with black New York that Shanker, even if he had possessed the fire in the belly to attempt a cross-class, interracial assault on the champions of fiscal austerity, would have found few friends there. Black New Yorkers were as angry about the decimated schools as Shanker, but they viewed him, and the union he led, as an enemy. The UFT had acquiesced in the shortening of the school day, a symbol to them of callous disregard. Community control in black neighborhoods was dead, replaced by a decentralization structure that gave the UFT more influence than black parents. And, above all, Ocean Hill–Brownsville's shadow loomed over everything Shanker said or did. Under the circumstances, the failure of the UFT and black citizens to work together to oppose school service cuts was as predictable as it was tragic. The union would now cast its lot with the banks. And the black community, politically marginalized, economically expendable—and no longer in control of the language of "community"—would be unable to do any-thing about it.[32]

The other municipal unions followed the UFT's lead when their turns came to negotiate with the EFCB. They too acquiesced in service cuts and work-rule tight-ening, and invested their pension funds in MAC bonds. Like the UFT, they were now stakeholders in the city's financial solvency, and as such, partners with the banking community. Union leaders began meeting regularly with EFCB members in what one observer described as a "bank/union nexus," working together to set the city's economic agenda. Both sides compromised a little. The unions agreed to accept small wage increases, usually limited to "Cost of Living Adjustments," or "COLAS," tied to productivity, deferring larger raises until solvency had been achieved. The banks agreed to permit these raises and protect the jobs of the more senior city employees. And both sides agreed to pay for the COLAs and senior job protections with layoffs of junior workers and social service spending cuts. The EFCB mandated a balanced city budget by 1981. To achieve this objective, it ended a thirty-year period in which assistance to impoverished New Yorkers had increased almost annually. Between 1975 and 1981, the city's basic welfare grant was frozen as New York's cost of living rose 68 percent, costing the poor-est segment of the population an estimated $2 billion in real purchasing power.[33] Housing allowances were also frozen during this time, even as rents rose rapidly. After growing explosively in the late 1960s and early 1970s, the welfare rolls were stabilized, then rolled back for the first time in twenty years, through stricter en-forcement of eligibility standards.[34] Social service spending declined 20 percent during the ten years following the onset of the fiscal crisis, a total of $1.4 billion in all.[35] Taking into account the rise in the cost of living during this period, it was the sharpest cut in assistance to New York's poor in the city's modern history.

Black New York, then was caught once again on the wrong side of an elemen-tal economic shift. The post–fiscal crisis city, with its emphasis on private devel-opment and its determination to rein in its traditionally generous services to the poor, would break with the New York of La Guardia, Wagner, and Lindsay. And, thanks in no small measure to the fallout from Ocean Hill–Brownsville, black New Yorkers lacked the political clout to fight back. Community control, insofar as it provided a route to power outside the traditional avenue of electoral politics, offered blacks a mixed blessing. By the onset of the fiscal crisis in 1975, many middle-class blacks in New York had used the community action and antipoverty apparatus as a rich source of jobs and patronage, in the process eclipsing old-line black machine politicians with ties to Tammany Hall. But since their power did not rest on a mass electoral base, community action leaders had little incentive to get out the vote in local contests. Throughout the 1960s and 1970s, whites, not blacks, dominated electoral politics in New York. In 1969, for example, 79 percent of the voters in the city's mayoral election were white, even though whites represented only 63 percent of the population.[36]

Black community action leaders who did not have to rely on gathering votes to stay in power never saw the need to get "their people" to the polls. As long as the sympathetic John Lindsay was mayor, and federal and state funds flowed into the city, this scarcely mattered. But by 1975, Lindsay was gone, and the Washington/Albany aid spigot had slowed to a trickle. Mayor Beame, who had cut his teeth in the Tammany Hall machine, listened to people who voted, or people who could deliver votes. Since blacks did not vote in great numbers, he saw no reason to listen to them. The negotiations over service cuts during the fiscal crisis took place almost as if blacks did not exist. By relying on community action at the expense of traditional electioneering, then, black leaders ignored a basic fact of life in city politics. While they might not have needed votes to obtain their jobs, the man who ultimately controlled those jobs — the mayor — did. Ultimately, they were beholden to an elected official, and unless they could credibly threaten to punish him at the polls, they were at his mercy.

Thus, when the EFCB budget ax started falling in 1975, black leaders could only respond with empty rhetoric, as when the head of the city's Community Development Agency complained about welfare cuts while "middle-income people and businessmen" escaped unscathed.[37] Thanks to the double-edged sword of community action, blacks could not reward their friends and punish their enemies at the polls, in the time-honored tradition of New York City group politics. "Community," once again, had played black New York false.

The reaction of middle-class whites in the city to the fiscal crisis mirrored that of the UFT and other public employee unions. Angry at budget cuts and resentful of the bankers who appeared to be running New York, they were nonetheless unwilling to animate an interracial alliance to prevent the cuts, and eventually, acquiesced in them. They did so largely because they viewed the cuts as aimed primarily at the city's black population. White middle-class New Yorkers had a number of choices in dealing with the crisis. One option was to permit an increase in taxes, thereby obviating the need for deep social service spending cuts. But antitax sentiment was so strong among white middle-class New Yorkers that city leaders never seriously considered it. Whites associated taxes and spending with black communities, not their own, whatever the actual facts may have been. In the words of one commenter, "in most of the middle-class sections of the city, increased taxes were perceived as being caused by welfare and other forms of assistance to blacks. That much of the money was going to their neighborhoods—policemen, firemen, teachers, and other civil servants—did not seem as obvious. There was little political support for new taxes." By the time of the fiscal crisis, "New Yorkers as taxpayers [had become] the fundamental electoral base, not New Yorkers as service consumers." Whites viewed blacks not only as the prime consumers of social services in the city, but as ungrateful ones at that. "The increasingly important middle class," an observer noted, "generally supported cutbacks in welfare, day care, and jobs programs, or the closing of some municipal hospitals. They were all identified with the poor and minorities." "The tone of politics," he concluded, "had changed in New York."[38]

The pent-up anger of Ocean Hill–Brownsville eventually translated into white middle-class support for economic measures that struck at the heart of the city's black community. These measures, moreover, could be couched in the outwardly race-neutral language of "fiscal responsibility," and thus sanitized for public consumption. The city's financial crisis was severe, of course, and choices were not unlimited. Some degree of municipal belt-tightening was inevitable. But the relative equanimity with which New York's white middle class accepted the option best designed to harm the city's black poor is significant. For New York's sour middle-class whites, indeed, the fiscal crisis presented itself as a kind of "equation," to be solved almost mechanically. Certain reductions were necessary for this "equation" to once again work, and they accepted them. The impact of the reductions on black citizens was unfortunate, but necessary. After all, the blacks lived in another New York.

Ultimately, it would fall to Edward Koch, New York's mayor from 1978 to 1989, to complete the post–Ocean Hill–Brownsville encirclement of the city's black population by uniting the outer-borough white middle class with its erstwhile opponents among Manhattan business, media, and professional elites. Koch's journey across the political spectrum during the late 1960s and 1970s was a microcosm of that of his white middle-class constituency.

Koch began his career as a liberal reform Democrat; he was, in fact, the man who toppled the last leader of Tammany Hall, Carmine DeSapio, in a Greenwich Village district leadership election in 1963. He was a strong supporter of the southern phase of the civil rights movement in the early 1960s, traveling to Mississippi during the Freedom Summer of 1964 to assist in voter registration drives. His racial disillusionment began there, when he claimed that civil rights leaders seemed less interested in publicizing assaults on white volunteers than on black ones. Ocean Hill–Brownsville reinforced Koch's emerging racial conservatism. He was outraged at what he considered the antiwhite, anti-Semitic atmosphere in the black community during the school strikes. By the time of the Forest Hills controversy in 1972, which he would describe as his "rubicon," Koch had become a strong supporter of the right of whites in outer-borough neighborhoods to live as they chose. Effectively, this meant living apart from poor blacks.[39]

Koch used his increased popularity among outer-borough whites to seek the mayoralty. After an abortive attempt in 1973, he defeated six candidates, including the incumbent, Beame, as well as a black and a Puerto Rican, in the 1977 Democratic primary — a "tribal election" that divided the voting population almost precisely along racial and ethnic lines.[40] He then won the mayoralty by outpolling Mario Cuomo, whose career had also received a boost from the Forest Hills dispute, in the general election.

While at first glance the mayor's working-class Jewish roots appeared to make him an unlikely candidate for an alliance with Manhattan elites, the late 1970s were a propitious time for this to occur. The city was still in the grip of the fiscal crisis, and desperately trying to regain solvency. The EFCB still controlled the city's finances. Many of the same Manhattanites who had supported McCoy and the Ocean Hill–Brownsville local board in 1968 now had other matters on their minds. Believing the economic survival of the city was at stake, they forged a coalition, through Koch, with like-minded middle-class whites. "It was the fiscal crisis," wrote Martin Shefter, a leading authority on the politics of the austerity years,

> that altered the priorities of many people who had formerly allied with blacks, thereby making it feasible for Koch to forge a support coalition composed not only of those who backed him because of his attacks on black leaders but also of those who were prepared to back him despite these attacks. . . . The elite civic associations and newspapers, which only a few years before had joined in a call for opening the city's political system to blacks, did not press [government officials] to accede to the demand[s] of [blacks]. Evidently, they regarded the municipal government regaining access to the market as more important than the concerns that had animated them in . . . the Ocean Hill–Brownsville controversy.[41]

The *Times,* for example, now supported the EFCB's austerity measures, as it had backed the Ocean Hill–Brownsville local board a decade earlier, "for the good of the city." Koch's political skills were such that he brought Manhattan and outer-borough whites — the *New York Times* and the UFT — together.

Koch identified proudly and unapologetically with the city's middle class population.[42] He also had the middle-class striver's grudging admiration for the well-to-do and powerful, despite his cultural unease with them. His main interest, in a break from previous New York City mayors, lay in the private, not the public, sector; he felt the future of the city was bound up with growth and job creation in private industry. He believed in competition, property, and equality of treatment. "You know," he once said, seeking to define his administration, "there are some people, the ideologues, who believe it's a sin to make a buck, that somehow or other the government should own all the property. I am not one of those people. I believe that government sets the climate for jobs and profits in the private sector. That's what this administration is seeking to do, so you can get jobs for people."[43] "It's not the function of government," he said on another occasion, "to create jobs on the public payroll."[44]

The two themes animating Koch's political career—disillusionment with blacks and respect for the private sector—came together in his approach to the city's ongoing fiscal crisis during his first term in office, from 1978 to 1981. He continued Beame's austerity policies, working closely with the EFCB to extend the freeze on welfare benefits and housing allowances that his predecessor had instituted. Koch closed numerous municipally owned hospitals, virtually all of them in black neighborhoods. He raised tuition at the City University, which by the late 1970s had a largely minority clientele. He reduced the level of basic municipal services—including sanitation and fire—that were especially important in poor black neighborhoods. And he took special delight in attacking black "poverty pimps," as he termed them, in the city's community action apparatus. Proving once again how precarious power derived from community action agencies could be, Koch moved to "reorganize" the city's antipoverty program so that he could control it personally. Ignoring charges of "genocide" from outraged black leaders, he made virtually every position of responsibility in a community action or antipoverty organization a mayoral appointment. Koch established a special office of patronage in City Hall so he could reward or punish according to circumstances. By the end of his first term, Koch appointees served in every black neighborhood in the city.[45]

At the same time, Koch was working to satisfy both his white middle- and upper-class constituencies. He lowered general municipal taxes, and reduced property taxes on the one- to three-family homes owned by many of his outer-borough supporters. He sought to aid real estate developers and financial interests with lowered business taxes and favorable zoning regulations.[46] During the Koch years, the city "gave priority in public investment, tax relief, and economic development to the central business district, while leaving outlying areas . . . to fend for themselves."[47] These growth-oriented policies, reminiscent of those of Robert Moses, sparked a real estate construction boom in the city's downtown during the 1980s. Koch increased development spending 72 percent during his first term alone, stimulating enormous growth in the city's "service" sector—real estate, banking, finance, law, and insurance.[48] By 1981, the city budget was balanced, and the EFCB disbanded, its mission complete.

Black New Yorkers waited in vain for white elites to offer support in their unsuccessful battle against Koch's austerity policies. In boardrooms and editorial offices, Ocean Hill–Brownsville was now a distant memory. As Martin Shefter observed, the black community "received little support from their upper middle-class and upper-class allies of the 1960s in fighting against Koch's reorganization of the city's poverty program, his closing of municipal hospitals, and his efforts to control the costs of redistributive programs. . . . [T]he support of those whites who had had a standing alliance with blacks in the 1960s [was] a prerequisite for the political victories of nonwhite New Yorkers. Such alliances [were] uncommon [after] 1975, however. . . . [T]his political isolation of blacks . . . largely neutralized the opposition of nonwhites to the city's post–fiscal crisis regime."[49] By the late 1970s, the same Manhattan whites who had backed Rhody McCoy and the Ocean Hill–Brownsville local board had become fixated on restoring the economic health of the city. They believed that support for the black community was a luxury they could not afford. Money—or the lack thereof—was talking.

The black community now stood virtually alone in New York City. The *Times,* the businessmen of the New York Urban Coalition, the Manhattan political class— all had edged away. In the decade following Ocean Hill–Brownsville, the city's politics and culture had undergone a profound change, what one historian has described as "a wholesale shift in power and normative values."[50] White New Yorkers of all classes now agreed generally on the rules and definitions of social, economic, and political life in New York—on the way the city should "work." And white middle-class definitions—Edward Koch's definitions, and Albert Shanker's as well—had carried the day. "Equality," according to these definitions, meant identical treatment under the law, but not equal group outcomes. Koch would use this understanding of equality often during his three mayoral terms, as he fought to limit the city's affirmative action program. Koch's conceptions of competition and individualism also dominated the city during the 1980s, as real estate and financial interests, turned loose by the mayor, helped create a culture of open, unapologetic acquisitiveness. Koch's New York fit the title of a book authored by two of his *Village Voice* critics—"city for sale"—even better than they knew. Except to deny the title's implication of ethical impropriety, Koch would have had no quarrel with this description. After all, it was not "a sin to make a buck."[51]

By the early 1980s, the private sector had achieved, at the very least, parity with the public sector in New York's economic and political culture. While the city had not abandoned its tradition of government assistance to its poorest residents, that commitment had been compromised in a way that would have given pause to Fiorello La Guardia, had he been alive to see it, and which did indeed give pause to John Lindsay. In the words of historian Joshua Freeman, "the social, ethical, and political environment of the city had been forever changed. In a few short years, financial leaders, politicians allied with them, and conservative intellectuals had succeeded in at least partially prying the city from its working-class, social democratic heritage."[52] Whites had even appropriated the idea of "community," as the events at Forest Hills and Canarsie had so graphically shown. Wherever one looked in the city—in politics, in economic policy, in cultural life—white New York had triumphed.

The 1980s were a bitter, frustrating decade for the city's black population. As the city's financial outlook brightened, Koch restored the budget cuts of the fiscal crisis years, and even expanded social service spending. But black anger now transcended economics—it was cultural, and when directed at Koch personally, visceral.[53] Isolated in Edward Koch's New York, many blacks began to refer derisively to the city as "up South." In the latter part of the decade, however, a new coalition of blacks and white liberals began to form around David Dinkins, a moderate black "pol" who had spent much of his career aligned with the regular Democratic organization in the city. Dinkins challenged Koch, who was running for an unprecedented fourth term, in the 1989 Democratic mayoral primary. Aided by Koch's abrasive personal style, which, after twelve years, had begun to grate on the voters, and by the racially motivated murder of a black teenager named Yusuf Hawkins by a group of white Brooklyn thugs, Dinkins defeated Koch. He then squeaked through in the general election against Republican Rudolph Giuliani to become New York's first African-American mayor.

Dinkins's single term in office, however, would be the exception that proved the rule of outer-borough white middle-class dominance in the city. White, not black, voters provided Dinkins with his slim margin of victory. He was the black candidate least calculated to threaten New York's whites, largely because he was a veteran of "retail" politics, having attended more white ethnic festivals, parades, and celebrations than any other politician in the city. And the Yusuf Hawkins murder, coming only two weeks before the Democratic primary with Koch, lent an aura of racial expiation to the Dinkins victory. But as mayor, Dinkins was unable to overcome the same attitudes that had fueled white middle-class anger during the Ocean Hill–Brownsville controversy, the fiscal crisis, and the Koch years. In August 1991, an Orthodox Jew driving in the Crown Heights section of Brooklyn accidentally struck and killed a black youngster playing on the sidewalk. When neighborhood blacks took to the streets in protest, Dinkins held police back for three nights, fearing that their presence would only provoke the demonstrators further. He lost his gamble. The protest turned violent, with Jews assaulted on the streets, sometimes in full view of television cameras. One, Yankel Rosenbaum, was pinned against a parked car and stabbed to death by a black youth, as the mob surrounding him shouted "kill the Jew!" By the time Dinkins belatedly ordered the police into the neighborhood in full force, his reputation among whites as a racial conciliator lay in ruins.

A second racially charged incident, in which Dinkins again hesitated to act decisively, further eroded his credibility with New York's white population. In January 1990, an argument between the Korean owner of a grocery store in a Brooklyn ghetto neighborhood and his black customer sparked a lengthy protest and boycott by black activists, organized by erstwhile Brooklyn CORE leader Sonny Carson—who had been among those threatening to carry white teachers out "in pine boxes" during the Ocean Hill–Brownsville dispute. The grocery owner and the customer gave widely divergent accounts of the precipitating incident. The Korean accused the customer of shoplifting, while the latter claimed she had merely been "haggling" over the price, and that the owner had struck her. Carson and his supporters marched in front of the grocery for almost a year, demanding that the "Korean bloodsucker" leave their community. Dinkins worked quietly behind the scenes to compromise the issue, without success. He refused, however, to take the step demanded by white supporters of the grocery owner—that he cross the picket line and make a symbolic purchase in the store—till eight months had passed, and even then, grudgingly and reluctantly. The grocery eventually left the neighborhood.

By 1993, when Dinkins ran for reelection, opposed once again by Rudolph Giuliani, most middle-class whites in the city viewed him as an apologist for black reverse bigotry and for according blacks "special treatment." He was now just another symbol of the black New York whites mistrusted and feared. Enough of the middle-class whites who had supported him in 1989 now recrossed the color line to elect Giuliani.

The two incidents that destroyed the mayoralty of David Dinkins—the Crown Heights riot and the Korean grocery boycott—also proved that, twenty-five years after Ocean Hill–Brownsville, black and white New Yorkers continued to view the same events, the same ideas, the same words, in markedly different ways. Whites, for example, saw the events at Crown Heights as a simple case of black racism, in which blacks sank to the same level as the white bigots who had murdered Yusuf Hawkins two years earlier. To blacks, however, the killing of a poor black boy by an Orthodox Jew, accidental as it may have been, symbolized the disparate power relations between blacks and Jews in Crown Heights, where a well-organized, politically well-connected Orthodox community controlled more than its fair share of services and influence. Whites saw the Korean grocery boycott as a black attempt to destroy a hardworking small businessman, and an example of the black community's own lack of initiative. Why, they asked, didn't blacks open such stores themselves? Blacks, in turn, cited Asian domination of small businesses in black neighborhoods. Why, they asked, didn't blacks have the same access to capital and credit as did Koreans? Well intentioned as he was, David Dinkins could not convince black and white New Yorkers to answer these questions in mutually acceptable ways. Driven by the forces of race and memory that Ocean Hill–Brownsville unleashed, they pulled ever farther apart.

Rudolph Giuliani was elected mayor in 1993 with 5 percent of the black vote. A native of Brooklyn, whose philosophy, in the words of a contemporary observer, "was largely shaped in white ethnic neighborhoods and Catholic schools," Giuliani set up the quintessential white middle-class regime. He moved quickly to cut Al Sharpton, an influential street organizer and black spokesman known for racially incendiary rhetoric, out of the city's political equation; for years, Giuliani refused even to utter his name in public. He ended affirmative action programs for minority contractors doing business with the city, cut welfare rolls by 250,000 during the first two years of his administration, and, most notably, used aggressive policing techniques to drastically lower the city's violent crime rate.[54]

In so doing, Giuliani moved issues relating to culture to the center of the city's political debate. And he did not hesitate to make questions of black lower-class behaviors, whether they involved crime, welfare, education, or the idea of individual initiative generally, into symbolic cultural dividing lines for the entire city. He thus replicated the racially stratified perceptual fault lines of Ocean Hill–Brownsville. Most white New Yorkers viewed Giuliani as a strong, fair leader unwilling to permit what they considered to be the flawed values of the black poor to filter into the city's cultural mainstream. Black New York, which bitterly opposed his successful 1997 reelection campaign, regarded him as a racist, intent on delegitimizing its values. White and black New Yorkers differed markedly in their reactions to the most incendiary issue of the Giuliani administration, that of police behavior. Blacks regarded the 1997 sodomizing of Abner Louima, and the fatal shootings of Amadou Diallo in 1999 and Patrick Dorismond in 2000, as products of a culture of violence against black males that, they felt, Giuliani encouraged. Most whites viewed these incidents as regrettable aberrations, and in no way indicative of ongoing patterns of racist behavior within the city's police department.

Despite his apotheosis in the eyes of the national media in the wake of his leadership of the city after the September 11, 2001, attacks on the World Trade

Center, Rudolph Giuliani has been no more successful in escaping the ghosts of Ocean Hill–Brownsville than his predecessors. The controversies of his mayoralty, as well as the Crown Heights disturbance and the Korean grocery boycott, showed that while the specific identities of the contending parties had changed since Ocean Hill–Brownsville—with the exception of the ubiquitous Sonny Carson—the issues dividing black and white New Yorkers had not. At Ocean Hill–Brownsville, blacks offered alternative definitions of equality, racism, and pluralism and different understandings of the role of competition and individualism, and raised questions about the place of "middle-class" values in city life. Whites rejected these alternative approaches. At Ocean Hill–Brownsville and in the years beyond, they imposed their own definitions and understandings on the civic culture by dint of greater numbers and influence. In so doing, whites appropriated the idea of "community" that had once appeared so promising to blacks, and forged a link between "middle-class" values and whiteness.

These divisions were profound enough to survive even in the emotional aftermath of the September 11 attacks. As outside observers spoke of a city suddenly united by tragedy, a bitter mayoral race belied their words. During the Democratic primary campaign in September, candidate Fernando Ferrer, who was supported by Al Sharpton, claimed to represent "the other New York," composed of minorities and the poor, against the white, prosperous New York of Rudolph Giuliani.[55] Ferrer was defeated by a white candidate, Mark Green, who, despite his own liberal credentials, capitalized on white fears of the extent of Sharpton's influence in a potential Ferrer administration. In November's general election, Green, now perceived as the "black" candidate by the city's white community, lost to Republican Michael Bloomberg, who had received Giuliani's endorsement. Black and white voting patterns in the election were sharply bifurcated. Green won the city's black vote by 71 to 25 percent, but lost among whites by 60 to 38 percent.[56] In the midst of what was being hailed as a period of unprecedented racial amity, black and white New Yorkers continued to define themselves against each other. Their perceptual differences, it was clear, would outlive the Giuliani administration in the new, post–September 11 city.

Regardless of the outcome of individual mayoral elections, the values of black New Yorkers will not disappear. They will be a crucial element in the battle for control of the culture and politics of the city in the coming decades. These decades threaten to be the most racially fractious in city history. Like Jews in the 1960s, Latinos and Asians are making their peace with New York's white population, creating the potential for blacks to become more isolated than ever. In the future, white New Yorkers must decide if it is in the best interests of the city—or even their own more narrowly defined interests—for this to occur. Perhaps the most important service white New Yorkers can perform for the city and for themselves is to allow blacks to carve out their own definition of what it means to be black and middle-class. Whites must accept the possibility that this definition will be different, perhaps substantially so, from theirs.

Black New Yorkers also have responsibilities in this regard. They were themselves partially complicit in the process by which middle-class values became linked with white identity, at Ocean Hill–Brownsville and elsewhere. They must do more than offer a critique of the cultural weaknesses of white New York. They must begin to reclaim an array of values from their primary association with whiteness, even in the face of charges of "Uncle Tomism" from some of their own brethren. Black New Yorkers cannot afford to allow their struggle to define a middle-class identity to be sidetracked into ambiguity and indirection, as Albert Vann and Leslie Campbell did at Ocean Hill–Brownsville. The ATA's ambivalence about endorsing "whiteness" is a luxury black New York simply cannot afford in the city of the twenty-first century.

It is also unrealistic for both blacks and whites to put their faith, as some contemporary critics, activists, and historians appear to do, in the disappearance of the category of "whiteness" itself as a solution to the city's and the nation's racial problems.[57] Neither the events of the Ocean Hill–Brownsville controversy, nor the decades that followed, offer much encouragement in this regard. Black and white New Yorks will continue to exist for the foreseeable future, not least because black and white New Yorkers may need them more than they will admit. The claims of race and memory are powerful and ongoing.

9

OCEAN HILL–BROWNSVILLE,

NEW YORK, AMERICA

Perhaps more than any other single event in any American city, the Ocean Hill–Brownsville controversy encapsulated the angst and irony of our nation's race relations in the 1960s and 1970s. Virtually every city in the nation had its own version of Ocean Hill–Brownsville during these years, a moment when blacks and whites realized, whether in the course of a busing crisis, an outbreak of urban unrest, a police brutality dispute, or a racially freighted electoral contest, that they lived in different worlds. These moments, taken as a whole, continue to affect the everyday transcripts of race relations in the United States—what are known as "infrapolitics"—today.[1] In this sense, New York, so often described as unique and unrepresentative of the rest of the nation, epitomized it. New York's story was America's story, too.

That story is, in many respects, one in which economic structures created a culture. In cities across the United States after World War II, the disappearance of industrial jobs and the creation of a segregated housing market by government officials and private developers trapped poor blacks in geographic, economic, and political isolation.[2] Out of this isolation grew an alternative culture, one that was sharply critical of the prevailing assumptions of the dominant white culture, and indeed, defined itself in terms of what white culture was not.

This black cultural critique was a powerful one. It exposed the weak underside of American national values: mindless materialism, rampant individualism, and invidious competition. Yet it would be a mistake to interpret the ideas of critics like Albert Vann and Leslie Campbell in New York and elsewhere as a blanket rejection of upward mobility and achievement in American society. Their message was more subtle. "White" values were harmful because they rewarded attributes which the white community privileged. Resources present in the black community, they argued, also deserved recognition as a form of currency in the American national marketplace. The nuances of this critique, however, may have been lost on both middle-class whites and lower-class blacks, who, each for their own reasons, assumed the incompatibility of black racial authenticity and middle-class status. By associating cooperative mutuality with black society and competitive individualism with whites, each helped define lower-class behaviors as essentially "black" in character, and middle-class behaviors as "white." Vann, Campbell, and other critics themselves contributed to this misapprehension through their anti-white rhetorical excesses, which often gave the appearance of endorsing a refusal to engage American values on any terms.

As a result, middle-class blacks, some thirty years after Ocean Hill–Brownsville and its equivalents around the United States, still struggle to define themselves in local and national culture. Ocean Hill–Brownsville's legacy is a black middle class distrustful of its own success, and ambivalent as to whether it is indeed possible, in W. E. B. Du Bois's famous words of almost a century ago, "for a man to be both a Negro and an American."[3] A culture in which high-achieving black students often ask themselves if they are "acting white," and in which middle-class black youth affect the "gangsta" posture of the hip-hop world, is a product of the misunderstanding, in both the black and white communities, of the message of men like Campbell and Vann.[4] Ocean Hill–Brownsville, and events like it nationwide, then, may have locked both races into a rigid and essentialist definition of what a "real" black American "should" be. They made it infinitely more difficult for Du Bois's dream of a full, mature black American identity, free of the stunting "doubleness" that limited its possibilities, to come true.[5]

But Vann and Campbell's message, however it may have been unjustly misinterpreted, had inherent flaws of its own. Neither man—nor many of the supporters of the Ocean Hill–Brownsville local board in the black community—could resist the siren call of anti-Jewish scapegoating, which ultimately offered that community so little. Local board supporters argued during the strikes that the UFT employed the issue of black anti-Semitism as a red herring, a distraction from the "real" educational questions that underlay the controversy. There was some truth to this.

Shanker eagerly, almost gleefully, circulated copies of some of the more egregious pieces of hate literature around the city to drum up support for the union. But there was enough other material in the public domain to go around, including the "Hey, Jew boy" poem read by Campbell on WBAI, and the outbursts that appeared under Vann's auspices in the *African-American Teachers Forum,* including attacks on "the Jew, our great liberal friend of yesterday, whose cries of anguish still resound from the steppes of Russia to the tennis courts at Forest Hills . . . [who] keeps our children ignorant."[6] Exaggerated by Shanker or not, black anti-Semitism was a real and deeply troubling issue in the Ocean Hill–Brownsville controversy. Vann, Campbell, and other progenitors and abettors of anti-Jewish sentiment in the city's black community during the Ocean Hill–Brownsville crisis must bear responsibility for their actions. The community control experiment epitomized black New York's quest for agency, for a leading role in shaping its destiny.[7] "Agency," of course, is a relative term, and the opportunities for black Americans to exercise it fully were historically circumscribed. But enough of it existed at Ocean Hill–Brownsville to make it justifiable to demand accountability from the black community. Black actors at Ocean Hill–Brownsville did not have the same degree of autonomy as white ones, but they had enough to be responsible for racist words and violent deeds, as well as for silence in the face of the racism and violence of others. Their choice to engage in or tolerate Jew-baiting was ultimately a human one, largely independent of the constraints of political and economic disempowerment. As human beings—as agents—they cannot elide the consequences of this choice.

The existence of anti-Jewish sentiment in the black community during the Ocean Hill–Brownsville dispute, while obviously reprehensible on its own terms, also damaged the community in a more basic way. It robbed black leaders of the moral authority they needed to give their message weight in the political dialogue of the city. It was, of course, unfair to ask black leaders to themselves be paragons of racial and ethnic tolerance in order to have their broader arguments taken seriously by whites, who had racial biases of their own. But it was the unique nature of the civil rights movement as, above all, a moral crusade, that made it difficult for black activists to exhibit the same weaknesses, inconsistencies, and prejudices as whites and still retain credibility in a white-dominated political landscape. The taint of anti-Semitism allowed white audiences in New York to write off men like Vann and Campbell on moral grounds, because they did not appear to live up to the principles of the movement they claimed to represent. Whites did not feel obligated to take seriously criticisms of their culture and values offered by black leaders whose own hands appeared to be unclean.

The issue of black anti-Semitism thus robbed New York's black community of essential strength during the Ocean Hill–Brownsville crisis by allowing whites to focus on the alleged moral imperfections of the messengers, and not their message itself. As a local and national phenomenon during the late 1960s, the anti-Jewish impulse was as tragic as it was unnecessary; it gave white New Yorkers, and white Americans, an excuse to ignore what was, for them, an uncomfortable message.

In particular, Ocean Hill–Brownsville gave Jewish New Yorkers, especially those residing in the outer boroughs, an excuse to ignore black New York's anguish, and turn toward unambiguous expressions of white identity. The crisis illustrated the historic power and attraction of "whiteness" in city and national life for marginalized nonblack groups. For decades, New York's Jews had straddled the white and nonwhite worlds of the city, attracted by aspects of each. The result was a form of cosmopolitanism that contributed to New York's uniquely open atmosphere in the twentieth century. But under the pressures of Ocean Hill–Brownsville, Jewish New Yorkers began to view this middle ground as exposed and vulnerable. The benefits of white identity—and white privilege—now became clear to them. Black leaders appeared indifferent to expressions of anti-Semitism at best, and, at worst, accomplices to it. The Jewish foothold in the city's economy appeared to be at risk. And white Catholics, after years of hostility, were offering a race-based safe haven from black attacks. Under these circumstances, it is not surprising that many outer-borough Jews chose "whiteness" over cosmopolitanism.[8]

In making this choice, Jews were following a familiar historical path, one that other non-Protestant whites, including the Irish, Italian, Polish, and Slavic Catholics with whom they were now aligning, had already traversed. Yet, unlike these Catholic groups, there was little sense of triumphalism in the journey of New York's Jews to whiteness. Jews chose this identity not so much because they wished to, but because they believed they had no choice. In truth, unlike other non-Protestant white groups who sought the privileges of whiteness, Jews came to it with ambivalence, almost with resignation. They must have realized that while whiteness had obvious economic, political, and social advantages, it also had its price. Whiteness, a cultural homogenizer, diminished the distinctive fabric of Jewish life in New York. Jews may have used whiteness, as other groups did before them, to define themselves against blacks; and thus gain acceptance and security in the mainstream of city life. But in so doing, they left behind some of their own unique identity, and robbed the city of a mediator between black and white New Yorks. "Whiteness" may have empowered New York's Jews, but it diminished them as well. And their journey to whiteness, which Ocean Hill–Brownsville completed, left the city much less able to cope with the consequences of racial difference.

Ocean Hill–Brownsville was also a local manifestation of a national cultural debate between black and white Americans during the late 1960s over the nature of "equality" in their society. The question of the meaning of "equality," of course, is central to the ongoing American struggle to define a national identity. It has been with us since the nation's beginnings, asked over and over, in many different guises, throughout our history. At Ocean Hill–Brownsville and elsewhere, black citizens took aim at the institutional barriers they viewed as impeding the realization of full "equality," a word they defined in terms of rough equivalence of group outcome. The issues of the fairness of civil service examinations and student "tracking" were perfect vehicles for black activists at Ocean Hill–Brownsville to express this results-oriented understanding of "equality." White teachers responded with a defense of competitive educational practices that explicitly provided for "winners" and "losers" in the race for distribution of rewards. Both sides, then, were articulating classic definitions of "equality" with deep roots in the American past.

But it was the presence of race that gave these arguments their harsh, vituperative edge. During the late 1960s, issues of equality and racial justice intersected in American life as they had not done since Reconstruction. In 1963, during his "I Have a Dream" speech at the March on Washington, Martin Luther King had won the hearts of white UFT teachers like Fred Nauman by defining equality in procedural and individual terms. By asking that blacks be judged by "the content of their character," he allowed whites like Nauman merely to reaffirm their already existing understandings of "equality." But by 1968, with civil rights leaders, including King, calling for a national commitment to an expanded definition of equality that promised substantive equivalence of condition, self-professed racial liberals like Fred Nauman began to pull away, setting the stage for a new debate during the succeeding three decades over equality and race in American life.

That debate, of course, would center around affirmative action, and its ground-level battles over jobs, promotions, and school admissions in thousands of localities across the United States would mark the fundamental racial dividing line in late twentieth-century America. Ocean Hill–Brownsville's struggle between black critics and white defenders of the Board of Examiners system, then, was an early, local manifestation of what would become a national argument. Today, the profound perceptual differences between blacks and whites over the meaning of equality threaten to overwhelm attempts at racial reconciliation. They are a bone in the throats of members of both races for reasons that go beyond their obvious practical consequences. The question of equality is built into the cultural fabric of our nation, and cannot be put to rest. Ocean Hill–Brownsville showed New Yorkers, and Americans, that the battle over this question would be racialized, vicious, and open-ended.

Another such national battle with roots in the Ocean Hill–Brownsville crisis involved what would eventually become known as multiculturalism. At Ocean Hill–Brownsville and elsewhere during the late 1960s, blacks and whites argued over the parameters of American pluralism. The ATA's "radical pluralist" challenge to the UFT was emblematic of the assault on the conceptions of broad cultural unity in which white Americans professed to believe, as well as an effort to distinguish the black experience in America from that of European immigrant groups. The black experience, the ATA argued, was unique. The involuntary nature of blacks' arrival, the ongoing reality of racial prejudice, and the historic privileges accorded whiteness in America made it impossible to project the story of white immigrants onto theirs. Radical pluralism demanded that the nation acknowledge a distinct group history of black Americans, one that could not be situated neatly within a common American narrative.

It is ironic that the immediate targets of the ATA's attacks—white UFT teachers—themselves professed a commitment to telling the "real" history of black Americans. The teachers had worked for the inclusion of black history in the curriculum of the New York City public schools, reversing years of neglect and stereotyping. Like many self-professed racial liberals, they were mystified and hurt by accusations of racism. What they may have only dimly realized at the time, however, and what would become clearer over the next thirty years, was how profoundly different their understandings of pluralism were from those of their critics in the black community. It was, indeed, as if blacks and whites were describing two separate Americas, each with its own distinct narrative of national identity.

The rivalry between these narratives would affect black and white Americans in other ways. Citizens who view themselves as occupying different cultural worlds will be much less likely to offer each other economic or political support in a crisis, as the actions of white middle-class New Yorkers during the city's fiscal retrenchment illustrated. Ocean Hill–Brownsville, then, was a harsh lesson in the practical consequences of cultural difference. Whether or not white New Yorkers were justified in their anger upon discovering the perceptual gap that separated them from the city's black population, this sense of cultural apartness translated into a denial of obligations toward the black community. The existence of cultural disconnection, then, destroyed a vital human connection. Ocean Hill–Brownsville showed that the social costs of competing cultural narratives in American life were high.

The alternative narratives offered by the ATA and similar groups would eventually engage the philosophical descendants of both Leslie Campbell and Fred Nauman. During the 1970s, 1980s, and 1990s, they would have as little success reconciling their versions of pluralism as did the protagonists at Ocean Hill–Brownsville. The questions of whether the United States will have a common culture, what that culture will look like, and, indeed, whether it even needs one, may well be the most important the nation will face in the twenty-first century. They will inevitably be intertwined with the question Du Bois famously predicted would be the most important in the America of the twentieth century—that of the "color line," or race—rendering them infinitely more complicated.[9]

Thus, Ocean Hill–Brownsville, which its supporters had hoped would symbolize the socially transformative potential of "community," instead illustrated the ways in which cultural disagreements could destroy community. Yet Ocean Hill–Brownsville may have given Americans a glimpse of the work necessary to achieve a new, more durable community in the future. In that sense it made a contribution to a truly "pluralistic" New York and nation, if only as a cautionary example.

Ocean Hill–Brownsville symbolized the closing of doors, the end of illusions, for both New York City and America. It taught liberals—as well as social democrats like Michael Harrington, Bayard Rustin, and A. Philip Randolph, who dreamed of a class-based alliance between the black poor and the white middle class—that race was more powerful than economics. It made it impossible for elite leaders like John Lindsay, McGeorge Bundy, and John Doar to address the aspirations and fears of middle-class whites.[10] It severely damaged the idea of community action as an instrument of social change. And, perhaps most harmful of all to the black community, it exposed local control's false promise of self-empowerment. Instead, in the words of Nicholas Lemann, it made the black poor "dependent on the largesse of the power structure [they] intended to confront."[11]

Ultimately, Ocean Hill–Brownsville epitomized the classic ironies of race relations in the United States during the late 1960s. Because of the historic effects of racism and poverty, blacks demanded and received special treatment in the form of community control. Community control was designed to facilitate black empowerment and self-respect. But whites, viewing special privilege as undeserved and illegitimate, refused to offer blacks this measure of respect, and indeed, interpreted community control as merely another badge of black inferiority. Moreover, since America is a procedurally egalitarian nation, it was only a matter of time before whites demanded and received the same treatment as blacks, and appropriated the mechanism of community control for their own uses. And this, of course, left blacks once again disadvantaged. Envisioned by blacks as an instrument of uplift, community control instead illustrated the distance they still needed to travel to achieve equality in America.

Yet by the 1960s, most white middle-class New Yorkers believed this "equality" had already been achieved. Indeed, they believed that New York was less racist, and more pluralistic, than at any time in its history. Ocean Hill–Brownsville's significance lay in the fundamentally opposed black and white understandings of the realities of daily life in New York, and the United States as a whole. All over the nation during the late 1960s and early 1970s, whites were discovering the dispiriting truth that despite civil rights legislation, nascent political empowerment, and the War on Poverty, blacks—regardless of class background—were deeply ambivalent about the state of race relations in the United States. Black and white Americans viewed the same events, the same institutions, the same words, the same ideas, in ways that had little or no relation to each other. In 1965, for example, as Watts burned only five days after the signing of the Voting Rights Act— a law which many whites assumed had completed the civil rights revolution in America—whites wondered how a city like Los Angeles without a ghetto that they could even discern could erupt, apparently spontaneously. Why didn't blacks see that this was their moment of triumph? In Chicago a year later, whites who assumed that the administration of Richard Daley had included the black community in its nexus of patronage and services were shocked by the anger that accompanied Martin Luther King's Chicago Freedom Movement. Why were blacks so discontented in a city that "worked" for all its citizens? And in Detroit, on the eve of that city's 1967 riot, whites pointed with pride to a city that was a magnet for Great Society funding, enjoyed a low unemployment rate, and was governed by a progressive municipal administration. Blacks saw a city rife with job and housing discrimination, dominated by a brutal, segregated police force. Much of Detroit's white population reacted to the riot with surprise and anger. Why would blacks riot when things were so good, or at the very least, getting better?

The answers, in all of these cities as well as New York, lay not in reality, but in perceived reality: blacks and whites inhabited different perceptual universes. Ocean Hill–Brownsville, once again, was a local manifestation of a national phenomenon. Whites had discovered that most blacks did not see the racial universe as they did. The work whites assumed had ended was only beginning.

American racial politics during the subsequent three decades were shaped largely by this racially demarcated perceptual chasm. It explained, for instance, why Edward Koch's expansion of social service spending levels during his second and third mayoral terms failed to increase his support in New York's black community. It also explained why Rudolph Giuliani probably was less popular among New York's black citizenry than any mayor in the city's history, despite his success in reducing the crime rate in black neighborhoods to a thirty-five-year low and creating jobs there, and notwithstanding his national status as "America's mayor" after the events of September 11. When blacks and whites argue over Giuliani's mayoralty, it is as if they are discussing two different men, just as the protagonists at Ocean Hill–Brownsville might as well have been reacting to two different sets of events. Like Fred Nauman and Rhody McCoy, they remain trapped by memory and by history's most heartbreaking lesson: it is perception, not reality, that matters most.

The identity of the city's mayor, in fact, may now be irrelevant to the two New Yorks that make up Ocean Hill–Brownsville's legacy. Having taken on a life of their own, they transcend him. They enmesh New Yorkers in a tangle of clashing attitudes and understandings that may well prove impervious even to changes in economic conditions. In the city today, blacks and whites work in the same offices, eat in the same restaurants, travel on the same subways, and, perhaps, even attend the same rap concerts, but afterwards, retreat to separate worlds. One is tempted to say that if these worlds can be reconciled anywhere, it will be in New York, city of eternal hope and renewal. But even in New York, all things are not possible. Ocean Hill–Brownsville's shadow remains a long one. Escaping it will require a degree of vision and fortitude that most of its citizens do not appear to possess at present. Until they do, Ocean Hill–Brownsville's heirs, both black and white, will search in half-light for elusive common ground, looking past each other, like strangers.

NOTES

The following source abbreviations are used throughout the notes. For full details, see the list of sources.

ATF	*African-American Teachers Forum*
Donovan Collection	Columbia Teachers College, Bernard Donovan Collection
Shapiro Collection	Columbia Teachers College, Rose Shapiro Collection
Stutz Collection	Columbia Teachers College, Rosalie Stutz Collection
UFT Collection	New York University, Elmer Holmes Bobst Library, United Federation of Teachers Collection

Introduction

1. Marilyn Gittell and Maurice Berube, eds., *Confrontation at Ocean Hill-Brownsville* (New York: Praeger, 1969), 33.
2. Henry Hampton and Steve Fayer, *Voices of Freedom: An Oral History of the Civil Rights Movement from the 1950s through the 1980s* (New York: Bantam Books, 1990), 495.
3. The first published historical scholarship on the Ocean Hill–Brownsville dispute was contained in Diane Ravitch's *The Great School Wars — New York, 1805-1973: A History of the Public Schools as Battlefield of Social Change* (New York: Basic Books, 1974), 251–398. Ravitch held supporters of the Ocean Hill–Brownsville local school board primarily responsible for the dispute, which she viewed as an example of the rise of racial extremism in New York's public education system during the 1960s. Tamar Jacoby, in the more recent *Someone Else's House: America's Unfinished Struggle for Integration* (New York: Free Press, 1998), 158–226, also blamed pro–community control supporters for the failure of interracialism in the city. Derek Edgell's *The Movement for Community Control of New York City's Schools, 1966-1970: Class Wars* (Lewiston, N.Y.: The Edwin Mellen Press, 1998), was generally more critical of the UFT position, which the author viewed as reactionary, and in some instances, racist. In "The 1968 New York City School Crisis: Teacher Politics, Racial Politics, and the Decline of Liberalism" (Ph.D. diss., Stanford University, 1994), Daniel H. Perlstein located the roots of the community control impulse in Old and New Left politics and the civil rights movement, and discussed the institutional and ideological limits to its growth. A nuanced account of John Lindsay's response to the Ocean Hill–Brownsville crisis is contained in Vincent J. Cannato, *The Ungovernable City: John Lindsay and His Struggle to Save*

New York (New York: Basic Books, 2001). Jane Anna Gordon's *Why They Couldn't Wait: A Critique of Black-Jewish Conflict Over Community Control in Ocean Hill-Brownsville* (New York: Routledge, 2001), is the most recent examination of this emotionally laden subject. See also the author's "'White' Values, 'Black' Values: The Ocean Hill–Brownsville Controversy and New York City Culture, 1965–1975," *Radical History Review* 59 (Spring 1994): 36–59, which places the dispute in the context of a broader cultural argument between black and white New Yorkers over the principles and ideas that would govern the city.

Useful participant accounts of the crisis include Rhody McCoy, "Analysis of Critical Issues and Incidents in the New York City School Crisis, 1967–1970, and Their Implications for Urban Education" (Ed.D. diss., University of Massachusetts, 1971); and Robert Rossner, *The Year Without An Autumn: Portrait of a School in Crisis* (New York: R. N. Baron, 1969). Of the numerous journalistic treatments of the Ocean Hill–Brownsville dispute, the following are the most valuable: Robert Campbell, *The Chasm* (Boston: Houghton Mifflin, 1974); Martin Mayer, *The Teachers Strike: New York, 1968* (New York: Harper & Row, 1969); Barbara Carter, *Pickets, Parents, and Power: The Story Behind the New York City Teachers' Strike* (New York: Citation Press, 1971); Miriam Wasserman, *The School Fix, NYC, USA* (New York: Outerbridge & Dienstfrey, 1970); and Naomi Levine, *Ocean Hill–Brownsville: Schools in Crisis* (New York: Popular Library, 1969). Oral histories are contained in Melvin Urofsky, ed., *Why Teachers Strike: Teachers' Rights and Community Control* (Garden City, N.Y.: Doubleday, 1970); and Hampton and Fayer, *Voices of Freedom*, 485–509. Gittell and Berube, *Confrontation at Ocean Hill-Brownsville*, provides basic primary documents, as well as contemporaneously produced articles, statements, and reports.

4. Nathan Glazer and Daniel Patrick Moynihan, *Beyond the Melting Pot: The Negroes, Puerto Ricans, Jews, Italians, and Irish of New York City* (Cambridge, Mass.: MIT Press, 1963), 299.

5. Ibid., 292–99.

6. Paul Ritterband, "Ethnic Power and the Public Schools: The New York City School Strike of 1968," *Sociology of Education* 47 (Spring 1974): 251–67.

7. See Wallace Sayre and Herbert Kaufman, *Governing New York City* (New York: Russell Sage Foundation, 1960); Jewell Bellush and Stephen David, eds., *Race and Politics in New York City: Five Studies in Policy-Making* (New York: Praeger, 1971), 3–24.

8. Nathan Glazer and Daniel Patrick Moynihan, *Beyond the Melting Pot: The Negroes, Puerto Ricans, Jews, Italians, and Irish of New York City,* 2d ed. (Cambridge: MIT Press, 1970), viii, xxix.

Chapter 1 Two New Yorks: New York City, 1945–1965

1. Joel Schwartz, *The New York Approach: Robert Moses, Urban Liberals, and Redevelopment of the Inner City* (Columbus: Ohio State University Press, 1993), 248; Harold X. Connolly, "The Economics of Blacks in Brooklyn" (unpublished paper, December 8, 1979, Brooklyn Historical Society, Brooklyn, N.Y.), 15.

2. Roger Starr, *The Rise and Fall of New York City* (New York: Basic Books, 1985), 68–70.

3. Schwartz, *The New York Approach,* 248; Connolly, "The Economics of Blacks in Brooklyn," 15.

4. Starr, *The Rise and Fall of New York City,* 68–70.

5. Judith Herman, ed., *The Schools and Group Identity: Educating for a New Pluralism* (New York: American Jewish Committee, 1974), 10–12.

6. See generally, Schwartz, *The New York Approach.*

7. See Robert A. Caro, *The Power Broker: Robert Moses and the Fall of New York* (New York: Alfred A. Knopf, 1974).

8. Eric Lichten, *Class, Power and Austerity: The New York City Fiscal Crisis* (South Hadley, Mass.: Bergin & Garvey, 1986), 75.

9. Schwartz, *The New York Approach,* xv–xxi, 108–260, 295–305; Starr, *The Rise and Fall of New York City,* 68–83.

10. Lichten, *Class, Power and Austerity,* 75; Connolly, "The Economics of Blacks in Brooklyn," 15.

11. Connolly, "The Economics of Blacks in Brooklyn," 14–16; Charles R. Morris, *The Cost of Good Intentions: New York City and the Liberal Experiment, 1960–1975* (New York: McGraw-Hill, 1980), 139. This trend was also a national one. White-collar jobs increased by approximately 8 million and blue-collar jobs declined by approximately 1.5 million in the United States between 1951 and 1962. *Wall Street Journal,* April 5, 1962, 1.

12. Morris, *The Cost of Good Intentions,* 140; Connolly, "The Economics of Blacks in Brooklyn," 16.

13. Morris, *The Cost of Good Intentions,* 140; Roger E. Alcaly and David Mermelstein, eds., *The Fiscal Crisis of American Cities* (New York: Random House, 1977), 62.

14. William Julius Wilson, *The Declining Significance of Race: Blacks and Changing America* (Chicago: University of Chicago Press, 1980), 93.

15. Starr, *The Rise and Fall of New York City,* 70.

16. This local trend also had a national parallel. Between 1952 and 1972, median American family income in inflation-adjusted dollars nearly doubled, and the percentage of American families earning over $25,000 per year grew from 3.2 to 20.5. Thomas Byrne Edsall and Mary D. Edsall, *Chain Reaction: The Impact of Race, Rights, and Taxes on American Politics* (New York: Norton, 1991), 95.

17. See Thomas Kessner, *Fiorello H. La Guardia and the Making of Modern New York* (New York: McGraw-Hill, 1984), xiv–xvi. Kessner, however, describes La Guardia as seeking to provide his bureaucracy with a "warm-hearted center to replace the boss and his machine" (xiv), an undertaking at which, as the events of the Ocean Hill–Brownsville controversy were to prove, he failed.

18. Schwartz, *The New York Approach,* 131–33, 159.

19. Starr, *The Rise and Fall of New York City,* 222; "Mitchell-Lama Act," Brownsville Community Council Papers, Folder II, Brooklyn Public Library, Brooklyn, N.Y.; David Rogers, *110 Livingston Street: Politics and Bureaucracy in the New York City School System* (New York: Random House, 1968), 62.

20. Schwartz, *The New York Approach,* xix–xx, 189–92, 198–203, 261–62, 294, 296.

21. "Metropolitan Council on Housing, 9th Annual Conference," November 18, 1967, Brownsville Community Council Papers, Folder II, Brooklyn Public Library, Brooklyn, N.Y.
22. Schwartz, *The New York Approach*, 261–62, 296.
23. Lichten, *Class, Power, and Austerity*, 85–86.
24. Starr, *The Rise and Fall of New York City*, 23.
25. See Gary Gerstle, *Working-Class Americanism: The Politics of Labor in a Textile City, 1914–1960* (Cambridge: Cambridge University Press, 1989).
26. Connolly, "The Economics of Blacks in Brooklyn," 17.
27. Stephen Cole, *The Unionization of Teachers* (New York: Praeger, 1969), 89.
28. Robert Douglas Ruth, "A Study of the Factors Affecting Teacher Attitudes and Participation in the New York City School Decentralization Controversy" (Ph.D. diss., Duke University, 1974), 162; New York City Board of Education, "Fiscal Aspects of Decentralization," June 16, 1967, 1, New York City Board of Education Papers, Bernard Donovan Collection, Box 13, Columbia Teachers College, Special Collections, Milbank Memorial Library, New York (hereafter Board of Education Papers, Donovan Collection); Naomi Levine, *Ocean Hill–Brownsville: Schools in Crisis* (New York: Popular Library, 1969), 19.
29. Morris, *The Cost of Good Intentions*, 136.
30. New York City Board of Education, "Fiscal Aspects of Decentralization," June 16, 1967, 1, Board of Education Papers, Donovan Collection; Levine, *Ocean Hill–Brownsville*, 19.
31. Diane Ravitch, *The Great School Wars—New York City, 1805–1973: A History of the Public Schools as Battleground of Social Change* (New York: Basic Books, 1974), 107–86.
32. Cole, *The Unionization of Teachers*, 95.
33. Philip Taft, *United They Teach: The Story of the United Federation of Teachers* (Los Angeles: Nash Publishing, 1974), 104, 107–51; "Reconnection for Learning: A Community School System for New York City—Report of the Mayor's Advisory Panel on Decentralization of the New York City Schools," November 9, 1967, 96, New York City Board of Education Papers, Rose Shapiro Collection, Box 8, Columbia Teachers College, Special Collections, Milbank Memorial Library, New York (hereafter "Board of Education Papers, Shapiro Collection"); Morris, *The Cost of Good Intentions*, 172; Barry Gottehrer, *The Mayor's Man: One Man's Struggle to Save Our Cities* (Garden City, N.Y.: Doubleday, 1975), 191.
34. Carlton Mabee, *Black Education in New York State* (Syracuse, N.Y.: Syracuse University Press, 1979), 285; Nathan Glazer and Daniel Patrick Moynihan, *Beyond the Melting Pot: The Negroes, Puerto Ricans, Jews, Italians, and Irish of New York City*, 2nd ed. (Cambridge, Mass.: MIT Press, 1970), xxxi.
35. Harold X. Connolly, *A Ghetto Grows in Brooklyn* (New York: New York University Press, 1977), 136, 141.
36. One of the relatively few opportunities for those without formal education to find gainful employment in postwar New York was in the construction field. The redevelopment boom sweeping the city was a fertile source of jobs for members of

the various construction trade unions. Blacks, however, were historically excluded from these unions, and black-owned firms were routinely shut out of bidding for contracts. As of 1968, not one major city contract had been awarded to a minority-owned firm. Given that 95 percent of all construction projects in New York City after World War II were publicly funded or subsidized, this effectively closed off the construction field as a window of opportunity for both black workers and firm owners. Alan A. Altshuler, *Community Control: The Black Demand for Participation in Large American Cities* (New York: Pegasus, 1970), 173; James Haughton, "The Role of the Board of Education in Perpetuating Racism in the Building Trades and Vice Versa," in *Schools Against Children: The Case for Community Control,* ed. Annette Rubinstein (New York: Monthly Review Press, 1970), 159–73.

37. For example, in 1950 over half the whites but only 18 percent of blacks in Brooklyn were classified as white-collar. Connolly, *A Ghetto Grows in Brooklyn,* 136, 141.

38. Nationally, 60 percent of the black labor force worked at unskilled or semiskilled jobs that were being liquidated at a rate of two million per year between 1947 and 1964. Speech, A. Philip Randolph, May 29, 1964, Richard Parrish Papers, Reel 1, Schomburg Center for Research in Black Culture, New York.

39. Jim Sleeper, *The Closest of Strangers: Liberalism and the Politics of Race in New York* (New York: Norton, 1990), 127–28, 142–50.

40. See Adina Back, "Up South in New York: The 1950s School Desegregation Struggles" (Ph.D. diss., New York University, 1997); Clarence Taylor, *Knocking on Our Own Door: Milton A. Galamison and the Struggle to Integrate New York City* (New York: Columbia University Press, 1997), 43, 44, 50–51.

41. Connolly, *A Ghetto Grows in Brooklyn,* 220–22; "Reconnection for Learning," 74–75, Board of Education Papers, Shapiro Collection, Box 8.

42. Marilyn Gittell and Maurice Berube, eds., *Confrontation at Ocean Hill–Brownsville* (New York: Praeger, 1969), 113, 138–40.

43. Melvin Urofsky, ed., *Why Teachers Strike: Teachers' Rights and Community Control* (Garden City, N.Y.: Doubleday, 1970), 179–80.

44. "Reconnection for Learning," 44–45, 74, Board of Education Papers, Shapiro Collection, Box 8; *New York Times,* June 7, 1966, 36; January 9, 1969, 67; Rogers, *110 Livingston Street,* 47, 62–66.

45. Barbara Carter, *Pickets, Parents, and Power: The Story Behind the New York City Teachers' Strike* (New York: Citation Press, 1971), 9; New York City Board of Education, "Achievements in Selected Areas of New York City Schools," 1968, United Federation of Teachers Collection, Record Group III, Sub-Group A, Series 2, Box 2, Folder 67, Robert F. Wagner Labor Archives, Elmer Holmes Bobst Library, New York University, New York (hereafter "UFT Collection"); "Reconnection for Learning," 90, Board of Education Papers, Shapiro Collection, Box 8; Teachers for Community Control, "Community Control is Community Responsibility," 1969, Teachers Action Caucus Papers, Box 1, Folder 1, Tamiment Institute Library, Elmer Holmes Bobst Library, New York University, New York; Vincent J. Cannato, *The Ungovernable City: John Lindsay and His Struggle to Save New York* (New York: Basic

Books, 2001), 290. Levine, *Ocean Hill–Brownsville,* 21–22; Tamar Jacoby, *Someone Else's House: America's Unfinished Struggle for Integration* (New York: Free Press, 1998), 167; *Newsweek,* October 28, 1968, 84.

46. *New York World-Telegram & Sun,* March 31, 1964, 31; Alter F. Landesman, *Brownsville: The Birth, Development and Passing of a Jewish Community in New York* (New York: Bloch Publishing, 1969).

47. Connolly, *A Ghetto Grows in Brooklyn,* 132.

48. Rogers, *110 Livingston Street,* 48.

49. Martin Mayer, *The Teachers Strike: New York, 1968* (New York: Harper & Row, 1969), 18.

50. Landesman, *Brownsville,* 371–74; Abraham P. Block, "Synagogues for Sale," *Jewish Spectator,* April 1966, 20–22; Brownsville Community Council, "Total Action Plan—1967–68," 2, Brownsville Community Council Papers, Folder II, Brooklyn Public Library, Brooklyn, N.Y.

51. Jonathan Rieder, *Canarsie: The Jews and Italians of Brooklyn Against Liberalism* (Cambridge, Mass.: Harvard University Press, 1985), 16–26, 79–80; Rogers, *110 Livingston Street,* 65–66; Sleeper, *The Closest of Strangers,* 137–38, 147.

52. Landesman, *Brownsville,* 371–74.

53. Mayer, *The Teachers Strike,* 18.

54. Only 60 percent of the eligible black population were registered to vote in Brooklyn during the 1960s. Glazer and Moynihan, *Beyond the Melting Pot,* xix.

55. Brownsville Community Council, "Total Action Plan, 1967–68," 2, Brownsville Community Council Papers, Folder II, Brooklyn Public Library, Brooklyn, N.Y.

56. Harold Savitch, "Powerless in the Urban Ghetto," *Polity* 5 (Fall 1972): 33; Gottehrer, *The Mayor's Man,* 186–87.

57. "Final Report of the Advisory Committee on Decentralization" (Niemeyer Report), July 1968, Table I, Board of Education Papers, Shapiro Collection, Box 1.

58. Gottehrer, *The Mayor's Man,* 186–87.

59. *Black Journal,* no. 5, October 1968 (WNEW-TV, New York); *New York Post,* November 5, 1966, 20; Carter, *Pickets, Parents, and Power,* 9.

60. *New York Times,* October 20, 1968, 38.

61. Urofsky, *Why Teachers Strike,* 255; *New York Times Magazine,* May 19, 1968, 66.

Chapter 2 The Rise of "Community"

1. "Reconnection for Learning: A Community School System for New York City—Report of the Mayor's Advisory Panel on Decentralization of the New York City Schools," November 9, 1967, 73–75, Shapiro Collection, Box 8.

2. Robert A. Caro, *The Power Broker: Robert Moses and the Fall of New York* (New York: Random House, 1974), 850–94; Charles R. Morris, *The Cost of Good Intentions: New York City and the Liberal Experiment, 1960–1975* (New York: McGraw-Hill, 1980), 19.

3. David Rogers, *110 Livingston Street: Politics and Bureaucracy in the New York City Schools* (New York: Random House, 1968), 266–323; Melvin Urofsky, ed., *Why Teachers Strike: Teachers' Rights and Community Control* (Garden City, N.Y.: Double-

day, 1970), 7. The educational bureaucracy at 110 Livingston Street was so vast and unruly that no exact determination of the number of administrators at work there could be made. Jewel Bellush and Stephen M. David, eds., *Race and Politics in New York: Five Studies in Policy-Making* (New York: Praeger, 1971), 139.

4. Rogers, *110 Livingston Street,* 274; Urofsky, *Why Teachers Strike,* 7–8.
5. Rogers, *110 Livingston Street,* 23, 49–50, 102–4.
6. Ibid., 17, 23–25; *New York Times,* February 4, 1964, 1.
7. Rogers, *110 Livingston Street,* 30.
8. *New York Times,* January 29, 1964, 43.
9. Rogers, *110 Livingston Street,* 25, 30–31, 238–39.
10. See Philip Bundick, "My People," *New York Recorder,* February 15, 1964, 2; March 14, 1964, 2.
11. Rogers, *110 Livingston Street,* 31–33, 75, 255, 397–99.
12. Ibid., 75–79, 82–83, 88–92, 398–99.
13. *New York Post,* September 20, 1964, 45; Rogers, *110 Livingston Street,* 79.
14. *New York Times Magazine,* September 20, 1964, 46.
15. Rogers, *110 Livingston Street,* 76; *New York Times Magazine,* September 20, 1964, 46; *New York Times,* March 13, 1964, 23.
16. *New York Times Magazine,* September 20, 1964, 48, 49.
17. Ibid., 48. See also Rogers, *110 Livingston Street,* 86–87, 89.
18. *New York Times Magazine,* September 20, 1964, 49; See also Kurt and Gladys Lang, "Resistance to School Desegregation: A Case Study of Backlash Among Jews," *Sociological Inquiry* 35 (Winter 1965): 104–6.
19. *New York Daily News,* August 30, 1964, 4.
20. PAT Press Release, n.d., Stutz Collection, Box 6; Rogers, *110 Livingston Street,* 87.
21. *New York Times Magazine,* September 20, 1964, 48.
22. The lives of PAT members may illustrate the separation of home and workplace that, some scholars argue, explains the political conservatism that has historically characterized many segments of white urban America. See Ira Katznelson, *City Trenches: Urban Politics and the Patterning of Class in the United States* (New York: Pantheon, 1981).
23. *New York Times Magazine,* September 20, 1964, 49. The second speaker's reference to "New York City" was characteristic of outer-borough residents who, although they themselves lived within the city limits, spoke of Manhattan as "the city."
24. Diane Ravitch, *The Great School Wars — New York City, 1805-1973: A History of the Public Schools as Battlefield of Social Change* (New York: Basic Books, 1974), 271; *New York Times,* October 3, 1963, 48; June 9, 1964, 52.
25. *New York Herald-Tribune,* September 15, 1964, 1, 5–6; *New York Times,* March 13, 1964, 1, 20; March 17, 1964, 1, 25; May 19, 1964, 1, 29.
26. *New York Times,* March 13, 1964, 20; March 17, 1964, 1.
27. *New York Herald-Tribune,* July 7, 1964, 7; August 14, 1964, 6; *New York Times.* September 25, 1964, 35; *New York World-Telegram & Sun,* January 27, 1964, 28; *New York Post,* May 14, 1964, 21.
28. *New York Herald-Tribune,* August 18, 1964, 8; October 20, 1964, 5; *New York Post,* September 8, 1963, 4.

29. *New York World-Telegram & Sun,* August 24, 1964, 19.

30. *New York Post,* May 14, 1964, 21.

31. *New York Times,* September 14, 1964, 1; October 6, 1964, 29; March 22, 1965, 35; May 17, 1965, 30; December 14, 1966, 37; Barbara Carter, *Pickets, Parents, and Power: The Story Behind the New York City Teachers' Strike* (New York: Citation Press, 1971), 147; Rogers, *110 Livingston Street,* 311.

32. *New York Times,* March 22, 1965, 35; December 14, 1966, 37.

33. Rogers, *110 Livingston Street,* 32–33, 93; *New York Times,* March 8, 1965, 30; July 3, 1967, 46; "Reconnection for Learning," 73–75, Shapiro Collection, Box 8.

34. *New York Times,* May 17, 1965, 37.

35. "Parent Leadership Training Program," n.d., Stutz Collection, Box 8; EQUAL, "Proposed Policy Statement for 1965," Stutz Collection, Box 10; Ellen Lurie, "School Integration in New York," September 1963, Stutz Collection, Box 11.

36. *New York Daily News,* August 30, 1964, 3; *New York Times,* October 3, 1963, 1; Rogers, *110 Livingston Street,* 94, 105; Ravitch, *The Great School Wars,* 271.

37. *New York Times,* October 4, 1963, 1; Rogers, *110 Livingston Street,* 94.

38. *New York Recorder,* February 1, 1964, 1; July 11, 1964, 1; Ravitch, *The Great School Wars,* 278–79; Rogers, *110 Livingston Street,* 116–21.

39. *New York Times,* January 20, 1964, 1; February 3, 1964, 1, 28; February 4, 1964, 1, 29; February 5, 1964, 1; March 13, 1964, 1, 20.

40. *New York Herald-Tribune,* January 27, 1964, 6; *New York Times,* October 3, 1963, 26

41. Martin Mayer, *The Teachers Strike: New York, 1968* (New York: Harper & Row, 1969), 17; Louis Harris and Bert E. Swanson, *Black-Jewish Relations in New York City* (New York: Praeger, 1970), xi; Rogers, *110 Livingston Street,* 93–94; Martin Shefter, *Political Crisis, Fiscal Crisis: The Collapse and Revival of New York City* (New York: Basic Books, 1985), 93; Nathan Glazer and Daniel Patrick Moynihan, *Beyond the Melting Pot: The Negroes, Puerto Ricans, Jews, Italians, and Irish of New York City,* 2nd ed. (Cambridge, Mass.: MIT Press, 1970), xix.

42. Rosalie Stutz, "Are There Any True Professionals?" EQUAL, September 21, 1967, Stutz Collection, Box 8. See also Pratt Area Community Council, "Discussion of Concepts Related to Decentratization," April 6, 1967, New York City Municipal Reference Center, "New York City Schools—Decentralization" Files, New York.

43. Pratt Area Community Council, "Discussion of Concepts Related to Decentratization."

44. See Allen J. Matusow, *The Unraveling of America: A History of Liberalism in the 1960s* (New York: Harper & Row, 1984); Nicholas Lemann, *The Promised Land: The Great Black Migration and How It Changed America* (New York: Alfred A. Knopf, 1991), 111–221.

45. Harlem Youth Opportunities Unlimited, *Youth in the Ghetto: A Study of the Consequences of Powerlessness and a Blueprint for Change* (New York: HARYOU, 1964).

46. Rogers, *110 Livingston Street,* 364–65; Ravitch, *The Great School Wars,* 294.

47. New York City Board of Education, "An Invitation to Education for a Modern World," n.d., Stutz Collection, Box 24.

48. Carter, *Pickets, Parents, and Power,* 7.

49. Ravitch, *The Great School Wars,* 280–83.

50. Mario Fantini, Marilyn Gittell, and Richard Magat, *Community Control and the Urban School* (New York: Praeger, 1970), 4.

51. *Negro Teachers Forum,* November 1966.

52. *Report of the National Advisory Commission on Civil Disorders* (Washington, D.C.: Government Printing Office, 1968), 1; Jim Sleeper, *The Closest of Strangers: Liberalism and the Politics of Race in New York* (New York: Norton, 1990), 148.

53. Barry Gottehrer, *The Mayor's Man: One Man's Struggle to Save Our Cities* (Garden City. N.Y.: Doubleday, 1975), 206.

54. See Roger Starr, *The Rise and Fall of New York City* (New York: Basic Books, 1985), 22; Shefter, *Political Crisis, Fiscal Crisis,* 84–85.

55. *New York Times,* November 2, 1968, 43.

56. Morris, *The Cost of Good Intentions, 116.*

57. Lindsay's fear of racial conflagration made him especially susceptible to the tactics of local black activists who coupled demands for financial support with predictions of street violence if they were not satisfied. Brooklyn CORE chairman Sonny Carson's June 1967 letter promising that Lindsay would "have a real cool summer" if funds for his organization were forthcoming was typical. Letter, Robert Carson to John V. Lindsay, June 7, 1967, Donovan Collection, Box 10. See also Tom Wolfe, *Radical Chic and Mau-Mauing the Flak-Catchers* (New York: Farrar, Straus & Giroux, 1970).

58. Transcript, "With Mayor Lindsay," June 9, 1968, WNEW-TV, Donovan Collection, Box 4.

59. *New York Review of Books,* June 6, 1968, 30.

60. Equal Employment Opportunity Commission, "White Collar Employment in 100 Major New York City Corporations," January 1968, 3, Brooklyn Historical Society, Brooklyn, N.Y.; Herman D. Bloch, *The Circle of Discrimination: An Economic and Social Study of the Black Man in New York* (New York: New York University Press, 1969), 237; Glazer and Moynihan, *Beyond the Melting Pot,* l, lv–lvi.

61. *New York Amsterdam News,* February 3, 1968, 4; February 17, 1968, 5; Mayer, *The Teachers Strike,* 45–46; Minutes of Meeting with Urban Coalition Education Task Force, April 29, 1968, Shapiro Collection, Box 8.

62. Ravitch, *The Great School Wars,* 346.

63. See Lawrence Cremin, *The Transformation of the School: Progressivism in American Education, 1876–1957* (New York: Knopf, 1968); Robert Westbrook, *John Dewey and American Democracy* (Ithaca, N.Y.: Cornell University Press, 1991), 506; *New York Review of Books,* October 10, 1968, 37–41.

64. Maurice R. Berube and Marilyn Gittell, "The Struggle for Community Control," in *Confrontation at Ocean Hill-Brownsville,* ed. Maurice R. Berube and Marilyn Gittell (New York: Praeger, 1969), 4, 6.

65. *New York Review of Books,* October 10, 1968, 40.

66. See Daniel H. Perlstein, "The 1968 New York City School Crisis: Teacher Politics, Racial Politics, and the Decline of Liberalism," (Ph.D. diss., Stanford University, 1994), 77–129; Celia Lewis Zitron, *The New York City Teachers Union, 1916–1964: A Story of Educational and Social Commitment* (New York: Humanities Press, 1968).

67. Perlstein, "The 1968 New York City School Crisis," 130–78.

68. *New York Times,* November 21, 1966, 34.

69. "Reconnection for Learning," 44–45, 79, Shapiro Collection, Box 8; Mayer, *The Teachers Strike,* 17.

70. *ATF,* November–December 1967; *New York Times,* September 20, 1967, 52; September 22, 1966, 34.

71. *Negro Teachers Forum,* November 1966.

72. *Report of the National Advisory Commission on Civil Disorders,* 2.

73. Maurice Isserman, *If I Had a Hammer. . . . The Death of the Old Left and the Birth of the New Left* (New York: Basic Books, 1987), 185–94; *Ramparts,* November 17, 1968, 17–25.

74. John O' Neill, "The Rise and Fall of the UFT," in *Schools Against Children: The Case for Community Control,* ed. Annette Rubinstein (New York: Monthly Review Press, 1970), 179, 180; *Ramparts,* November 17, 1968, 17–25.

75. O' Neill, "The Rise and Fall of the UFT," 177.

76. See Daniel Griffiths, *Teacher Mobility in New York: A Study of the Recruitment, Selection, Appointment, and Promotion of Teachers in the New York City Public Schools* (New York: New York University School of Education, 1963); Ramon Sanchez, "It's Hard to 'Turn On' Teachers," *Freedomways* 9 (Fall 1969): 367–72.

77. O'Neill, "The Rise and Fall of the UFT," 174–91.

78. Ibid., 177–78, 187–88; Philip Taft, *United They Teach: The Story of the United Federation of Teachers* (Los Angeles: Nash Publishing, 1974), 232–35.

79. O' Neill, "The Rise and Fall of the UFT," 178, 187.

80. "UFT Statement on Decentralization," December 11, 1967, 4, Shapiro Collection, Box 8.

81. Ibid.

82. Urofsky, *Why Teachers Strike,* 179.

83. Tamar Jacoby, "The Uncivil History of the Civilian Review Board," *City Journal* 3 (Winter 1993): 56–63.

84. Ravitch, *The Great School Wars,* 317.

85. Rogers, *110 Livingston Street,* 200; Ravitch, *The Great School Wars,* 317; "Notes on EQUAL Meeting," May 27, 1965, Stutz Collection, Box 10.

86. *Negro Teachers Forum,* November 1966.

87. Michael Parenti, "Assimilation and Counter-Assimilation: From Civil Rights to Black Nationalism," in *Power and Community: Dissenting Essays in Political Science,* ed. Philip Green and Sanford Levinson (New York: Pantheon, 1969), 186.

88. "A Plan for An Experimental School District: Ocean Hill–Brownsville," August 1967, 3, Shapiro Collection, Box 8; Mwlina Imiri Abubadika, *The Education of Sonny Carson* (New York: Norton, 1972), 9, 13, 19, 21, 82, 139, 141, 153, 158, 199; Ralph Poynter, "The UFT Against the Communities," March 15, 1968, 9, Stutz Collection, Box 25.

89. Philip Green, "Decentralization, Community Control, and Revolution: Reflections on Ocean Hill–Brownsville," in Green and Levinson, *Power and Community,* 253–54. See also, on the UFT's view of community control supporters as antidemocratic and potentially totalitarian, Rogers, *110 Livingston Street,* 199.

Chapter 3 "Black" Values, "White" Values:
Race and Culture in New York City During the 1960s

1. *New York Times*, November 2, 1968, 25; January 8, 1968, 97. The U.S. Bureau
   of Labor Statistics estimated that a family of four in New York City could live
   "modestly" for $10,195 a year in 1967. Ibid.
2. Nathan Glazer and Daniel Patrick Moynihan, *Beyond the Melting Pot: The Negroes,
   Puerto Ricans, Jews, Italians, and Irish of New York City*, 2nd ed. (Cambridge, Mass.:
   MIT Press, 1970), xxxi; John Hull Mollenkopf, *A Phoenix in the Ashes: The Rise
   and Fall of the Koch Coalition in New York City Politics* (Princeton, N.J.: Princeton
   University Press, 1992), 58; Martin Mayer, *The Teachers Strike: New York, 1968*
   (New York: Harper & Row, 1969), 17. New York maintained this high proportion
   of white residents despite losing 12.9 percent of its white population between
   1950 and 1960 and 5.3 percent between 1960 and 1965. *New York Times*, June 7,
   1966, 36; "Reconnection for Learning: A Community School System for New York
   City—Report of the Mayor's Advisory Panel on Decentralization of the New York
   City Schools," November 9, 1967, 74, New York City Board of Education Papers,
   Shapiro Collection, Box 8.
3. Roger Starr, *The Rise and Fall of New York City* (New York: Basic Books, 1985), 189;
   Ronald Formisano, *Boston Against Busing: Race, Class, and Ethnicity in the 1960s and
   1970s* (Chapel Hill: University of North Carolina Press, 1991), 12.
4. Roger Waldinger, "Changing Ladders and Musical Chairs: Ethnicity and Opportunity in Post-Industrial New York," *Politics and Society* 15 (1986–87): 383.
5. Eric Lichten, *Class, Power and Austerity: The New York City Fiscal Crisis* (South
   Hadley. Mass.: Bergin & Garvey, 1986), 67. Municipal spending on education
   doubled in New York between 1956 and 1967, and the number of educational
   personnel in the city grew by almost 60 percent in the first half of the 1960s. "Reconnection for Learning: A Community School System for New York City—Report
   of the Mayor's Advisory Panel on Decentralization of the New York City Schools,"
   November 9, 1967, 4, Shapiro Collection, Box 8; Charles R. Morris, *The Cost of
   Good Intentions: New York City and the Liberal Experiment, 1960–1975* (New York:
   McGraw-Hill, 1980), 136.
6. Daniel Griffiths, *Teacher Mobility in New York: A Study of the Recruitment, Selection,
   Appointment, and Promotion of Teachers in the New York City Public Schools* (New
   York: New York University School of Education, 1963), 35–36, 116–27.
7. Daniel N. Perlstein, "The 1968 New York City School Crisis: Teacher Politics,
   Racial Politics, and the Decline of Liberalism" (Ph.D. diss., Stanford University,
   1994), 353.
8. Christina Tree, "Grouping Pupils in New York City," *Urban Review* 3 (September
   1968): 8–15; Kenneth Clark, *Dark Ghetto: Dilemmas of Social Power* (New York:
   Harper & Row, 1965), 124.
9. Kurt Lang and Gladys Lang, "Resistance to School Desegregation: A Case Study of
   Backlash Among Jews," *Sociological Inquiry* 35 (Winter 1965): 104, 106.
10. *The Morningsider*, November 21, 1963, 9.

11. *New York Herald-Tribune,* March 26, 1964, 17, 19.
12. Tree, "Grouping Pupils in New York City," 8–15.
13. Harlem Youth Opportunities Unlimited, *Youth in the Ghetto: A Study of the Consequences of Powerlessness and a Blueprint for Change* (New York: HARYOU, 1964), 201–2.
14. Nathan Glazer, "Negroes and Jews: The New Challenge to Pluralism," *Commentary* 38 (December 1964): 32. See also Milton Himmelfarb, "How We Are," ibid., 39 (January 1965): 69–74.
15. See Nicholas Lemann, *The Big Test: The Secret History of the American Meritocracy* (New York: Farrar, Straus and Giroux, 1999).
16. Oscar Lewis, "The Culture of Poverty," *Scientific American* 215 (October 1966): 21, 25.
17. Daniel Patrick Moynihan, *The Negro Family: The Case for National Action,* (Washington, D.C.: U.S. Department of Labor, 1965); See also Nicholas Lemann, *The Promised Land: The Great Black Migration and How It Changed America* (New York: Knopf, 1991), 172–82.
18. Nathan Glazer and Daniel Patrick Moynihan, *Beyond the Melting Pot: The Negroes, Puerto Ricans, Jews, Italians, and Irish of New York City* (Cambridge, Mass.: MIT Press, 1963).
19. James Coleman et al., *Equality of Educational Opportunity* (Washington, D.C.: U.S. Office of Education, 1966); James Coleman, "Equal Schools or Equal Students?" *The Public Interest* 4 (Summer 1966): 73–74.
20. Albert Murray, "The Atomization of the New York Public Schools," January 22, 1968, 7–8, Shapiro Collection, Box 8.
21. Quoted in Jeremy Larner, "The New York School Crisis," in *The Urban School Crisis: An Anthology of Essays,* ed. Irving Howe (New York: League for Industrial Democracy/United Federation of Teachers, 1966), 11, 12.
22. United Federation of Teachers, "Plan for More Effective Schools," May 15, 1964, Stutz Collection, Box 4.
23. Joseph Alsop, "Ghetto Education," *New Republic,* November 18, 1967, 18–23; *United Teacher,* March 3, 1967, 8–9; Mayer, *The Teachers Strike,* 22.
24. Patrick Harnett, "Community Control: Solution or Sop?" *Village Voice,* November 14, 1968, 24.
25. United Federation of Teachers, "Statement on Decentralization," December 11, 1967, UFT Collection, Record Group III, Sub-Group A, Series 2, Box 2, Folder 42; *United Teacher,* December 6, 1967, 3; January 24, 1968, 26; February 17, 1967, 5; *New York Times,* September 20, 1967, 1, 36; Barbara Carter, *Pickets, Parents, and Power: The Story Behind the New York City Teachers' Strike* (New York: Citation Press, 1971), 163; Marjorie Murphy, *Blackboard Unions: The AFT and the NEA, 1900–1990* (Ithaca: Cornell University Press, 1990), 237.
26. See Gary Gerstle, *Working Class Americanism: The Politics of Labor in a Textile City, 1914–1960* (Cambridge: Cambridge University Press, 1989).
27. Glazer and Moynihan, *Beyond the Melting Pot,* 2nd ed., xxiii–xxiv.
28. New York City Board of Education, "Guidelines to Decentralization," November 8, 1961, 4, Shapiro Collection, Box 8.

29. New York City Board of Education, "Teaching About Integration," September 1966, in *Teaching About Minorities in Classroom Situations* (New York: New York City Board of Education Curriculum Bulletin, 1967–68), 1, 5, 55.

30. United Federation of Teachers, "More Effective Schools Plan," 1964, Richard Parrish Papers, Reel 3, Schomburg Center for Research in Black Culture, New York.

31. *New York Recorder,* June 8, 1966, 5, Brooklyn Historical Society, Brooklyn, N.Y.

32. UFT, "Urban Kit Program," February 6, 1967, UFT Collection, Record Group III, Sub-Group A, Series 2, Box 22, Folder 609.

33. Minutes, UFT Committee on African-American History, December 1, 1966, UFT Collection, Record Group III, Sub-Group A, Series 2, Box 22, Folder 608.

34. *United Teacher,* March 6, 1968, 9; UFT Negro History Week promotional photograph, PS 129, 1968, UFT Collection (Photographs).

35. *United Teacher,* February 3, 1967, 23.

36. UFT, "Negro History Week," PS 144, February 1969, UFT Collection, Record Group III, Sub-Group A, Series 2, Box 5, Folder 137.

37. See below, pp. 115–41. R. J. Papaleo, "How Is America Divided on the Question of Civil Rights?" (Lesson Plan, Social Studies Department, JHS 271, 1968), in author's possession.

38. Kenneth Clark, "Clash of Cultures in the Classroom," *Integrated Education* 1 (August 1963): 11, 13.

39. Richard A. Cloward and Lloyd Ohlin, *Delinquency and Opportunity: A Theory of Delinquent Gangs* (New York: Free Press, 1960); Lemann, *The Promised Land,* 122–23; Clark, *Dark Ghetto,* 54; Allen J. Matusow, *The Unraveling of America: A History of Liberalism in the 1960s* (New York: Harper & Row, 1984), 97–127, 243–71.

40. Jewel Bellush and Stephen M. David, eds., *Race and Politics in New York City: Five Studies in Policy-Making* (New York: Praeger, 1971), 26–27.

41. Clark, *Dark Ghetto,* 129, 131, 132.

42. Preston Wilcox, "The Controversy Over I.S. 201," *Urban Review* 1 (July 1966): 13–15.

43. Ibid, 15.

44. Edward Weaver, "The New Literature on Education of the Black Child," *Freedomways* 8 (Fall 1968): 375, 379.

45. Doxey Wilkerson, "Blame the Negro Child!" *Freedomways* 8 (Fall 1968), 342, 344, 346; Robert Rosenthal and Lenore Jacobson, *Pygmalion in the Classroom* (New York: Holt, Rinehart and Winston, 1968); Robert Rosenthal and Lenore Jacobson, "Teacher Expectations for the Disadvantaged," *Scientific American* 218 (April 1968): 19–23.

46. Brownsville Community Council, "A Challenge to Educational Genocide," 1968, Brownsville Community Council Papers, Folder II, Brooklyn Public Library, Brooklyn, N.Y.

47. Carter, *Pickets, Parents, and Power,* 11.

48. David McClintick and Art Sears, Jr., "Decentralized District in New York Ghetto Claims Gains in Schools," *Wall Street Journal,* April 10, 1969, 28.

49. Charles V. Hamilton, "Education in the Black Community: An Examination of the Realities," *Freedomways* 8 (Fall 1968): 319, 320, 321, 324.

50. Preston Wilcox, "Africanization: The New Input to Black Education," *Freedomways* 8 (Fall 1968): 396; *New York Amsterdam News,* May 18, 1968, 17.

51. Clark, *Dark Ghetto,* 78.

52. Clark, "Clash of Cultures in the Classroom," 13.

53. Stokely Carmichael and Charles V. Hamilton, *Black Power: The Politics of Liberation in America* (New York: Random House, 1967), 40, 65, vii.

54. Harold Cruse, *The Crisis of the Negro Intellectual* (New York: William Morrow, 1967), 89, 94, 258, 455; See also William L. Van Deburg, *New Day in Babylon: The Black Power Movement and American Culture, 1965–1975* (Chicago: University of Chicago Press, 1992), 260–72.

55. Milton Galamison, "Educational Values and Community Power," *Freedomways* 8 (Fall 1968): 311.

56. David Spencer, "A Harlem Parent Speaks," *NEA Journal* 57 (March 1968): 8–9. Spencer attempted to eliminate tracking in the IS 201 school district. Though he was unsuccessful, the district did end the public designation of "fast" and "slow" classes by number. *New York Times,* September 21, 1968, 20.

57. New York City Commission on Human Rights, "Report on Three Demonstration Projects in the City Schools," February–March 1968, 25, Donovan Collection, Box 13.

58. *Guardian,* November 30, 1968, 6.

59. *New York Amsterdam News,* December 7, 1968, 14.

60. *The Liberator,* September 1968, 2.

61. *New York Amsterdam News,* March 23, 1968, 2.

62. Mario Fantini and Gerald Weinstein, "Taking Advantage of the Disadvantaged," *Columbia Teachers College Record* 69 (November 1967): 2, 11.

63. *New York Daily News,* April 29, 1968, 10.

64. Teachers Freedom Party, "Community Control of Schools and the Interdicting of the Mass Society," 1968, 11, 16, UFT Collection, Record Group III, Sub-Group A, Series 2, Box 1, Folder 38.

65. Cruse, *The Crisis of the Negro Intellectual,* 283, 317.

66. Hamilton, "Education in the Black Community: An Examination of the Realities," 321.

67. Carmichael and Hamilton, *Black Power,* 49.

68. Wilcox, "Africanization: The New Input to Black Education," 397.

69. James Campbell, "Struggle: The Highest Form of Education," *Freedomways* 8 (Fall 1968): 413.

70. Rhody McCoy and Keith Baird, "Whose Schools?" in *The Black Experience: A Record of Summer Forums, July–August 1968* (New York: Forum of Columbia University, 1968), Schomburg Center for Research in Black Culture, New York; *New York Times,* September 18, 1968, 32.

71. Perlstein, "The 1968 New York City School Crisis," 343.

72. Ocean Hill–Brownsville Local School Board, "Report of Curriculum Advisory Committee," 1967, UFT Collection, Record Group III, Sub-Group A, Series 2, Box 1, Folder 38.

73. *Village Voice,* January 18, 1968, 40.

74. Galamison, "Educational Values and Community Power," 317.

75. *American Teacher,* April 1967, 13; *United Teacher,* January 20, 1967, 8, 9.

76. *United Teacher,* January 20, 1967, 8, 9; Edith Marlin, letter in *Changing Education,* Winter 1967, 34.

77. As reported in *United Teacher,* January 20, 1967, 6.

Chapter 4 The Ocean Hill–Brownsville Community Control Experiment

1. *New York Times,* December 20, 1966, 1, 49; December 21, 1966, 1, 32; December 22, 1966, 1, 27.

2. Barbara Carter, *Pickets, Parents, and Power: The Story Behind the New York City Teachers' Strike* (New York: Citation Press, 1971), 22–23; *United Teacher,* February 17, 1967, 5; Richard Karp, "School Decentralization in New York," *Interplay,* August–September 1968, 14.

3. Jack Bloomfield, "The Untold Story of Ocean Hill," *New York Daily Column,* 1968, 6; Carter, *Pickets, Parents, and Power,* 55; Diane Ravitch, "Community Control Revisited," *Commentary* 53 (February 1972): 74; Maurice Goldbloom, "The New York School Crisis," in *Confrontation at Ocean Hill–Brownsville,* ed. Marilyn Gittell and Maurice Berube (New York: Praeger, 1969), 256.

4. Bloomfield, "The Untold Story of Ocean Hill," 1–6; Goldbloom, "The New York School Crisis," 256.

5. Bloomfield, "The Untold Story of Ocean Hill," 1–6.

6. Henry Hampton and Steve Fayer, *Voices of Freedom: An Oral History of the Civil Rights Movement from the 1950s through the 1980s* (New York: Bantam Books, 1990), 488–89.

7. Martin Mayer, *The Teachers Strike: New York, 1968* (New York: Harper & Row, 1968), 21–23, 36–37.

8. "Community Action Bureau Proposal, 1968–69," Brownsville Community Corporation, Brownsville Community Council Papers, Folder I, Brooklyn Public Library, Brooklyn, N.Y.

9. Eugenia Kemble, "New York's Experiments in School Decentralization," 12.

10. Diane Ravitch, *The Great School Wars — New York City, 1805–1973: A History of the Public Schools As Battlefield of Social Change* (New York: Basic Books, 1974), 357.

11. Lindsay's dissatisfaction with funding notwithstanding, the New York City public school budget was the largest in the nation in 1967, at $1.2 billion. "Reconnection For Learning: A Community School System for New York City — Report of the Mayor's Advisory Panel on Decentralization of the New York City Schools," November 9, 1967, 4, New York City Board of Education Papers, Rose Shapiro Collection, Box 8, Columbia Teachers College, Special Collections, Milbank Memorial Library, New York (hereafter "Board of Education Papers, Shapiro Collection").

12. "Board of Education Statement of Policy on Decentralization," April 19, 1967, New York City Board of Education Papers, Bernard Donovan Collection, Box 15, Columbia Teachers College, Special Collections, Milbank Memorial Library, New York (hereafter "Board of Education Papers, Donovan Collection").

13. Ibid.

14. Mario Fantini, Marilyn Gittell, and Richard Magat, *Community Control and the Urban School* (New York: Praeger, 1970).

15. James Haughton, "The Role of the Board of Education in Perpetuating Racism in the Building Trades and Vice Versa," in *Schools Against Children: The Case for Community Control, ed.* Annette Rubinstein, (New York: Monthly Review Press, 1970), 159–73.

16. Charles V. Hamilton, "The Patron-Recipient Relationship and Minority Politics in New York City," *Political Science Quarterly* 94 (Summer 1979): 211–27; Martin Shefter, *Political Crisis, Fiscal Crisis: The Collapse and Revival of New York City* (New York: Basic Books, 1985), 92–95.

17. John Hull Mollenkopf, *A Phoenix in the Ashes: The Rise and Fall of the Koch Coalition in New York City Politics* (Princeton, N.J.: Princeton University Press, 1992), 58, 82, 91–92; Hamilton, "The Patron-Recipient Relationship," 219–27; Shefter, *Political Crisis, Fiscal Crisis,* 93; Mayer, *The Teachers Strike,* 17.

18. Letter, Bernard Donovan to John Powis, June 29, 1967, Board of Education Papers, Donovan Collection, Box 14.

19. "A Plan for An Experimental School District in District 17 (Ocean Hill–Brownsville)," June 1967, Board of Education Papers, Donovan Collection, Box 14.

20. Mayer, *The Teachers Strike,* 22; Naomi Levine, *Ocean Hill-Brownsville: Schools in Crisis* (New York: Popular Library, 1969), 32–33.

21. Letter, Bernard Donovan to Mario Fantini, June 30, 1967, Board of Education Papers, Donovan Collection, Box 14.

22. Donovan's tacit acceptance of the results of the August local board elections, which his office had not officially authorized, is another example of his accommodating attitude.

23. Kemble, "New York's Experiments in School Decentralization," 9; "Statement of the Teachers of the Ocean Hill–Brownsville Experimental District," September 27, 1967, Board of Education Papers, Donovan Collection, Box 14.

24. Derek Edgell, *The Movement for Community Control of New York City's Schools, 1966-1970: Class Wars* (Lewiston, N.Y.: Edwin Mellen Press, 1998), 101; Mayer, *The Teachers Strike,* 23–24; Hampton and Fayer, *Voices of Freedom,* 487, 491–92. This position would actually have been listed as "district superintendent," its practical equivalent in the rest of the city's public schools.

25. Kemble, "New York's Experiments in School Decentralization," 9; Mayer, *The Teachers Strike,* 23–24.

26. Mayer, *The Teachers Strike,* 24.

27. "A Plan for An Experimental School District: Ocean Hill–Brownsville," August 1967, Board of Education Papers, Shapiro Collection, Box 8.

28. Ibid.; Mayer, *The Teachers Strike,* 26; "Final Report of the Advisory Committee on Decentralization," July 1968, 11–12, Board of Education Papers, Shapiro Collection, Box 1; *New York Post,* October 26, 1968, 24.

29. "Final Report of the Advisory Committee on Decentralization," July 1968, 14, 20, Board of Education Papers, Shapiro Collection, Box 1; News Release, Ocean Hill–

Brownsville School Project, August 11, 1967, Board of Education Papers, Shapiro Collection, Box 8.

30. Ibid. While Wright did not share the views of his colleagues on the local board, he was a logical choice given his political stature in the community. Wright saw the Ocean Hill–Brownsville community control experiment in practical, not ideological terms: as a source of jobs for his political cronies.

31. Rhody McCoy and Keith Baird, "Whose Schools?" in *The Black Experience: A Record of Summer Forums, July–August 1968* (New York: Forum of Columbia University, 1968), 54, Schomburg Center for Research in Black Culture, New York.

32. Minutes, Meeting of Board of Education Ad Hoc Committee on Board of Examiners, February 15, 1965, Board of Education Papers, Shapiro Collection, Box 1.

33. There were, for example, only four blacks out of close to one thousand on the elementary school principals eligibility list. Mayer, *The Teachers Strike,* 28; *ATF,* January 1969, 1.

34. News Release, Ocean Hill–Brownsville School Project, August 11, 1967, Board of Education Papers, Donovan Collection, Box 14; Memorandum, Howard Kalodner to Rhody McCoy, August 10, 1967, Board of Education Papers, Donovan Collection, Box 14; Letter, Rhody McCoy to James Allen, July 28, 1968, Board of Education Papers, Donovan Collection, Box 18.

35. "Final Report of the Advisory Committee on Decentralization," July 1968, 19–22, Board of Education Papers, Shapiro Collection, Box 1; Memorandum, Howard Kalodner to Rhody McCoy, August 10, 1967, Board of Education Papers, Shapiro Collection, Box 8; "Eligibility Requirements for Principal of Demonstration Elementary School," March 19, 1968, Board of Education Papers, Shapiro Collection, Box 8; Letter, James Allen to Bernard Donovan, August 21, 1967, Board of Education Papers, Donovan Collection, Box 14; "Eligibility for Demonstration School Principal," December 1, 1967, Board of Education Papers, Donovan Collection, Box 14; Carter, *Pickets, Parents, and Power,* 36–37; *Council of Supervisory Associations v. Board of Education* 288 NYS2d 135, 56 Misc 2d 32 (Kings County, 1968).

36. *ATF,* September–October 1967, 1–3. Ferguson was eventually convicted and sentenced to prison.

37. Telegram, Albert Shanker to Shapiro, October 11, 1967, Board of Education Papers, Shapiro Collection, Box 8; "Statement of the Teachers of the Ocean Hill–Brownsville Experimental District," September 27, 1967, Board of Education Papers, Donovan Collection, Box 14; *New York Post,* October 26, 1968, 23; Kemble, "New York's Experiments in School Decentralization," 11.

38. Levine, *Ocean Hill–Brownsville: Schools in Crisis,* 33. See also Hampton and Fayer, *Voices of Freedom,* 490–91.

39. Rhody McCoy, "The Year of the Dragon," in Gittell and Berube, *Confrontation at Ocean Hill-Brownsville,* 56, 58, 60.

40. *United Federation of Teachers v. Board of Education,* September 26, 1967, Board of Education Papers, Shapiro Collection, Box 8; *Council of Supervisory Associations v. Board of Education,* September 26, 1967, Board of Education Papers, Shapiro Collection, Box 8; UFT press release, October 3, 1967, United Federation of

Teachers Collection, Record Group III, Sub-Group A, Series 2, Box 2, Folder 42, Robert F. Wagner Labor Archives, Elmer Holmes Bobst Library, New York University, New York (hereafter "UFT Collection"); *New York Law Journal,* November 19, 1967, 19.

41. UFT press release, October 3, 1967, UFT Collection, Record Group III, Sub-Group A, Series 2, Box 2, Folder 42; *New York Post,* November 24, 1967, 26.

42. Shanker need not have worried. By the time the election took place, the Ocean Hill–Brownsville local board's attempted termination of Nauman and his union colleagues had united the membership behind him. He was reelected president with over 90 percent of the vote. *United Teacher,* June 26, 1968, 3.

43. *Council of Supervisory Associations v. Board of Education,* 288 NYS2d 135, 56 Misc2d 32 (Kings County, 1968).

44. *New York Times,* November 16, 1968, 1, 26; Carter, *Pickets, Parents, and Power,* 127; *New York Daily News,* November 17, 1968, 3; *United Teacher,* November 20, 1968, 17.

45. *Council of Supervisory Associations v. Board of Education,* January 15, 1969, Board of Education Papers, Donovan Collection, Box 10; *New York Times,* January 16, 1969, 1, 48.

46. The "disruptive child" issue is discussed below, pp. 160–64.

47. *New York Times,* September 19, 1967, 1, 36; September 20, 1967, 1, 36.

48. Mayer, *The Teachers Strike,* 31; African-American Teachers Association, "Guidelines for Black Teachers During and After the UFT Strike," September 1967, UFT Collection, Record Group III, Sub-Group A, Series 2, Box 3, Folder 95.

49. *ATF,* September–October 1967, 4; *New York Times,* September 21, 1967, 1, 53; September 22, 1967, 1, 40.

50. "Reconnection for Learning," November 9, 1967, 26–27, 51, Board of Education Papers, Shapiro Collection, Box 8.

51. *New York Times,* November 9, 1967, 34.

52. *New York Post,* November 11, 1967, 29.

53. *New York Amsterdam News,* November 11, 1967, 16.

54. "UFT Statement on Decentralization," December 11, 1967, Board of Education Papers, Shapiro Collection, Box 8.

55. Ibid.

56. Ibid.

57. *New York Post,* November 24, 1967, 26; Mayer, *The Teachers Strike,* 31.

58. Letter, Theodore Lang to Rhody McCoy, September 8, 1967, Board of Education Papers, Donovan Collection, Box 14; Sandra Feldman, "Dear Colleague," November 17, 1967, UFT Collection, Record Group III, Sub-Group A, Series 2, Box 2, Folder 42; Mayer, *The Teachers Strike,* 40.

59. Mayer, *The Teachers Strike,* 32; McCoy, "The Year of the Dragon," 60–61.

60. Interview, Fred Nauman, October 15, 1991, Albany, N.Y.

61. Daniel E. Griffiths, *Teacher Mobility in New York City: A Study of the Recruitment, Selection, Appointment, and Promotion of Teachers in the New York City Public Schools* (New York: New York University School of Education, 1963), 32–33.

62. Interview, Fred Nauman, October 15, 1991, Albany, N.Y.

63. Hampton and Fayer, *Voices of Freedom,* 492, 507–8; *New York Post,* November 24, 1967, 26.

64. John W. Hughes, "Ocean Hill: A Modern Tragedy," 11, 1969, UFT Collection, Record Group III, Sub-Group A, Series 2, Box 2, Folder 63.

65. Ibid., 10.

66. Mayer, *The Teachers Strike,* 34–35.

67. Ibid., 36; telegram, Project Method to Bernard Donovan, April, 25, 1968, Board of Education Papers, Donovan Collection, Box 18.

68. Hampton and Fayer, *Voices of Freedom,* 485–86; Maurice Goldbloom, "The New York School Crisis," in Gittell and Berube, *Confrontation at Ocean Hill–Brownsville,* 271.

69. Letter, Thomas Rooney to Bernard Donovan, April 6, 1968, Board of Education Papers, Donovan Collection, Box 10.

70. Press Release, Ocean Hill–Brownsville Local School Board, March 5, 1968, Board of Education Papers, Donovan Collection, Box 18.

71. *New York Amsterdam News,* April 27, 1968, 25; Mayer, *The Teachers Strike,* 36; *New York Daily News,* April 11, 1968, 5.

72. *United Teacher,* February 21, 1968, 17; April 3, 1968, 7; May 29, 1968, 3; *New York Amsterdam News,* February 10, 1968, 7.

73. Bylaws of the Board of Education of the City of New York, Article II, Sections 101.1 and 105a.1; Agreement between the Board of Education of the City of New York and United Federation of Teachers, Local 2, American Federation of Teachers, AFL-CIO, 1967–69; New York City Board of Education, "Transfer of Teachers," October 11, 1968, Board of Education Papers, Shapiro Collection, Box 7; Minutes, Board of Education Meeting, October 11, 1968, Board of Education Papers, Shapiro Collection, Box 7; Levine, *Ocean Hill-Brownsville,* 53; Ravitch, *The Great School Wars,* 346, 423.

74. Ibid. Intradistrict transfers, in contrast, were at the discretion of the district superintendent and did not require hearings.

75. The UFT dropped the Fucillo case after the Ocean Hill–Brownsville local board's termination of Fred Nauman and his colleagues. Interview, Lewis Friedman, December 7, 1993, Brooklyn, N.Y.

76. *United Teacher,* June 26, 1968, 3.

77. *New York Times,* March 26, 1968, 34; Ravitch, *The Great School Wars,* 337; Memorandum, David Seeley to John Lindsay, March 9, 1968, Office of the Mayor (Lindsay, John V.), Subject Files, 1966–1973, Box 34, New York City Municipal Reference Center, New York.

78. Minutes, Meeting of Board of Education and Education Task Force of New York Urban Coalition, April 29, 1968, Board of Education Papers, Shapiro Collection, Box 8; Mayer, *The Teachers Strike,* 45–46; Karp, "School Decentralization in New York," 14.

79. Mayer, *The Teachers Strike,* 46–50; Interview, Fred Nauman, October 15, 1991, Albany, N.Y.

80. *New York Times,* May 10, 1968, 38; "Report to Governing Board by Clara Marshall, Chair, Personnel Committee, Ocean Hill–Brownsville School District," May 1968,

Board of Education Papers, Donovan Collection, Box 18; Mayer, *The Teachers Strike,* 47–50.

81. Gittell and Berube, *Confrontation at Ocean Hill–Brownsville,* 33.

82. Mayer, *The Teachers Strike,* 50; "Report to Governing Board by Clara Marshall, Chair, Personnel Committee, Ocean Hill–Brownsville School District," May 1968, Board of Education Papers, Donovan Collection, Box 18.

Chapter 5 The Strikes

1. Interview, Fred Nauman, October 15, 1991, Albany, N.Y.

2. Martin Mayer, *The Teachers Strike: New York, 1968* (New York: Harper & Row, 1969), 43–44; Diane Ravitch, *The Great School Wars—New York City, 1805–1973: A History of the Public Schools as Battlefield of Social Change* (New York: Basic Books, 1974), 355–58.

3. Interview, Fred Nauman, October 15, 1991, Albany, N.Y.

4. Ravitch, *The Great School Wars,* 358; Melvin Urofsky, ed., *Why Teachers Strike: Teachers' Rights and Community Control* (Garden City, N.Y.: Doubleday, 1970), 37.

5. *New York Daily News,* July 14, 1968, 12.

6. Urofsky, *Why Teachers Strike,* 37; *New York Times,* May 15, 1968, 44.

7. *New York Times,* May 15, 1968, 44.

8. Urofsky, *Why Teachers Strike,* 187–88.

9. Sol Stern, "The New 'Scabs,'" *Ramparts,* November 17, 1968, 23.

10. Ravitch, *The Great School Wars,* 354–55; Interview, Fred Nauman, October 15, 1991, Albany, N.Y.; *New York Times Magazine,* May 23, 1968, 38.

11. Ravitch, *The Great School Wars,* 358.

12. Ibid., 364–65; Marilyn Gittell and Maurice Berube, eds., *Confrontation at Ocean Hill–Brownsville* (New York: Praeger, 1969), 100.

13. Gittell and Berube, *Confrontation at Ocean Hill–Brownsville,* 91, 94, 96–98.

14. Urofsky, *Why Teachers Strike,* 38; Ravitch, *The Great School Wars,* 358.

15. Mayer, *The Teachers Strike,* 63; Gittell and Berube, *Confrontation at Ocean Hill–Brownsville,* 338; "Announcement," Rhody McCoy, May 21, 1968, Donovan Collection, Box 17.

16. Ravitch, *The Great School Wars,* 356, 358.

17. *New York Times,* May 15, 1968, 44.

18. *New York Daily News,* May 14, 1968, 5.

19. *Fortune,* January 1968, 37.

20. UFT Flyer, September 19, 1968, UFT Collection, Record Group III, Sub-Group A, Series 2, Box 2, Folder 46.

21. Nathan Glazer and Daniel Patrick Moynihan, *Beyond the Melting Pot: The Negroes, Puerto Ricans, Jews, Italians, and Irish of New York City* (Cambridge, Mass.: MIT Press, 1963), 298.

22. Charles R. Morris, *The Cost of Good Intentions: New York City and the Liberal Experiment, 1960–1975* (New York: McGraw-Hill, 1980), 71.

23. *1966 Annual Report,* Police Department of the City of New York. 29; *New York Daily News,* July 12, 1968, 30.

24. Tamar Jacoby, "The Uncivil History of the Civilian Review Board," *City Journal* 3 (Winter 1993): 56–63; Godfrey Hodgson, *America in Our Time* (New York: Doubleday, 1976), 416, 419.

25. Louis Harris and Bert E. Swanson, *Black-Jewish Relations in New York City* (New York: Praeger, 1970), 131–58.

26. Ibid., xvii; Mayer, *The Teachers Strike,* 89.

27. Mayer, *The Teachers Strike,* 62; Ravitch, *The Great School Wars,* 363; *New York Daily News,* August 18, 1968, 5.

28. Mayer, *The Teachers Strike,* 63; Ravitch, *The Great School Wars,* 364–65; Gittell and Berube, *Confrontation at Ocean Hill-Brownsville,* 83–101. Technically, Rivers's ruling was only advisory, but it was viewed as definitive by Donovan, the UFT, and the city's white population.

29. Ravitch, *The Great School Wars,* 365–66.

30. Ibid., 367; Mayer, *The Teachers Strike,* 64–65.

31. Mayer, *The Teachers Strike,* 35, 66.

32. *New York Times,* September 12, 1968, 52.

33. *United Teacher,* September 18, 1968, 6; *New York Times,* September 19, 1968, 57.

34. Ibid., September 16, 1968, 52.

35. Mayer, *The Teachers Strike,* 69–70; Ravitch, *The Great School Wars,* 367–68.

36. Morris, *The Cost of Good Intentions,* 28–29, 91–92, 212–13; Barry Gottehrer, *The Mayor's Man: One Man's Struggle to Save Our Cities* (Garden City, N.Y.: Doubleday, 1975), xi, 205.

37. *New York Post,* November 26, 1968, 24; *New York Times Magazine,* April 20, 1969, 63.

38. *United Teacher,* November 6, 1968, 15.

39. Ibid.; Mayer, *The Teachers Strike,* 73–74.

40. *New York Times,* September 11, 1968, 37.

41. Mayer, *The Teachers Strike,* 77–80; Ravitch, *The Great School Wars,* 368–70; Urofsky, *Why Teachers Strike,* 41.

42. Mayer, *The Teachers Strike,* 79–89; Ravitch, *The Great School Wars,* 371–75.

Chapter 6 Like Strangers: The Third Strike and Beyond

1. *Nation,* November 18, 1968, 524.

2. Diane Ravitch, *The Great School Wars—New York City, 1805-1973: A History of the Public Schools as Battlefield of Social Change* (New York: Basic Books, 1974), 370; Rabbi Ronald Millstein, "The Jew: Man in the Middle," September 1968, UFT Collection, Record Group III, Sub-Group A, Series 2, Box 2, Folder 71; OAAU Releases, October 3, 1968 and January 22, 1969, Shapiro Collection, Box 7; *ATF,* November 1968, 1.

3. "If African American History . . ." (1968), Shapiro Collection, Box 8; Jonathan Kaufman, *Broken Alliance: The Turbulent Times Between Blacks and Jews in America* (New York: Scribner, 1988), 153–57; Henry Hampton and Steve Fayer, *Voices of Freedom: An Oral History of the Civil Rights Movement from the 1950s through the 1980s* (New York: Bantam, 1990), 504–6; Murray Friedman, *What Went Wrong?:*

The Creation and Collapse of the Black-Jewish Alliance (New York: Free Press, 1995), 260–61; Jim Sleeper, *The Closest of Strangers: Liberalism and the Politics of Race in New York* (New York: Norton, 1990), 98–101.

4. Jewish leaders were also disappointed by Lindsay's tepid reaction to the anti-Semitic material. "What does Shanker want? For the police vans to come, arrest [anti-Semites] and send them to New Jersey?" he asked testily. *I. F. Stone's Review,* November 4, 1968; *United Teacher,* October 24, 1968, 5.

5. *New York Amsterdam News,* November 14, 1968, 13.

6. "If African American History . . . ," n.a., 1968, Shapiro Collection, Box 8; Naomi Levine, *Ocean Hill–Brownsville: Schools in Crisis* (New York: Popular Library, 1969), 79–80; *Time,* January 31, 1969, 58.

7. Preston Wilcox, quoted in Lillian Calhoun, "New York: Schools and Power — Whose?," *Integrated Education* 7 (January–February 1969): 23.

8. *ATF,* November 1968, 2.

9. Robert Campbell, *The Chasm* (Boston: Houghton Mifflin, 1974), xx.

10. *Liberator,* March 1968, 19.

11. Louis Harris and Bert E. Swanson, *Black-Jewish Relations in New York City* (New York: Praeger, 1970), xxii–xxiii, 74, 131–68; *New York Times,* November 2, 1968, 43.

12. *New York Post,* October 30, 1968; Martin Mayer, *The Teachers Strike: New York, 1968* (New York: Harper & Row, 1969), 88.

13. *New York Times,* November 2, 1968, 43.

14. *United Teacher,* November 20, 1968, 3, 9.

15. *New York Times,* September 25, 1968, 30; *United Teacher,* October 7, 1968, 3; *New York Times,* October 16, 1968, 32.

16. *New York Times,* November 5, 1968, 43; November 15, 1968, 34.

17. Ibid., October 16, 1968, 1, 32, 46; October 15, 1968, 34.

18. Ibid., October 16, 1968, 1, 32, 46.

19. Ibid; Barry Gottehrer, *The Mayor's Man: One Man's Struggle to Save Our Cities* (Garden City, N.Y.: Doubleday, 1975), 200–201.

20. *New York Times,* October 18, 1968, 1, 50; *New York Post,* September 26, 1968, 23; October 1, 1968, 24; Ravitch, *The Great School Wars,* 370.

21. *Village Voice,* October 31, 1968, 62.

22. Although the UFT, while officially supporting Hubert Humphrey, printed a letter of support for the teachers from Republican candidate Richard Nixon. *United Teacher,* November 6, 1968, 16.

23. Charles R. Morris, *The Cost of Good Intentions: New York City and the Liberal Experiment, 1960-1975* (New York: McGraw-Hill, 1980), 116; Sleeper, *The Closest of Strangers*; Roger Starr, *The Rise and Fall of New York* (New York: Basic Books, 1985); Gottehrer, *The Mayor's Man,* 202. See the account of a meeting between Italians and blacks early in Lindsay's first term in his aide Barry Gottehrer's autobiography, for an insight into the administration's attitude toward the city's white middle class: "The young blacks arrived in their best clothes, neat enough for Sunday school. The Italian teenagers drove up mainly in souped-up Cadillacs, each

with the obligatory pack of cigarettes tucked up under the sleeve of his T-shirt."
Gottehrer, *The Mayor's Man,* 23.

24. Mayer, *The Teachers Strike,* 92, 99–100; *New York Times,* October 21, 1968, 44.

25. *New York Times,* November 1, 1968, 32; Melvin Urofsky, ed., *Why Teachers Strike: Teachers' Rights and Community Control* (Garden City, N.Y.: Doubleday, 1970), 44.

26. *United Teacher,* November 6, 1968, 18; Mayer, *The Teachers Strike,* 93–94, 98; *New York Times,* November 2, 1968, 35.

27. *New York Times,* October 22, 1968, 50; November 14, 1968, 39.

28. Ibid., September 19, 1968, 39.

29. Letter, William Bowe to John V. Lindsay, October 16, 1968, New York Central Labor Council Papers, Box 19, Robert F. Wagner Labor Archives, Elmer Holmes Bobst Library, New York University, New York.

30. Letter, William Cross to Harry Van Arsdale, November 2, 1968, New York Central Labor Council Papers, Box 19, Robert F. Wagner Labor Archives, Elmer Holmes Bobst Library, New York University, New York.

31. *New York Times,* October 22, 1968, 50; September 22, 1968, 65.

32. Press Release, IS 201, October 21, 1968, Shapiro Collection, Box 8; Levine, *Ocean Hill-Brownsville,* 78.

33. Mayer, *The Teachers Strike,* 101.

34. Derek Edgell, *The Movement for Community Control of New York City's Schools, 1966-1970: Class Wars* (Lewiston, N.Y.: Edwin Mellen Press, 1998), 253.

35. Mayer, *The Teachers Strike,* 99–102; Urofsky, *Why Teachers Strike,* 45–46; Ravitch, *The Great School Wars,* 376–77.

36. Mayer, *The Teachers Strike,* 100; *United Teacher,* November 20, 1969, 17.

37. Mayer, *The Teachers Strike,* 100–103; *New York Times,* November 18, 1968, 1, 50, 51; *New York Daily News,* November 13, 1968, 3; November 17, 1968, 3.

38. Mayer, *The Teachers Strike,* 101.

39. *United Teacher,* December 4, 1968, 2; Urofsky, *Why Teachers Strike,* 46; *New York Daily News,* November 30, 1968, 4.

40. *New York Times,* November 18, 1968, 1, 51; Urofsky, *Why Teachers Strike,* 46. An indication of the perceptual gulf between blacks and whites at this point was the comment of a black local board supporter that the Delegate Assembly had rejected the settlement out of "guilt," when in fact the delegates did not believe it went far enough to punish the local board. *New York Amsterdam News,* November 23, 1968, 1.

41. *New York Times,* November 18, 1968, 1, 50, 51; November 19, 1968, 1, 38; *United Teacher,* November 20, 1968, 2, 8, 9.

42. *Council of Supervisory Associations v. Board of Education,* January 15, 1969, Donovan Collection, Box 10; *New York Times,* January 16, 1969, 1.

43. See *New York Teacher News,* January 18, 1964, 3.

44. See Perlstein, "The 1968 New York City School Crisis," 100–101, 124; Derek Edgell, *The Movement for Community Control of New York City's Schools, 1966-1970: Class Wars* (Lewiston, N.Y.: Edwin Mellen Press, 1998), 364; Herbert Hill, letter in *Issues in Industrial Society* 1 (1970): 68, 70–71.

45. "Doesn't Anybody Care?" 1969, UFT Collection, Record Group III, Sub-Group A, Series 2, Box 5, Folder 140; *New York Times*, March 16, 1969, 44; June 25, 1969, 44; John W. Hughes, "Ocean Hill: A Modern Tragedy," 1969, UFT Collection, Record Group III, Sub-Group A, Series 2, Box 2, Folder 63; interview, Fred Nauman, October 15, 1991, Albany, N.Y.

46. Urofsky, *Why Teachers Strike*, 257.

47. Harris and Swanson, *Black-Jewish Relations in New York City*, 72–73.

48. Ibid., 13–15.

49. Hampton and Fayer, *Voices of Freedom*, 507; "Anti-Semitism," Sia Berhan, December 26, 1968, UFT Collection, Record Group III, Sub-Group A, Series 2, Box 1, Folder 17; Naomi Levine, *Ocean Hill–Brownsville*, 104–5.

50. *New York Times*, January 23, 1969, 1, 51; January 17, 1969, 1, 28; January 18, 1969, 1, 32; January 28, 1969, 27; January 31, 1969, 1, 77; Vincent J. Cannato, *The Ungovernable City: John Lindsay and His Struggle to Save New York* (New York: Basic Books, 2001), 358–59.

51. *New York Times*, January 17, 1969, 1, 19; January 23, 1969, 1, 51.

52. Harris and Swanson, *Black-Jewish Relations in New York City*, 165, 166, 168.

53. Godfrey Hodgson, *America in Our Time* (New York: Doubleday, 1976), 416; Gottehrer, *The Mayor's Man*, 202; Sleeper, *The Closest of Strangers*, 150; John Hull Mollenkopf, *A Phoenix in the Ashes: The Rise and Fall of the Koch Coalition in New York City Politics* (Princeton, N.J.: Princeton University Press, 1992), 65, 88–89, 100–110.

54. Jonathan Rieder, *Canarsie: The Jews and Italians of Brooklyn Against Liberalism* (Cambridge, Mass.: Harvard University Press, 1985), 73.

55. Ravitch, *The Great School Wars*, 381–88; *New York Times*, January 29, 1969, 38; May 3, 1969, 1, 43; *New York Daily News*, May 1, 1969, 3; Barbara Carter, *Pickets, Parents, and Power: The Story Behind the New York City Teachers' Strike* (New York: Citation Press, 1971), 148–52; "A Summary of the 1969 School Decentralization Law for New York City," 1969, UFT Collection, Record Group III, Sub-Group A, Series 2, Box 4, Folder 109.

56. Ravitch, *The Great School Wars*, 388–91; Carter, *Pickets, Parents and Power*, 160–64; "Important Message to Parents of Ocean Hill–Brownsville," Rhody McCoy, March 1970, UFT Collection, Record Group III, Sub-Group A, Series 2, Box 5, Folder 138.

57. "Important Message to Parents of Ocean Hill–Brownsville," Rhody McCoy, March 1970, UFT Collection, Record Group III, Sub-Group A, Series 2, Box 5, Folder 138.

58. "A Letter to Para-Professionals of Ocean Hill–Brownsville School District," C. Herbert Oliver, April 22, 1970, UFT Collection, Record Group III, Sub-Group A, Series 2, Box 5, Folder 138.

59. *New York Times*, March 21, 1970, 1, 38; July 3, 1970, 35; July 30, 1970, 37; *New York Daily News*, July 8, 1970, 28.

60. Morris, *The Cost of Good Intentions*, 148.

61. Michael A. Rebell and Arthur R. Block, *Educational Policy Making and the Courts: An Empirical Study of Judicial Activism* (Chicago: University of Chicago Press,

1982), 75–122; Michael A. Rebell and Arthur R. Block, *Equality and Education: Federal Civil Rights Enforcement in the New York City School System* (Princeton, N.J.: Princeton University Press, 1985), 79; Jerald E. Podair, "Like Strangers: Blacks, Whites, and New York City's Ocean Hill–Brownsville Crisis, 1945–1980" (Ph.D. diss., Princeton University, 1997), 258.

62. Rebell and Block, *Equality and Education,* 78–133, 146–50, 169–70.

63. Diane Ravitch, "Community Control Revisited," *Commentary* 53 (February 1972): 74.

Chapter 7 Culture War

1. *Negro Teachers Forum,* November 1966, 2, 4. Membership in the ATA was not restricted to New York City public school teachers; anyone "interested in what the Negro educator has to say" could join. This policy enabled the group to broaden its base of support to include college professors, clergymen, and political activists.

2. "Reconnection for Learning: A Community School System for New York City— Report of the Mayor's Advisory Panel on Decentralization of the New York City Schools," November 9, 1967, 74, Shapiro Collection, Box 8.

3. David Rogers, *110 Livingston Street: Politics and Bureaucracy in the New York City School System* (New York: Random House, 1968), 23–35, 196, 199, 311–16.

4. "Reconnection for Learning," 74, Shapiro Collection, Box 8.

5. *Black Journal* no. 5, October 1968 (WNEW-TV, New York); *New York Post,* November 5, 1966, 20; Barbara Carter, *Pickets, Parents, and Power: The Story Behind the New York City Teachers' Strike* (New York: Citation Press, 1971), 9; Teachers for Community Control, "Community Control Is Community Responsibility," 1969, Teachers Action Caucus Papers, Box 1, Folder 1, Tamiment Institute Library, Elmer Holmes Bobst Library, New York University, New York; Albert Vann to Esther Swanker, May 1, 1967, UFT Collection, Record Group III, Sub-Group A, Series 2, Box 1, Folder 9; Jason Epstein, "The Politics of School Decentralization," *New York Review of Books,* June 6, 1968, 29; Kenneth Clark, *Dark Ghetto: Dilemmas of Social Power* (New York: Harper & Row, 1965), 122; Negro Teachers Association, "Crisis in Our Schools," May 27, 1967, UFT Collection, Record Group III, Sub-Group A, Series 2, Box 1, Folder 9.

6. Harlem Youth Opportunities Unlimited, *Youth in the Ghetto: A Study of the Consequences of Powerlessness and a Blueprint for Change* (New York: HARYOU, 1964), 210.

7. See, for example, *New York Recorder,* May 28, 1966, 20.

8. Interview, C. Herbert Oliver, in Henry Hampton and Steve Fayer, *Voices of Freedom: An Oral History of the Civil Rights Movement from the 1950s through the 1980s* (New York: Bantam Books, 1990), 488–89.

9. *Negro Teachers Forum,* November 1966, 1; December 1966, 2–3.

10. "Reconnection for Learning," 44–45, 74, Shapiro Collection, Box 8; Martin Mayer, *The Teachers Strike: New York, 1968* (New York: Harper & Row, 1969), 17; *New York Times,* June 7, 1966, 1, 36.

11. Mayer, *The Teachers Strike,* 17.

12. *New York Times,* June 7, 1966, 36.

13. Ellen Lurie, *How to Change the Schools* (New York: Random House, 1970), 110–13; Daniel Griffiths, *Teacher Mobility in New York: A Study of the Recruitment, Selection, Appointment, and Promotion of Teachers in the New York Public Schools* (New York: New York University School of Education, 1963), 209–10.

14. Marjorie Murphy, *Blackboard Unions: The AFT and the NEA, 1900–1980* (Ithaca, N.Y.: Cornell University Press, 1990), 264; Rogers, *110 Livingston Street,* 285–97; "Reconnection for Learning," 47, Shapiro Collection, Box 8.

15. The Negro Teachers Association changed its name to the African-American Teachers Association in 1967. *ATF,* May–August 1967.

16. Interview, Jitu Weusi, January 27, 1994, Brooklyn, N.Y.; Jim Sleeper, *The Closest of Strangers: Liberalism and the Politics of Race in New York* (New York: Norton, 1990), 69, 246.

17. Interview, Jitu Weusi, January 27, 1994, Brooklyn, N.Y.

18. *Negro Teachers Forum,* December 1966, 3.

19. *ATF,* May–August 1967, 2.

20. Sleeper, *The Closest of Strangers,* 59, 69; Griffiths, *Teacher Mobility in New York,* 209–10.

21. *New York Times,* September 23, 1966, 24. IS 201 cost an almost unprecedented five million dollars to build, and its projected class size was well below the city average. *New York Post,* November 5, 1966, 20.

22. *New York Times,* September 22, 1966, 1, 50; September 23, 1966, 1, 24; *New York Post,* September 21, 1966, 24.

23. *New York Times,* September 20, 1966, 1, 36; September 21, 1966, 1, 34, 35.

24. Albert Shanker to chapter chairmen, September 22, 1966, UFT Collection, Record Group III, Sub-Group A, Series 2, Box 1, Folder 9.

25. *New York Times,* September 20, 1966, 1, 36; September 21, 1966, 34.

26. Ibid., September 21, 1966, 1.

27. Albert Shanker to chapter chairmen, September 22, 1966, UFT Collection, Record Group III, Sub-Group A, Series 2, Box 1, Folder 9.

28. *Negro Teachers Forum,* November 1966, 3–4.

29. Ibid., 1, 4.

30. Carter, *Pickets, Parents, and Power,* 119; Philip Taft, *United They Teach: The Story of the United Federation of Teachers* (Los Angeles: Nash Publishing Co., 1974), 138.

31. *New York Amsterdam News,* May 4, 1968, 27.

32. *United Teacher,* January 24, 1967, 25–27; Edward Gottlieb, "Ghetto Schools Need the Power of Blackness," *WIN,* November 1968, 5.

33. *United Teacher,* January 24, 1967, 25–27.

34. *New York Times,* September 10, 1967, 79.

35. Albert Vann to Albert Shanker, August 1967, UFT Collection, Record Group III, Sub-Group A, Series 2, Box 1, Folder 9.

36. Albert Shanker to Albert Vann, August 15, 1967, UFT Collection, Record Group III, Sub-Group A, Series 2, Box 1, Folder 9; Albert Vann to Albert Shanker, August 1967, UFT Collection, Record Group III, Sub-Group A, Series 2, Box 1, Folder 9.

37. *ATF,* May–August 1967, 3.

38. *New York Times,* September 16, 1967, 32.

39. See discussion of the More Effective Schools program above, pp. 55–56.

40. "Teachers Merit Your Support in Their Battle for Quality Education," September 1967, UFT Collection, Record Group III, Sub-Group A, Series 2, Box 4, Folder 115.

41. Telegram, Martin Luther King to Albert Shanker, September 13, 1967, UFT Collection, Record Group III, Sub-Group A, Series 2, Box 4, Folder 115.

42. Telegram, Albert Shanker to Martin Luther King, September 13, 1967, UFT Collection, Record Group III, Sub-Group A, Series 2, Box 4, Folder 115.

43. *New York Post,* September 14, 1967, 28.

44. Rhody McCoy and Keith Baird, "Whose Schools?" in *The Black Experience: A Record of Summer Forums, July–August 1968* (New York: Forum of Columbia University, 1968); Telegram, ATA to UFT, May 23, 1967, UFT Collection, Record Group III, Sub-Group A, Series 2, Box 1, Folder 9; *New York Times,* September 28, 1967, 50.

45. *New York Amsterdam News,* February 3, 1968, 22.

46. Brooklyn CORE, "The Institute for Learning (for the 'disruptive child')," January 1968, Donovan Collection, Box 10.

47. "The New Coalition," August 1968, 3, UFT Collection, Record Group III, Sub-Group A, Series 2, Box 1, Folder 9.

48. *New York Amsterdam News,* February 10, 1968, 7.

49. Minutes, Meeting of UFT Representatives with Ralph Rogers, PS 144, Brooklyn, N.Y., March 22, 1968, UFT Collection, Record Group III, Sub-Group A, Series 2, Box 5, Folder 133.

50. *Negro Teachers Forum,* November 1966, 4; December 1966, 2.

51. *ATF,* November–December 1967, 1, 3.

52. Ibid. This attitude was also exemplified by the response of Mildred Vann, an ATA member (and the wife of Albert Vann) to a black teacher who claimed that "we didn't get any inferiority complex" in white-run schools: "No, you just began to think you were white." *New York Times,* September 21, 1967, 52.

53. Ibid. The UFT claimed these numbers were exaggerated, and that only about one-quarter of the black teachers in the city belonged to the ATA. Paul Ritterband, "Ethnic Power and the Public Schools: The New York City School Strike of 1968," *Sociology of Education* 47 (Spring 1974): 264.

54. Marilyn Gittell and Maurice Berube, eds., *Confrontation at Ocean Hill–Brownsville* (New York: Praeger, 1969), 33.

55. Edmund Gordon, "Decentralization and Educational Reform," *IRCD Bulletin,* November 1968–January 1969, 3, 4.

56. Sleeper, *The Closest of Strangers,* 219.

57. *New York Daily News,* November 20, 1968, 3; *New York Times,* November 20, 1968, 1, 32; *Newsday,* November 23, 1968, 6W-8W; *New York Amsterdam News,* November 23, 1968, 1.

58. *Community,* December 1, 1968, 4.

59. *Newsday,* November 23, 1968, 7W.

60. *Community Control* (Newsreel Films, October 1968).

61. *New York Times,* November 11, 1968, 55; March 16, 1969, E10.

62. Vincent J. Cannato, *The Ungovernable City: John Lindsay and His Struggle to Save New York* (New York: Basic Books, 2001), 345.

63. Dwight Macdonald, "An Open Letter to Michael Harrington," *New York Review of Books,* December 5, 1968, 49; Annette T. Rubinstein, "Visiting Ocean Hill–Brownsville in November 1968 and May 1969," in *Schools Against Children: The Case for Community Control,* ed. Annette T. Rubinstein (New York: Monthly Review Press, 1970), 228–46; I. F. Stone, "The Mason-Dixon Line Moves to New York," *I. F. Stone's Weekly,* November 4, 1968.

64. McCoy and Baird, "Whose Schools?"

65. Derek Edgell, *The Movement for Community Control of New York City's Schools, 1966-1970: Class Wars* (Lewiston, N.Y.: Edwin Mellen Press, 1998), 318–19; John W. Hughes, "Ocean Hill: A Modern Tragedy," 1969, 19–20, UFT Collection, Record Group III, Sub-Group A, Series 2, Box 2, Folder 63.

66. *New York Times Magazine,* November 24, 1968, 64.

67. Hampton and Fayer, *Voices of Freedom,* 491–92.

68. Luther Seabrook, "Proposal for the Recruitment and Training of Teachers for Disadvantaged Areas," December 1, 1967, UFT Collection, Record Group III, Sub-Group A, Series 2, Box 1, Folder 9.

69. *New York Amsterdam News,* November 30, 1968, 15; December 21, 1968, 7.

70. *New York Times,* October 21, 1968, 42.

71. *Village Voice,* June 6, 1968, 5.

72. *ATF,* January–April 1968, 4.

73. Robert Browne, "The Challenge of Black Student Organizations," *Freedomways* 8 (Fall 1968): 333.

74. Michael Parenti, "Assimilation and Counter-Assimilation: From Civil Rights to Black Nationalism," in *Power and Community: Dissenting Essays in Political Science,* ed. Philip Green and Sanford Levinson (New York: Pantheon, 1969), 186.

75. *Community Control.*

76. Ruben Maloff, letter to *New York Times,* September 26, 1968, UFT Collection, Record Group III, Sub-Group A, Series 2, Box 2, Folder 55.

77. Marc Trop to UFT, 1968, UFT Collection, Record Group III, Sub-Group A, Series 2, Box 6, Folder 1.

78. Copal Mintz, letter to *New York Times,* July 15, 1968, UFT Collection, Record Group III, Sub-Group A, Series 2, Box 1, Folder 5.

79. Lillian Schreiber, letter to *New Republic,* November 23, 1968, 40.

80. Dorothy Harris, letter to *United Teacher,* October 7, 1968, 11.

81. See, for example, *United Teacher,* April 3, 1968.

82. Robert Rossner, *The Year Without an Autumn: Portrait of a School in Crisis* (New York: R. W. Baron, 1969), 214.

83. Patrick Harnett, "Why Teachers Strike: A Lesson for Liberals," *Village Voice,* October 31, 1968, 62.

84. *New York Post,* November 26, 1968, 75.

85. Melvin Urofsky, ed., *Why Teachers Strike: Teachers' Rights and Community Control* (Garden City, N.Y.: Doubleday, 1970), 180.

86. David Selden, "Don't Give Up on 'Compensatory Education,'" *PFT Reporter,* May 1969, 2.

87. Albert Murray, "The Atomization of the New York Public Schools," January 22, 1968, 8, Shapiro Collection, Box 8.

88. Patrick Harnett, "Community Control: Solution or Sop?" *Village Voice,* November 14, 1968, 20.

89. Leo Shapiro, letter to *United Teacher,* October 24, 1968, 8.

90. *New York Post,* June 29, 1968, 46.

91. *New York Amsterdam News,* October 26, 1968, 39; Edgell, *Movement for Community Control,* 476.

92. *New York Post,* November 26, 1968, 75.

93. *ATF,* November–December 1972, 6; March–April 1972, 14–15.

94. Burton Zwiebach, "Democratic Theory and Community Control," *Community Issues,* March 1969, 11.

95. Lurie, *How to Change the Schools,* 51, 54–55, 73, 173.

96. *ATF,* December 1970, 13; Summer 1971, 1; November–December 1972, 43; April 1971, 2.

97. Ibid., February 1971, 3.

98. Rhody McCoy, "Analysis of Critical Issues and Incidents in the New York City School Crisis, 1967–1970 and Their Implications for Urban Education in the 1970s" (Ed.D. diss., University of Massachusetts, 1971), 62.

99. Lurie, *How to Change the Schools,* 51.

100. *ATF,* November 1970, 4–5.

101. Charles B. McMillan, "The Changing Schools: A Look at Community Control," *Freedomways* 13 (1973): 67.

102. *ATF,* January–February, 1972, 6.

103. James Watkins, "Pilot Project: Teacher Recruitment and Training," July 1970, 6, UFT Collection, Record Group III, Sub-Group A, Series 2, Box 1, Folder 10.

104. McCoy, "Analysis of Critical Issues and Incidents in the New York City School Crisis," 135.

105. *ATF,* February 1971, 12.

106. Ibid., November–December 1972, 9–15.

107. Ibid., 11.

108. The UFT's reliance on the culture of poverty theory as the justification for these compensatory programs is illustrated by Shanker's insistence that the MES program be evaluated only by its success rate with "culturally deprived" children as measured against other such children, and not middle-class children. See Carter, *Pickets, Parents, and Power,* 120.

109. United Federation of Teachers, *The History of Black Americans: A Study Guide and Curriculum Outline* (New York: United Federation of Teachers, 1972), 86–87, 99, 102, 110–11, UFT Collection, Record Group III, Sub-Group A, Series 2, Box 22, Folder 611.

110. Albert Shanker, "The Real Meaning of the New York City Teachers' Strike," *Phi Delta Kappan* 50 (1969): 440.

111. David Allen Miller, letter to *New York Times Magazine,* December 8, 1968, 150.

112. Sleeper, *The Closest of Strangers,* 219.
113. *ATF,* December 1970, 2; March–April 1972, 6–7.
114. John W. Hughes, "Ocean Hill: A Modern Tragedy," 1969, 20, UFT Collection, Record Group III, Sub-Group A, Series 2, Box 2, Folder 63.
115. See generally, John H. McWhorter, *Losing the Race: Self-Sabotage in Black America* (New York: Free Press, 2000).
116. Interview, Jitu Weusi, January 27, 1994, Brooklyn, N.Y.
117. *ATF,* September 1969, 5.
118. Seymour Graubard to Elliott Richardson, February 29, 1972; Albert Shanker to Richard Nixon, March 23, 1972; Albert Shanker to Theodore Kheel, March 24, 1972; Trude Lash to Albert Shanker, April 3, 1972; all UFT Collection, Record Group III, Sub-Group A, Series 2, Box 1, Folder 10.
119. Robert P. Moore, memorandum, February 17, 1972; ATA Memorandum to "Members and Friends," May 21, 1973; "UFT/ATA One Million Dollar Suit," New York City African-American Teachers Convention, April 21–23, 1972; all UFT Collection, Record Group III, Sub-Group A, Series 2, Box 1, Folder 10. *New York Amsterdam News,* April 22, 1972, C-1.
120. *New York Amsterdam News,* October 7, 1967, 14.
121. *New York Daily News,* June 20, 1968, 10; Minutes, New York City Board of Education, June 19, 1968, Donovan Collection, Box 18; *New York Post,* September 14, 1968, 14; *United Teacher,* November 20, 1968, 2.
122. *New York Amsterdam News,* February 3, 1968, 22.
123. McCoy, "Analysis of Critical Issues and Incidents in the New York City School Crisis," 115.
124. *Village Voice,* December 12, 1968, 14.

Chapter 8 After the Crisis

1. *New York Times,* November 18, 1968, 46; *New York Review of Books,* December 5, 1968, 49.
2. *New York Times,* September 20, 1968, 29.
3. *United Teacher,* November 6, 1968, 8.
4. Letter, Laura Schectman to Albert Shanker, December 15, 1968, UFT Collection, Record Group III, Sub-Group A, Series 2, Box 1, Folder 17.
5. Letter, Morris Silver to Albert Shanker, November 1968, UFT Collection, Record Group III, Sub-Group A, Series 2, Box 1, Folder 17.
6. *New York Times,* October 21, 1968, 41.
7. *Village Voice,* December 12, 1968, 14.
8. Minutes, American Civil Liberties Union Board of Directors Meeting, April 19–20, 1969, 11, American Civil Liberties Union Papers, Volume X, F6002 1969, Box 22, Folder 5; Memoranda, "On Equality and Community Control," March 30, 1969, and "Decentralization and Community Control," March 31, 1969, American Civil Liberties Union Papers, Volume X, F6002 1969, Box 22, Folder 6; Memorandum, "NYCLU Statement on Equality and Community Control," April 14, 1969, American Civil Liberties Union Papers, Volume XI, F6002 1969, Box 22, Folder 6;

Minutes, American Civil Liberties Union Equality Committee, January 22, 1969, American Civil Liberties Union Papers, Volume XI, F6100 1969, Box 93, Folder 5, Seeley G. Mudd Manuscript Library, Princeton University, Princeton, N.J.

9. *New Leader,* June 12, 1972, 10.

10. Marilyn Gittell, "Educational Achievements and Community Control," *Community Issues,* November 1, 1968, 11.

11. Jim Sleeper, *The Closest of Strangers: Liberalism and the Politics of Race in New York* (New York: Norton, 1990), 150.

12. *New York Times,* August 20, 1972, 1, 32; September 6, 1972, 31.

13. Ibid., September 21, 1972, 34. See generally, Mario Cuomo, *Forest Hills Diary* (New York: Random House, 1974).

14. *Teachers Action Caucus Newsletter,* November–December 1972, 3, Teachers Action Caucus Papers, Box 1, Folder 6, Tamiment Library, Elmer Holmes Bobst Library, New York University, New York (hereafter *"TAC Newsletter"* and "TAC Papers").

15. Jonathan Rieder, *Canarsie: The Jews and Italians of Brooklyn Against Liberalism* (Cambridge, Mass.: Harvard University Press, 1985), 216.

16. Ibid., 217, 227.

17. *ATF,* November–December 1972, 2, 3.

18. *TAC Newsletter,* November–December 1972, 3, Box 1, Folder 6, TAC Papers.

19. *ATF,* November–December 1972, 4.

20. *TAC Newsletter,* November–December 1972, 3, TAC Papers, Box 1, Folder 6.

21. *ATF,* November–December 1972, 2.

22. *TAC Newsletter,* November–December 1972, 3, TAC Papers, Box 1, Folder 6; TAC, "UFT Rank-and-File Teachers and Paraprofessionals Charge: Shanker's Attack on Dr. Clark is Support for Racist Forces in Canarsie and Throughout New York City," June 12, 1973, TAC Papers, Box 1, Folder 6.

23. *TAC Newsletter,* November–December 1972, 3, TAC Papers, Box 1, Folder 6.

24. Ibid.

25. EQUAL, "The Corona Victory," May 1971, 1, UFT Collection, Record Group III, Sub-Group A, Series 2, Box 1, Folder 10.

26. Thomas Kessner, *Fiorello H. La Guardia and the Making of Modern New York* (New York: McGraw-Hill, 1989), xiv.

27. See generally, Charles R. Morris, *The Cost of Good Intentions: New York City and the Liberal Experiment, 1960–1975* (New York: McGraw-Hill, 1980).

28. George Sternlieb and James M. Hughes, "Metropolitan Decline and Inter-Regional Job Safety," in *The Fiscal Crisis of American Cities,* ed. Roger E. Alcaly and David Mermelstein (New York: Random House, 1977), 158; Alcaly and Mermelstein, *The Fiscal Crisis of American Cities,* 4; Eric Lichten, *Class, Power, and Austerity: The New York City Fiscal Crisis* (South Hadley, Mass.: Bergin & Garvey, 1986), 75.

29. Robert Zevin, "New York City Crisis: First Act in a New Age of Reaction," in Alcaly and Mermelstein, *The Fiscal Crisis of American Cities,* 24; Lichten, *Class, Power, and Austerity,* 74; Ken Auletta, *The Streets Were Paved With Gold* (New York: Random House, 1975), 213.

30. Mark H. Maier, *City Unions: Managing Discontent in New York City* (New Brunswick, N.J.: Rutgers University Press, 1987), 175–177, 191; Joshua B. Freeman,

Working-Class New York: Life and Labor Since World War II (New York: The New Press, 2000), 265–66.

31. *United Teacher,* September 21, 1975, 3.

32. Maier, *City Unions,* 177.

33. John Hull Mollenkopf, *A Phoenix in the Ashes: The Rise and Fall of the Koch Coalition in New York City Politics* (Princeton, N.J.: Princeton University Press, 1992), 138; Martin Shefter, *Political Crisis, Fiscal Crisis: The Collapse and Revival of New York City* (New York: Basic Books, 1985), 147, 189, 256.

34. Shefter, *Political Crisis, Fiscal Crisis,* 147–48.

35. Mollenkopf, *A Phoenix in the Ashes,* 138.

36. Ibid., 82; Freeman, *Working-Class New York,* 277–79.

37. *New York Amsterdam News,* February 26, 1977, B-1.

38. Robert W. Bailey, *The Crisis Regime: The Municipal Assistance Corporation, the Emergency Financial Control Board, and the Political Impact of the New York City Financial Crisis* (Albany, N.Y.: SUNY Press, 1984), 58–59, 100, 126–27, 138. See also Roger Starr, *The Rise and Fall of New York City* (New York: Basic Books, 1985).

39. Edward I. Koch, *Politics* (New York: Simon & Schuster, 1985), 129–35; Mollenkopf, *A Phoenix in the Ashes,* 88; Sleeper, *The Closest of Strangers,* 110–11; Arthur Browne, Dan Collins, and Michael Goodwin, *I, Koch: A Decidedly Unauthorized Biography of the Mayor of New York City, Edward I. Koch* (New York: Dodd, Mead, 1985), 109–14; Jack Newfield and Wayne Barrett, *City for Sale: Edward Koch and the Betrayal of New York* (New York: Harper & Row, 1988), 116–23.

40. Chris McNickle, *To Be Mayor of New York: Ethnic Politics in the City* (New York: Columbia University Press, 1993), 267.

41. Shefter, *Political Crisis, Fiscal Crisis,* 181.

42. See, generally, Mollenkopf, *A Phoenix in the Ashes.*

43. Ibid., 141–42.

44. Shefter, *Political Crisis, Fiscal Crisis,* 175.

45. Ibid., 147, 176, 180–81, 184, 256.

46. Ibid., 197; Mollenkopf, *A Phoenix in the Ashes,* 163.

47. Freeman, *Working-Class New York,* 277.

48. Shefter, *Political Crisis, Fiscal Crisis,* 176.

49. Ibid., 184, 185.

50. Freeman, *Working-Class New York,* 335.

51. Newfield and Barrett, *City for Sale.*

52. Freeman, *Working-Class New York,* 287.

53. Fred Siegel, *The Future Once Happened Here: New York, D.C., L.A., and the Fate of America's Big Cities* (New York: Free Press, 1997), 208, 215.

54. Andrew Kirtzman, *Rudy Giuliani: Emperor of the City* (New York: William Morrow, 2000), 55, 73, 74, 88, 171–72, 174, 180–81, 186.

55. See *New York Times,* September 23, 2001, A52.

56. Ibid., November 8, 2001, D4.

57. See David R. Roediger, *The Wages of Whiteness: Race and the Making of the American Working Class* (London: Verso, 1991); Noel Ignatiev, *How the Irish Became White*

(New York: Routledge, 1995); John Garvey and Noel Ignatiev, eds., *Race Traitor* (New York: Routledge, 1996).

Chapter 9 Ocean Hill-Brownsville, New York, America

1. James C. Scott, *Domination and the Arts of Resistance: Hidden Transcripts* (New Haven, Conn.: Yale University Press, 1990); James C. Scott, *Weapons of the Weak: Everyday Forms of Peasant Resistance* (New Haven, Conn.: Yale University Press, 1985); Robin D. G. Kelley, *Race Rebels: Culture, Politics, and the Black Working Class* (New York: Free Press, 1994), 8–9; Robin D. G. Kelley, "'We Are Not What We Seem': Rethinking Black Working Class Opposition in the Jim Crow South," in *The New African-American Urban History*, ed. Kenneth W. Goings and Raymond A. Mohl (Thousand Oaks, Calif.: Sage Publications, 1996), 187–239.
2. See Thomas J. Sugrue, *The Origins of the Urban Crisis: Race and Inequality in Postwar Detroit* (Princeton, N.J.: Princeton University Press, 1996); Arnold Hirsch, *Making the Second Ghetto: Race and Housing in Chicago, 1940–1960* (Cambridge: Cambridge University Press, 1983); John F. Bauman, *Public Housing, Race, and Renewal: Urban Planning in Philadelphia, 1920–1974* (Philadelphia: Temple University Press, 1987); Nicholas Lemann, *The Promised Land: The Great Black Migration and How It Changed America* (New York: Alfred A. Knopf, 1991).
3. W. E. B. Du Bois, *The Souls of Black Folk* (New York: Vintage, 1990), 9.
4. See John H. McWhorter, *Losing the Race: Self-Sabotage in Black America* (New York: Free Press, 2000).
5. Du Bois, *The Souls of Black Folk,* 7–15.
6. *ATF,* November 1968, 2.
7. See Goings and Mohl, *The New African-American Urban History;* Eric Foner, *Reconstruction: America's Unfinished Revolution, 1863–1877* (New York: Harper & Row, 1988); and Aldon Morris, *The Origins of the Civil Rights Movement: Black Communities Organizing for Change* (New York: Free Press, 1984), for uses of the theme of agency by historians of the African-American past.
8. See in particular Jonathan Rieder, *Canarsie: The Jews and Italians of Brooklyn Against Liberalism* (Cambridge, Mass.: Harvard University Press, 1985).
9. Du Bois, *The Souls of Black Folk,* 16.
10. See generally, in the context of another eastern city, J. Anthony Lukas, *Common Ground: A Turbulent Decade in the Lives of Three American Families* (New York: Knopf, 1985), and Ronald Formisano, *Boston Against Busing: Race, Class, and Ethnicity in the 1960s and 1970s* (Chapel Hill: University of North Carolina Press, 1991).
11. Lemann, *The Promised Land,* 123.

SOURCES

Archives and Manuscript Collections

Brooklyn Historical Society
　Brooklyn Local Press Collections
Brooklyn Public Library
　Brownsville Community Council Papers
Columbia Teachers College, Milbank Memorial Library
　New York City Board of Education Papers
　　Nathan Brown Collection
　　Bernard Donovan Collection
　　Seymour Lachman Collection
　　Isaiah Robinson Collection
　　Rose Shapiro Collection
　　Rosalie Stutz Collection
Ford Foundation
　Ford Foundation Grant File
Museum of Television and Radio
　Ocean Hill–Brownsville broadcast videotapes
New York City Municipal Reference Center
　New York City Schools—Decentralization Files
　Office of the Mayor (Lindsay, John V.) Subject Files
New York University, Elmer Holmes Bobst Library
　Robert F. Wagner Labor Archives
　　New York Central Labor Council Papers
　　United Federation of Teachers Collection
　Tamiment Institute Library
　　Teachers Action Caucus Papers
Princeton University
　American Civil Liberties Union Papers
Schomburg Center for Research in Black Culture
　Richard Parrish Papers
Wayne State University
　American Federation of Teachers Papers

Newspapers and Periodicals

African-American Teachers Forum
American Teacher
Black News
Changing Education
Commentary
Commonweal
Community
Community Issues
Dissent
Freedomways
Guardian
I. F. Stone's Review
Interplay
Integrated Education
IRCD Bulletin
Jewish Spectator
Liberator
Nation
National Review
NEA Journal
Negro Teachers Forum
New Leader
New Republic
Newsweek
New York
New York Amsterdam News
New York Daily Column
New York Herald-Tribune
New York Law Journal
New York Post
New York Recorder
New York Review of Books
New York Teacher News
New York Times
New York World-Telegram & Sun
New York World-Journal-Tribune
Newsday
Newsweek
PFT Reporter
Ramparts
Teachers Action Caucus Newsletter
Time
United Teacher

Village Voice
Wall Street Journal

Interviews and Oral Histories

Keith Baird
Wayne Barrett
Simon Beagle
Abraham Beame
Norma Becker
Beverly Chernoff
Merton Chernoff
Charles Cogen
Richard Easton
Ronald Evans
Ann Filardo
Lewis Friedman
Bernard Gordon
Robert Greenberg
Fred Nauman
John O'Neill
Roger Parente
Rose Shapiro
Harold Siegel
Rebecca Simonson
Albert Vann
Samuel Wallach
Jitu Weusi (Leslie Campbell)
Jack Zuckerman

Books and Articles

Abubadika, Mwlina Imiri. *The Education of Sonny Carson.* New York: Norton, 1972.
Alcaly, Roger, and David Mermelstein, eds. *The Fiscal Crisis of American Cities.* New York: Random House, 1977.
Altshuler, Alan A. *Community Control: The Black Demand for Participation in Large American Cities.* New York: Pegasus, 1970.
Auletta, Ken. *The Streets Were Paved With Gold.* New York: Random House, 1975.
Back, Adina. "Up South in New York: The 1950s School Desegregation Struggles." Ph.D. diss., New York University, 1997.
Bailey, Robert W. *The Crisis Regime: The Municipal Assistance Corporation, the Emergency Financial Control Board, and the Political Impact of the New York City Financial Crisis.* Albany, N.Y.: SUNY Press, 1984.
Baltzell, E. Digby. *The Protestant Establishment: Aristocracy and Caste in America.* New Haven, Conn.: Yale University Press, 1964.

Bauman, John W. *Public Housing, Race, and Renewal: Urban Planning in Philadelphia, 1920–1974.* Philadelphia: Temple University Press, 1987.

Bell, Daniel. *The End of Ideology: On the Exhaustion of Political Ideas in the Fifties and Sixties.* Glencoe, Ill.: Free Press, 1960.

Bellush, Jewel, and Stephen M. David, eds. *Race and Politics in New York City: Five Studies in Policy-Making.* New York: Praeger, 1971.

Bloch, Herman D. *The Circle of Discrimination: An Economic and Social Study of the Black Man in New York.* New York: New York University Press, 1969.

Bloom, Alexander. *Prodigal Sons: The New York Intellectuals and Their World.* New York: Oxford University Press, 1986.

Braun, Robert J. *Teachers and Power: The Story of the American Federation of Teachers.* New York: Simon & Schuster, 1972.

Browne, Arthur, Dan Collins, and Michael Goodwin. *I, Koch: A Decidedly Unauthorized Biography of the Mayor of New York City, Edward I. Koch.* New York: Dodd, Mead, 1985.

Browne, Robert. "The Challenge of Black Student Organizations." *Freedomways* 8 (Fall 1968): 325–33.

Campbell, James. "Struggle: The Highest Form of Education." *Freedomways* 8 (Fall 1968): 407–14.

Campbell, Robert. *The Chasm.* Boston: Houghton-Mifflin, 1974.

Cannato, Vincent J. *The Ungovernable City: John Lindsay and His Struggle to Save New York.* New York: Basic Books, 2001.

Carmichael, Stokely, and Charles V. Hamilton. *Black Power: The Politics of Liberation in America.* New York: Random House, 1967.

Caro, Robert A. *The Power Broker: Robert Moses and the Fall of New York.* New York: Knopf, 1974.

Carter, Barbara. *Pickets, Parents, and Power: The Story Behind the New York City Teachers' Strike.* New York: Citation Press, 1971.

Clark, Kenneth. "Clash of Cultures in the Classroom," *Integrated Education* 1 (August 1963): 7–14.

————. *Dark Ghetto: Dilemmas of Social Power.* New York: Harper & Row, 1965.

Cloward, Richard, and Lloyd Ohlin. *Delinquency and Opportunity: A Theory of Delinquent Gangs.* New York: Free Press, 1960.

Cohen, S. Alan. "Local Control and the Cultural Deprivation Fallacy." *Phi Delta Kappan* 50 (1969): 255–58.

Cole, Stephen. *The Unionization of Teachers.* New York: Praeger, 1969.

Coleman, James S., et al. *Equality of Educational Opportunity.* Washington, D.C.: U.S. Office of Education, 1966.

————. "Equal Schools or Equal Students?" *The Public Interest* 4 (Summer 1966): 70–75.

Connolly, Harold X. *A Ghetto Grows in Brooklyn.* New York: New York University Press, 1977.

————. "The Economics of Blacks in Brooklyn." Unpublished paper, Brooklyn Historical Society, December 8, 1979.

Cremin, Lawrence. *The Transformation of the School: Progressivism in American Education, 1876-1957*. New York: Knopf, 1968.

Cruse, Harold. *The Crisis of the Negro Intellectual*. New York: William Morrow, 1967.

Cuomo, Mario. *Forest Hills Diary*. New York: Random House, 1974.

Demas, Bouton H. *The School Elections: A Critique of the 1969 New York City School Decentralization Law*. New York: Institute for Community Studies, 1971.

Dionne, E. J. *Why Americans Hate Politics*. New York: Simon & Schuster, 1991.

Du Bois, W. E. B. *The Souls of Black Folk*. New York: Vintage, 1990.

Edgell, Derek. *The Movement for Community Control of New York City's Schools, 1966-1970: Class Wars*. Lewiston, N.Y.: Edwin Mellen Press, 1998.

Edsall, Thomas Byrne. *The New Politics of Inequality*. New York: Norton, 1984.

Edsall, Thomas Byrne, and Mary D. Edsall. *Chain Reaction: The Impact of Race, Rights, and Taxes on American Politics*. New York: Norton, 1991.

Eisenberg, Carolyn. "The Parents' Movement at I.S. 201: From Integration to Black Power, 1958-1966." Ed.D. diss., Columbia University Teachers College, 1971.

Fantini, Mario, Marilyn Gittell, and Richard Magat. *Community Control and the Urban School*. New York: Praeger, 1970.

Fantini, Mario, and Gerald Weinstein. "Taking Advantage of the Disadvantaged." *Columbia Teachers College Record* 69 (November 1967): 1-14.

Foner, Eric. *Reconstruction: America's Unfinished Revolution, 1863-1877*. New York: Harper & Row, 1988.

Formisano, Ronald. *Boston Against Busing: Race, Class, and Ethnicity in the 1960s and 1970s*. Chapel Hill: University of North Carolina Press, 1991.

Fraser, Steve, and Gary Gerstle, eds. *The Rise and Fall of the New Deal Order, 1930-1980*. Princeton, N.J.: Princeton University Press, 1989.

Freeman, Joshua B. *Working-Class New York: Life and Labor Since World War II*. New York: The New Press, 2000.

Friedman, Murray. *Overcoming Middle-Class Rage*. Philadelphia: Westminster Press, 1971.

———. *What Went Wrong? The Creation and Collapse of the Black-Jewish Alliance*. New York: Free Press, 1995.

Galamison, Milton. "Educational Values and Community Power." *Freedomways* 8 (Fall 1968): 311-18.

Galbraith, John Kenneth. *The Affluent Society*. Boston: Houghton-Mifflin, 1958.

Garvey, John, and Noel Ignatiev, eds. *Race Traitor*. New York: Routledge, 1996.

Gelfand, Donald, and Russell D. Lee, eds. *Ethnic Conflicts and Power: A Cross-National Perspective*. New York: Wiley, 1973.

Gerstle, Gary. *Working-Class Americanism: The Politics of Labor in a Textile City, 1914-1960*. Cambridge: Cambridge University Press, 1989.

Gitlin, Todd. *The Sixties: Years of Hope, Days of Rage*. New York: Bantam Books, 1987.

Gittell, Marilyn. *Participants and Participation: A Study of School Policy in New York City*. New York: Center for Urban Education, 1967.

———. *Local Control in Education: Three Demonstration School Districts in New York City*. New York: Praeger, 1972.

————. *School Boards and School Policy: An Evaluation of School Decentralization in New York City.* New York: Praeger, 1973.

Gittell, Marilyn, and Maurice Berube, eds. *Confrontation at Ocean Hill–Brownsville.* New York: Praeger, 1969.

Glazer, Nathan. "Negroes and Jews: The New Challenge to Pluralism." *Commentary* 38 (December 1964): 29–34.

Glazer, Nathan, and Daniel Patrick Moynihan. *Beyond the Melting Pot: The Negroes, Puerto Ricans, Jews, Italians, and Irish of New York City.* Cambridge: MIT Press, 1963; 2d ed., 1970.

Goings, Kenneth W., and Raymond A. Mohl, eds. *The New African-American Urban History.* Thousand Oaks, Calif.: Sage Publications, 1996.

Gordon, Jane Anna. *Why They Couldn't Wait: A Critique of Black-Jewish Conflict Over Community Control in Ocean Hill–Brownsville.* New York: Routledge, 2001.

Gottehrer, Barry. *The Mayor's Man: One Man's Struggle to Save Our Cities.* Garden City, N.Y.: Doubleday, 1975.

Graham, Hugh Davis. *The Civil Rights Era: Origins and Development of National Policy, 1960-1972.* New York: Oxford University Press, 1990.

Green, Philip, and Sanford Levinson, eds. *Power and Community: Dissenting Essays in Political Science.* New York: Pantheon, 1969.

Grier, William, and Price Cobbs. *Black Rage.* New York: Basic Books, 1968.

Griffiths, Daniel. *Teacher Mobility in New York City: A Study of the Recruitment, Selection, Appointment, and Promotion of Teachers in the New York Public Schools.* New York: New York University School of Education, 1963.

Halpern, Ben. *Jews and Blacks: The Classic American Minorities.* New York: Herder & Herder, 1971.

Hamilton, Charles V. "Education in the Black Community: An Examination of the Realities." *Freedomways* 8 (Fall 1968): 319–24.

————. "The Patron-Recipient Relationship and Minority Politics in New York City." *Political Science Quarterly* 94 (Summer 1979): 211–27.

Hampton, Henry, and Steve Fayer. *Voices of Freedom: An Oral History of the Civil Rights Movement from the 1950s through the 1980s.* New York: Bantam Books, 1990.

Harlem Youth Opportunities Unlimited. *Youth in the Ghetto: A Study of the Consequences of Powerlessness and a Blueprint for Change.* New York: HARYOU, 1964.

Harrington, Michael. *The Long-Distance Runner: An Autobiography.* New York: Holt, 1988.

Harris, Louis, and Bert E. Swanson. *Black-Jewish Relations in New York City.* New York: Praeger, 1970.

Hartz, Louis. *The Liberal Tradition in America.* New York: Harcourt Brace, 1955.

Haskins, James. *Diary of a Harlem Schoolteacher.* New York: Grove Press, 1969.

Haughton, James. "The Role of the Board of Education in Perpetuating Racism in the Building Trades and Vice Versa." In *Schools Against Children: The Case for Community Control,* edited by Annette Rubinstein, 159–73. New York: Monthly Review Press, 1970.

Hentoff, Nat. *A Political Life: The Education of John Lindsay.* New York: Knopf, 1969.

Herman, Judith, ed. *The Schools and Group Identity: Educating for a New Pluralism.* New York: American Jewish Committee, 1974.

Himmelfarb, Milton. "How We Are." *Commentary* 39 (January 1965): 69–74.

———. "Jewish Class Conflict?" *Commentary* 49 (January 1970): 37–42.

———. "Are Jews Becoming Republican?" *Commentary* 72 (August 1981): 27–31.

Hirsch, Arnold. *Making the Second Ghetto: Race and Housing in Chicago, 1940–1960.* Cambridge: Cambridge University Press, 1983.

Hochschild, Jennifer. *What's Fair?: American Beliefs About Distributive Justice.* Cambridge: Harvard University Press, 1981.

———.*Thirty Years After Brown.* Washington, D.C.: Joint Center for Political Studies, 1985.

Hodgson, Godfrey. *America in Our Time.* New York: Doubleday, 1976.

Horton, Raymond. *Municipal Labor Relations in New York City: Lessons of the Lindsay-Wagner Years.* New York: Praeger, 1973.

Howe, Irving. *World of Our Fathers.* New York: Harcourt Brace Jovanovich, 1976.

Howe, Irving, ed. *The Urban School Crisis: An Anthology of Essays.* New York: League for Industrial Democracy/United Federation of Teachers, 1966.

Huggins, Nathan Irvin. *Harlem Renaissance.* London: Oxford University Press, 1971.

Ignatiev, Noel. *How the Irish Became White.* New York: Routledge, 1995.

Isserman, Maurice. *If I Had a Hammer . . . : The Death of the Old Left and the Birth of the New Left.* New York: Basic Books, 1987.

Jacoby, Tamar. "The Uncivil History of the Civilian Review Board." *City Journal,* 3 (Winter 1993): 56–63.

———. *Someone Else's House: America's Unfinished Struggle for Integration.* New York: Free Press, 1998.

Jencks, Christopher. *Inequality: A Reassessment of the Effect of Family and Schooling in America.* New York: Harper & Row, 1972.

Katz, Michael. *In the Shadow of the Poorhouse: A Social History of Welfare in America.* New York: Basic Books, 1986.

Katz, Michael, ed. *The "Underclass" Debate: Views From History.* Princeton, N.J.: Princeton University Press, 1993.

Katznelson, Ira. *City Trenches: Urban Politics and the Patterning of Class in the United States.* New York: Pantheon, 1981.

Kaufman, Jonathan. *Broken Alliance: The Turbulent Times Between Blacks and Jews in America.* New York: Scribner, 1988.

Kelley, Robin D. G. *Race Rebels: Culture, Politics, and the Black Working Class.* New York: Free Press, 1994.

Kessner, Thomas. *Fiorello H. La Guardia and the Making of Modern New York.* New York: McGraw-Hill, 1984.

King, Martin Luther, Jr. *Why We Can't Wait.* New York: New American Library, 1964.

Kirtzman, Andrew. *Rudy Giuliani: Emperor of the City.* New York: William Morrow, 2000.

Klein, Woody. *Lindsay's Promise: The Dream That Failed.* New York: Macmillan, 1970.

Koch, Edward I. *Politics.* New York: Simon & Schuster, 1985.

Kozol, Jonathan. *Death at an Early Age.* New York: Bantam Books, 1967.

Landesman, Alter F. *Brownsville: The Birth, Development, and Passing of a Jewish Community in New York.* New York: Bloch Publishing, 1969.

Lang, Gladys Engel. *Responses to a Decentralization Crisis.* New York: Center for Urban Education, 1968.

Lang, Kurt, and Gladys Lang. "Resistance to School Desegregation: A Case Study of Backlash Among Jews." *Sociological Inquiry* 35 (Winter 1965): 94–106.

Larner, Jeremy. "The New York School Crisis." In *The Urban School Crisis: An Anthology of Essays,* edited by Irving Howe. New York: League for Industrial Democracy/United Federation of Teachers, 1966,

Lemann, Nicholas. *The Promised Land: The Great Black Migration and How It Changed America.* New York: Knopf, 1991.

————.*The Big Test: The Secret History of the American Meritocracy.* New York: Farrar, Straus and Giroux, 1999.

Lester, Julius. *Look Out Whitey! Black Power's Gon' Get Your Mama!* New York: Grove Press, 1969.

Levine, Naomi. *Ocean Hill–Brownsville: Schools in Crisis.* New York: Popular Library, 1969.

Levy, Gerald. *Ghetto School: Class Warfare in an Elementary School.* New York: Pegasus, 1970.

Lewis, Oscar. *La Vida: A Puerto Rican Family in the Culture of Poverty—New York and San Juan.* New York: Random House, 1965.

————. "The Culture of Poverty." *Scientific American* 215 (October 1966): 19–25.

Libarle, Marc, and Tom Seligson, eds. *The High School Revolutionaries.* New York: Random House, 1970.

Lichten, Eric. *Class, Power, and Austerity: The New York City Fiscal Crisis.* South Hadley, Mass.: Bergin & Garvey, 1986.

Lindsay, John. *The City.* New York: Norton, 1969.

Lukas, J. Anthony. *Common Ground: A Turbulent Decade in the Lives of Three American Families.* New York: Knopf, 1985.

Lurie, Ellen. *How to Change the Schools.* New York: Random House, 1970.

Mabee, Carlton. *Black Education in New York State.* Syracuse, N.Y.: Syracuse University Press, 1979.

Maier, August, and Elliott Rudwick. *CORE: A Study in the Civil Rights Movement, 1942–1968.* Urbana: University of Illinois Press, 1975.

Maier, Mark H. *City Unions: Managing Discontent in New York City.* New Brunswick, N.J.: Rutgers University Press, 1987.

Marable, Manning. *How Capitalism Underdeveloped Black America: Problems in Race, Political Economy, and Society.* Boston: South End Press, 1987.

Matusow, Allen J. *The Unraveling of America: A History of Liberalism in the 1960s.* New York: Harper & Row, 1984.

Mayer, Martin. *The Teachers Strike: New York, 1968.* New York: Harper & Row, 1969.

McCoy, Rhody. "Analysis of Critical Issues and Incidents in the New York City School Crisis, 1967–1970 and Their Implications for Urban Education." Ed.D. diss., University of Massachusetts, 1971.

McMillan, Charles. "The Changing Schools: A Look at Community Control."
  Freedomways 13 (1973): 63–68.

McNickle, Chris. *To Be Mayor of New York: Ethnic Politics in the City.* New York:
  Columbia University Press, 1993.

McWhorter, John H. *Losing the Race: Self-Sabotage in Black America.* New York: Free
  Press, 2000.

Mills, C. Wright. *The Power Elite.* New York: Oxford University Press, 1956.

Mollenkopf, John Hull. *A Phoenix in the Ashes: The Rise and Fall of the Koch Coalition in
  New York City Politics.* Princeton, N.J.: Princeton University Press, 1992.

Morris, Aldon. *The Origins of the Civil Rights Movement: Black Communities Organizing
  for Change.* New York: Free Press, 1984.

Morris, Charles R. *The Cost of Good Intentions: New York City and the Liberal
  Experiment, 1960–1975.* New York: McGraw-Hill, 1980.

Moynihan, Daniel Patrick. *The Negro Family: The Case for National Action.*
  Washington, D.C.: U.S. Department of Labor, 1965.

———. *Maximum Feasible Misunderstanding: Community Action in the War on Poverty.*
  New York: Free Press, 1969.

Murphy, Marjorie. *Blackboard Unions: The AFT and the NEA, 1900–1990.* Ithaca, N.Y.:
  Cornell University Press, 1990.

Murray, Charles. *Losing Ground: American Social Policy, 1950–1980.* New York: Basic
  Books, 1984.

National Advisory Commission on Civil Disorders. *Report of the National Advisory
  Commission on Civil Disorders.* Washington, D.C.: Government Printing Office,
  1968.

Newfield, Jack, and Wayne Barrett. *City for Sale: Edward Koch and the Betrayal of New
  York.* New York: Harper & Row, 1988.

New York City Board of Education. *Teaching About Minorities in Classroom Situations.*
  New York: New York City Board of Education, 1967–68.

Novak, Michael. *The Rise of the Unmeltable Ethnics.* New York: Macmillan, 1972.

O'Neill, William L. *Coming Apart: An Informal History of America in the 1960s.* New
  York: Random House, 1971.

Patterson, James T. *America's Struggle Against Poverty.* Cambridge, Mass.: Harvard
  University Press, 1981.

Patterson, Orlando. *Ethnic Chauvinism: The Reactionary Impulse.* New York: Stein &
  Day, 1977.

Perlstein, Daniel H. "The 1968 New York City School Crisis: Teacher Politics, Racial
  Politics, and the Decline of Liberalism." Ph.D. diss., Stanford University, 1994.

Phillips, Kevin. *The Emerging Republican Majority.* New Rochelle, N.Y.: Arlington
  House, 1969.

Piven, Frances Fox, and Richard Cloward. *The Politics of Turmoil: Poverty, Race, and the
  Urban Crisis.* New York: Pantheon, 1974.

———. *Poor People's Movements: Why They Succeed, How They Fail.* New York: Vintage
  Books, 1979.

———. *Regulating the Poor: The Functions of Public Welfare.* New York: Vintage, 1993.

Podair, Jerald E. "'White' Values, 'Black' Values: The Ocean Hill–Brownsville

Controversy and New York City Culture, 1965–1975." *Radical History Review* 59 (Spring 1994): 36–59.

———. "Like Strangers: Blacks, Whites, and New York City's Ocean Hill–Brownsville Crisis, 1945–1980." Ph.D. diss., Princeton University, 1997.

Podhoretz, Norman. "My Negro Problem—and Ours." *Commentary* 35 (February 1963): 93–101.

Pritchett, Wendell E. *Brownsville, Brooklyn: Blacks, Jews, and the Changing Face of the Ghetto.* Chicago: University of Chicago Press, 2002.

Rainwater, Lee, and William Yancey. *The Moynihan Report and the Politics of Controversy.* Cambridge, Mass.: MIT Press, 1967.

Ravitch, Diane, "Community Control Revisited" *Commentary* 53 (February 1972): 69–74.

———. *The Great School Wars—New York, 1805–1973: A History of the Public Schools as Battleground of Social Change.* New York: Basic Books, 1974.

———. *The Troubled Crusade: American Education, 1945–1980.* New York: Basic Books, 1983.

Rebell, Michael A., and Arthur R. Block. *Educational Policy Making and the Courts: An Empirical Study of Judicial Activism.* Chicago: University of Chicago Press, 1982.

———. *Equality and Education: Federal Civil Rights Enforcement in the New York City School System.* Princeton, N.J.: Princeton University Press, 1985.

Rieder, Jonathan. *Canarsie: The Jews and Italians of Brooklyn Against Liberalism.* Cambridge, Mass.: Harvard University Press, 1985.

Ritterband, Paul. "Ethnic Power and the Public Schools: The New York City School Strike of 1968." *Sociology of Education* 47 (1974): 251–67.

Rodgers, Daniel T. *Contested Truths: Keywords in American Politics since Independence.* New York: Basic Books, 1987.

Roediger, David R. *The Wages of Whiteness: Race and the Making of the American Working Class.* London: Verso, 1991.

Rogers, David. *110 Livingston Street: Politics and Bureaucracy in the New York City School System.* New York: Random House, 1968.

Rosenthal, Robert, and Lenore Jacobson. *Pygmalion in the Classroom.* New York: Holt, Rhinehart & Winston, 1968.

———. "Teacher Expectations for the Disadvantaged" *Scientific American* 218 (April 1968): 19–23.

Rossner, Robert. *The Year Without An Autumn: Portrait of a School in Crisis.* New York: R. W. Baron, 1969.

Rubinstein, Annette, ed. *Schools Against Children: The Case for Community Control.* New York: Monthly Review Press, 1970.

Rustin, Bayard. "From Protest to Politics: The Future of the Civil Rights Movement." *Commentary* 39 (February 1965): 25–31.

———. *Down the Line: The Collected Writings of Bayard Rustin.* Chicago: Quadrangle, 1971.

Ruth, Robert Douglas. "A Study of the Factors Affecting Teacher Attitudes and Participation in the New York City Decentralization Controversy." Ph.D. diss., Duke University, 1974.

Ryan, William. "Blaming the Victim: The Folklore of Cultural Deprivation." *This Magazine Is About Schools!* 3 (1971): 97–117.

Savitch, Harold, "Powerless in the Urban Ghetto," *Polity,* 5 (Fall 1972): 19–56.

Sayre, Wallace, and Herbert Kaufman. *Governing New York City.* New York: Russell Sage Foundation, 1960.

Scammon, Richard, and Ben Wattenberg. *The Real Majority.* New York: Coward-McCann, 1970.

Schierenbeck, Jack. *Union Made a World of Difference: Reflections on the "Revolution" at 40.* New York: United Federation of Teachers, 2000.

Schwartz, Joel. *The New York Approach: Robert Moses, Urban Liberals, and Redevelopment of the Inner City.* Columbus: Ohio State University Press, 1993.

Scott, James C. *Weapons of the Weak: Everyday Forms of Peasant Resistance.* New Haven, Conn.: Yale University Press, 1985.

———. Domination and the Arts of Resistance: Hidden Transcripts. New Haven, Conn.: Yale University Press, 1990.

Sexton, Patricia Cayo. *Class Struggles in the Schools.* New York: League for Industrial Democracy / United Federation of Teachers, 1966.

Shanker, Albert. "The Real Meaning of the New York City Teachers' Strike." *Phi Delta Kappan* 50 (1969): 434–41.

Shefter, Martin. *Political Crisis, Fiscal Crisis: The Collapse and Revival of New York City.* New York: Basic Books, 1985.

Siegel, Fred. *The Future Once Happened Here: New York, D.C., L.A., and the Fate of America's Big Cities.* New York: Free Press, 1997.

Silberman, Charles E. *Crisis in Black and White.* New York: Random House, 1964.

Sitkoff, Harvard. *The Struggle for Black Equality, 1954–1980.* New York: Hill & Wang, 1993.

Sleeper, Jim. *The Closest of Strangers: Liberalism and the Politics of Race in New York.* New York: Norton, 1990.

Stack, Carol. *All Our Kin: Strategies for Survival in a Black Community.* New York: Harper & Row, 1974.

Spencer, David. "A Harlem Parent Speaks." *NEA Journal* 57 (March 1968): 8–9.

Starr, Roger. *The Rise and Fall of New York City.* New York: Basic Books, 1985.

Stone, I. F. The Mason-Dixon Line Moves to New York." *I. F. Stone's Weekly,* November 4, 1968.

Sugrue, Thomas J. *The Origins of the Urban Crisis: Race and Inequality in Postwar Detroit.* Princeton, N.J.: Princeton University Press, 1996.

Swanson, Bert E. *The Struggle for Equality: The School Integration Controversy in New York City.* New York: Hobbs, Dorman, 1966.

Taft, Philip. *United They Teach: The Story of the United Federation of Teachers.* Los Angeles: Nash Publishing, 1974.

Taylor, Clarence. *Knocking on Our Own Door: Milton A. Galamison and the Struggle to Integrate New York City.* New York: Columbia University Press, 1997.

Trachtenberg, Paul, ed. *Selection of Teachers and Supervisors in Urban School Systems.* New York: Agathon Publication Services, Inc., 1972.

Tree, Christina. "Grouping Pupils in New York City." *Urban Review* 3 (September 1968): 8–15.

Tyack, David. *The One Best System: A History of American Urban Education.* Cambridge, Mass.: Harvard University Press, 1974.

United Federation of Teachers. *The History of Black Americans: A Study Guide and Curriculum Outline.* New York: United Federation of Teachers, 1972.

Urofsky, Melvin, ed. *Why Teachers Strike: Teachers' Rights and Community Control.* Garden City, N.Y.: Doubleday, 1970.

Van Deburg, William L. *New Day in Babylon: The Black Power Movement and American Culture, 1965–1975.* Chicago: University of Chicago Press, 1992.

Waldinger, Roger. "Changing Ladders and Musical Chairs: Ethnicity and Opportunity in Post-Industrial New York." *Politics and Society* 15 (1986–87): 369–401.

Wasserman, Miriam. *The School Fix, NYC, USA.* New York: Outerbridge & Dienstfrey, 1970.

Weaver, Edward. "The New Literature on Education of the Black Child." *Freedomways* 8 (Fall 1968): 367–79.

Weilk, Carol A. *The Ocean Hill–Brownsville School Project: A Profile.* New York: Institute for Community Studies, 1969.

Weisbord, Robert, and Arthur Stein. *Bitter-Sweet Encounter: The Afro-American and the American Jew.* Westport, Conn.: Negro Universities Press, 1970.

Weisbrot, Robert. *Freedom Bound: A History of America's Civil Rights Movement.* New York: Norton, 1990.

Westbrook, Robert. *John Dewey and American Democracy.* Ithaca, N.Y.: Cornell University Press, 1991.

Wilcox, Preston. "The Controversy Over I.S. 201." *Urban Review* 1 (July 1966): 12–16.

———. "Africanization: The New Input to Black Education." *Freedomways* 8 (Fall 1968): 395–98.

Wilentz, Sean. "Against Exceptionalism: Class Consciousness and the American Labor Movement." *International Labor and Working Class History* 26 (1984): 1–24.

Wilkerson, Doxey. "Blame the Negro Child!" *Freedomways* 8 (Fall 1968): 340–46.

Wilkins, Roy. *Standing Fast: The Autobiography of Roy Wilkins.* New York: Viking, 1982.

Wilson, William Julius. *The Declining Significance of Race: Blacks and Changing America.* Chicago: University of Chicago Press, 1980.

Wolfe, Tom. *Radical Chic and Mau-Mauing the Flak-Catchers.* New York: Farrar, Straus & Giroux, 1970.

X, Malcolm, and Alex Haley. *The Autobiography of Malcolm X.* New York: Grove Press, 1964.

Zagoria, Sam, ed. *Public Works and Public Unions.* Englewood Cliffs, N.J.: Prentice-Hall, 1972.

Zeluck, Stephen. "The UFT Strike: Will It Destroy the AFT?" *Phi Delta Kappan* 50 (1969): 250–54.

Zimet, Melvin. *Decentralization and School Effectiveness: A Case Study of the 1969 School Decentralization Law in New York City.* New York: Teachers College Press, 1973.

Zitron, Celia Lewis. *The New York City Teachers Union, 1916–1964: A Story of Educational and Social Commitment.* New York: Humanities Press, 1968.

INDEX

ability tracking: black intellectuals' criticism of, 63–64, 228n.56; educational achievement and, 154–56; "equality" paradigm and, 210–11; liberals' rejection of, 30; reduction in use of, 151; support for, 27–28, 52–53

Addabbo, Joan, 27

affective learning, ATA introduction of, 168–71

affirmative action, equality paradigm and, 210–11

African-American Teachers Association (ATA), 35, 41–42, 49, 78, 190–91, 205; class politics and, 157, 159, 178–82; community control experiment and, 91–92, 96, 98, 152, 185, 190–92; cultural values debate and, 41, 153–82, 211–14; demise of, 180–82; "disruptive child" provision controversy, 160–64; dominance of Ocean Hill–Brownsville schools, 167–71; educational achievement of blacks as focus of, 154–56; hostility to Jews within, 155–56, 165, 167; Lisser appointment controversy and, 159–60; McCoy supported by, 104; membership demographics, 167, 239n.1, 241n.53; origins, 153, 156, 167; strike of 1967 and, 162–64; strikes of 1968 and, 116, 142; UFT clashes with, 180–82

African-American Teachers Forum, 165–67, 176–78, 209

African culture, curriculum development including, 67–70. *See also* black culture and history

AFT. *See* American Federation of Teachers

AFSCME. *See* American Federation of State, County, and Municipal Employees

agency, community control as tool of, 208–14

Agricultural Adjustment Administration, 15

Allen, James: community control issue and, 34–35; decentralization plan and, 149; principals' appointments and, 88, 142; strikes of 1968 and, 137–39

American Civil Liberties Union, 127. *See also* New York Civil Liberties Union

American Federation of State, County, and Municipal Employees (AFSCME), 134

American Federation of Teachers (AFT), 68, 149, 172

"Analysis of Critical Issues and Incidents in the New York City School Crisis, 1967–1970," 216n.3

Anti-Defamation League, 143

anti-semitism: black expression of, 165–66; as excuse for racism, 207–10; strikes of 1968 and, 124–52

Antonetty, Evelina, 175

A. Philip Randolph Institute, 42, 112, 134–35

ATA. *See* African-American Teachers Association

Baird, Keith, 67

Baldwin, James, 125

Beame, Abraham (Mayor), 193–99

Bedford-Stuyvesant, black migration to Ocean Hill–Brownsville from, 17–18

Bedford-Stuyvesant Restoration Corporation, 110

Benjamin Franklin High School, 60

Bereiter-Engelmann reading program, 169–71

Beyond the Melting Pot, 6–8, 54, 57, 113

Birbach, Jerry, 187–205

black culture and history: affective learning curriculum and, 170–71; cultural pluralism and, 57–58, 67–70; Ocean Hill–Brownsville experiment and, 96–97; race-class politics and, 156–59, 164–74; Teachers Union lesson plans, 142. *See also* African culture

black educators: community control supported by, 41; cultural values debate and, 7–8, 165–66, 174–82

black intellectuals and activists, 32, 41–42; anti-semitism among, 124–26, 164–67; cultural values debate and, 49–50, 58–70; fiscal crisis in New York City and, 194–205; national race relations and, 207–14; strikes of 1968 and, 123–52

Black Power, 32, 63, 66

Black Power movement, 32–35

"blockbusting," housing segregation and, 16

Bloomberg, Michael, 204

Bloomfield, Jack, 74–77

Board of Education (New York City): bureaucratic structure of, 23–24, 39, 221n.3; centralization of, 14–15, 23–24; community control movement and, 31–32, 49, 79–82; cultural pluralism policy of, 57–58; decentralization plan and, 92–94, 114–15, 148–49; demonstration principals issue and, 138–40; discriminatory hiring practices of, 151, 155–56; "disruptive child" provision controversy and, 161–64; fiscal crisis in New York City and, 194–200; integration proposals, 22–23, 33, 153–54; Intermediate School 201 development and, 34–35; Lindsay appointments to, 110–12; media criticism of, 40; Ocean Hill–Brownsville experiment and, 74–102; parent sit-in at, 71–73; power delegation by, 110; school pairing plan, 25–30; strike

negotiations by, 115–22; teacher transfer hearings, 108–14; UFT relations with, 43–47, 71

Board of Examiners (New York City), 50–51, 53, 85; black educators' attacks on, 165–66; decentralization plan and, 92–93, 114, 148–49; discriminatory recruitment practices of, 155–56; GASing system, 95; merit-based values of, 171–74; principals' eligibility list, 87–88, 94–95, 231n.33; suit against, 150–51

Breslin, Jimmy, 40, 126–28

Bronx High School of Science, 30

Brooklyn College, 29

Brotherhood of Sleeping Car Porters, 134–35

Brownsville Boys Club, 17

Brownsville Community Corporation, 75

Brownsville Community Council, 62, 72

Brown v. Board of Education, 22, 24

Bundy, McGeorge, 38, 40, 212; community control issue and, 79–80, 91–92, 100–102, 149, 152; strikes of 1968 and, 127–28, 132; teacher transfer controversy and, 109–10

Bundy Report (Report of the Mayor's Advisory Panel on Decentralization of the New York City Schools), 91–94, 100

Burrus, John, 181–82

business community: community control supported by, 37–38; fiscal crisis in New York City and union alliances with, 192–200

busing, school desegregation and use of, 24–25, 28–30, 188–92

Campbell, James, 67

Campbell, Leslie (Jitu Weusi), 41, 58, 96–97, 142–43, 205; ATA and, 156–59, 167, 174; becomes Jitu Weusi, 181; cultural values debate and, 175, 179, 182, 207–8; Lisser appointment controversy and, 160

Canarsie integration controversy, 188–92